SCHOLASTIC
ATLAS
OF THE
WORLD

SCHOLASTIC ATLAS OF THE WORLD

SCHOLASTIC
REFERENCE

Library of Congress Cataloging-in-Publication Data
Steele, Philip, 1948–
Scholastic atlas of the world/by Philip Steele
p.cm.
Includes index.
1. Atlases [1.Atlases. 2. Geography.] I. Title.
G1021.S687 2001
912—dc21   00-030064

ISBN 0-439-47435-3

Produced by Miles Kelly Publishing Ltd
Bardfield Centre, Great Bardfield, Essex, CM7 4SL, UK

Project Manager: Anne Marshall
Design: Jo Brewer, Alex Charles, Digital Wisdom
Design Assistance: Andy Knight
Cartography: Digital Wisdom (Nicholas Rowland)
Consultants: Clive Carpenter, Keith Lye

Text: Philip Steele, Jane Walker
Editors: Neil de Cort, Belinda Gallagher
Assistant Editors: Mark Darling, Helen Parker, Liz Tortice

Proofreader: Sarah Doughty
Statistics: Clive Carpenter, Luke Seaber
Index: Jane Parker, Textype Typesetters
Picture Research: Lesley Cartlidge, Kate Miles, Liberty Newton
Artwork Commissioner: Janice Bracken
Publishing Director: Jim Miles

Color reproduction: DPI Colour, Saffron Walden, Essex, UK

10 9 8 7 6 5 4 3 2 1   02 03 04 05

Printed in the U.S.A.   08
First paperback printing, September 2002

Scholastic Reference Staff

Editorial Director: Wendy Barish
Associate Editor: Mary Varilla Jones
Editorial Assistant: Elysa Jacobs
Curriculum Consultant: Bob Stremme
Flag Consultant: Dr. Whitney Smith,
  Flag Research Center

Creative Director: David Saylor
Art Director: Nancy Sabato

Managing Editor: Manuela Soares
Associate Production Editor: Victoria Washington Maher

Manufacturing Vice President: Angela Biola
Manufacturing Manager: Alison Forner

Population and life expectancy figures used in this book are from the International Database of the U.S. Census Bureau. The source used to identify area, language, and religion was the CIA World Factbook. Statistics on motor vehicle use were obtained from the American Automobile Manufacturer's Association.

The population statistics for the United States are the numbers released from the U.S. Census Bureau from Census 2000. The life facts statistics for the United States are based on the U.S. Census Bureau population projections for the year 2000.

Countries

Contents

How to Use this Atlas

The *Scholastic Atlas of the World* presents information in a new and exciting way. Comparisons are made between countries and the United States—land area, time difference, life expectancy, car ownership, how long it takes to travel between distant cities—and many more features. How does the height of Mount McKinley, the highest mountain in the United States, compare with other mountains around the world? How does the length of different rivers compare? All these exciting and unique features are contained within this atlas.

Understanding the maps

This key shows the different features, labels, and symbols included in the maps, and helps you to read and understand them.

	forest and grassland
	desert
	mountainous region
	ice
	country border
	disputed border
	state/province border
✪Paris	national capital
●Darwin	state/province capital
Santa Cruz ●	town
Sardinia (ITALY)	dependency/ territory
Dnieper	river
▲ *Pico Bolívar 16,411 ft (5,001 m)*	mountain
Chichén Itzá	place of interest

The projection used for these maps is cylindrical—see page 11.

Country listing

Countries featured on the page are listed in order of their physical size.

Political map

This shows the countries and how they relate to the surrounding land area.

Important words

Difficult words that need more explanation are listed in the glossary on page 206.

Discover more

Did you know that Europe has a longer coastline than anywhere else in the world or that the Dead Sea is actually a lake? Find out more fascinating world facts in these boxes.

Abbreviations

FED.	Federation
Gt	Great
I.	island
Is/IS	islands
L.	lake
Mt	Mount
MTS	mountains
n.a.	not available
St.	Saint
cm	centimeter
cu	cubic
ft	feet
in	inch
l	liter
lb	pound
kg	kilogram
km	kilometer
m	meter
mi	mile
mm	millimeter
sq	square
t	metric ton

Continent tabs

The world maps are arranged within continents (see page 16), shown by these index tabs. Each continent has its own page background color.

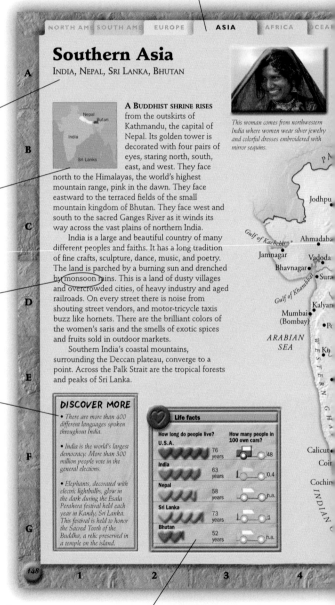

Life facts

How does life in the United States compare with the rest of the world? How long does the average person expect to live? How many people own cars? Find out here.

In the North American section of this atlas on pages 40–67, state and province facts are compared (as on the right). Find out how populated each state is and who lives there.

(Note: Figures in the Life facts boxes do not always add up to 100 because some people fall into more than one type. The term American Indian is used in line with the U.S. Census Bureau figures.)

Scale and compass rose

The scale allows you to find out how large an area on a map is (see page 12). The compass rose helps you to find north.

Highest mountains

The world's tallest mountains are compared with Mount McKinley, the tallest in the United States. The symbol is used on the map to show where the featured mountain is situated.

Where in the world?

Look at

 the area of the United States compared with that of other country groupings.

 the time difference between Washington, DC, the featured city, and GMT (Greenwich mean time, see page 15).

Find out

 where the featured countries are on the globe (highlighted in red).

 latitude (drawn in a west–east direction and shown in blue) and longitude (drawn between the North Pole and the South Pole and shown in red) lines that pinpoint the featured city (see page 13).

 how far away the featured city is from Washington, DC, and how long it takes to fly there, traveling at 520 mph (835 kmh).

Longest rivers

Some of the countries' longest rivers are compared with the Nile (the world's longest) and the Mississippi (the longest in the United States). The symbol is used on the map to show you where the featured river is situated.

Flags

Each country has its own flag. In the United States and Canada, the state and province flags are also shown.

Search and find

Here you can find the cities and towns featured on the map. Use the grid references to locate their exact position.

Map within page

Highest mountains

Mount Everest 29,028 ft (8,848 m)
Mount McKinley 20,320 ft (6,194 m)

Where in the world?

7 A.M. noon 5:30 P.M.
Washington, DC GMT Delhi

Washington, DC to Delhi
7,480 mi (12,038 km)
14 hr 25 min

Delhi lies on
28° 54'N latitude
77° 13'E longitude

Longest rivers

Nile	4,145 mi (6,670 km)
Mississippi	3,741 mi (6,020 km)
Ganges	1,560 mi (2,510 km)

Country facts

	Area sq mi (sq km)	Population	Language	Religion	Currency
India	1,222,243 (3,165,609)	1,000,848,550	Hindi	Hindu	Rupee
Nepal	56,827 (147,182)	24,302,653	Nepali	Hindu	Rupee
Sri Lanka	25,332 (65,610)	19,144,875	Sinhala	Buddhist	Rupee
Bhutan	18,417 (47,000)	1,951,965	Dzongkha	Lamaistic Buddhist	Ngultrum

The Taj Mahal was built in India at Agra by Emperor Shāh Jāhān for his wife in the 1600s. It took over 20,000 workers 23 years to build.

Search and find

India	
Capital: Delhi	B5
Agra	C5
Ahmadabad	C4
Ajmer	C5
Allahabad	C6
Bangalore	F5
Bhavnagar	D4
Bhopal	C5
Calcutta	D7
Calicut	F4
Chennai (Madras)	F5
Cochin	F4
Coimbatore	F5
Cuttack	D7
Guwahati	C8
Haora	D7
Hubli-Dharwar	E4
Hyderabad	E5
Imphal	C8
Indore	C5
Jabalpur	D6
Jaipur	C5
Jamnagar	C4
Jamshedpur	D7
Jodhpur	C5
Kalyan	D4
Kanpur	C6
Kolhapur	E4
Kurnool	E5
Lalitpur	C5
Lucknow	C6
Ludhiana	B5

Madurai	F5
Mumbai (Bombay)	D4
Mysore	F5
Nagpur	D5
Nellore	E5
Patna	C7
Poona	D4
Raipur	D6
Solapur	D5
Srinagar	A5
Surat	D4
Tiruchchirappalli	F5
Udaipur	C5
Vadodara	D4
Varanasi	C6
Vijayawada	E6
Vishakhapatnam	E6

Nepal	
Capital: Kathmandu	C7
Biratnagar	C7

Sri Lanka	
Capital: Colombo	G5
Galle	G5
Jaffna	F5
Kandy	G5
Trincomalee	G5

Bhutan	
Capital: Thimphu	C8
Phuntsholing	C8

Physical maps

The key on the left will help you to identify the different towns, land features, and borders included on each map. Towns where most people live have been included as well as those places that are important for other reasons, such as trade and tourism. The longest rivers, the highest mountains, and the most notable physical features are shown.

Fact box

Find out more about each country—its area, population, language, religion, and currency. On continent spreads you will also find the largest country by area and population within that continent. For the United States and Canada, state and province information, such as the state flower, is given. (Sources for the statistics can be found on the copyright page.)

Map grid references

The letters and numbers that are contained within this border help you to find places on the map. For example, look for Calcutta in the Search and find—its grid reference is D7. Trace with your finger a line across from D and down from 7 and you will find Calcutta on the map. The index at the back of the book lists the grid references of all towns, cities, rivers, mountains, and other map features. Using this method you can find any of them on the maps.

Making Maps

ABOUT 4,500 YEARS AGO A SKILLED WORKER IN Babylon was making detailed markings on a clay tablet. The markings he made probably showed some buildings in a nearby river valley. The worker was making one of the very first maps.

The ancient Egyptians and Greeks made maps, too. One Egyptian-Greek astronomer who was named Ptolemy (365–283 B.C.) wrote down everything that was known about the world, and drew maps to illustrate his words, in a huge book called *Geography*. Later, during the Middle Ages, the mapmaking skills of Chinese and Arab scholars were ahead of the rest of the world. The first map ever to be printed appeared in a Chinese encyclopedia in about 1155—more than 300 years before Europeans knew how to print.

Maps became more available in the 1500s. At this time Europeans were discovering new areas of the world. In 1492, when Columbus set sail and discovered the New World, the latest world map did not even show North or South America. After the invention of the printing press, probably by Johann Gutenberg in the mid–1400s, maps were produced more cheaply.

As people discovered new places, they needed new maps. Trail maps were made for the pioneers who traveled west across America in the late 1700s and early 1800s. During the world wars, the invention of the airplane helped armies, because accurate maps could be drawn using photos taken from the air.

Today, most of our maps are produced by computers. Material is collected from surveys of Earth, and aerial photos and satellite images. Computers arrange this material to draw the highly accurate maps you use today.

Peeling the orange
If you could peel off Earth's surface like the skin of an orange, you would be left with segments similar to those shown here. Mapmakers fill the gaps between the segments by digitally stretching them.

▲ *Ptolemy's map of the world first appeared in about A.D. 150 in ancient Egypt. Over 1,300 years later it was finally printed in an atlas in Germany.*

Map of the 13 colonies
In the 1600s and 1700s, 13 colonies were set up along the east coast of North America by people arriving mainly from England. These 13 colonies eventually became the founding states of the United States of America.

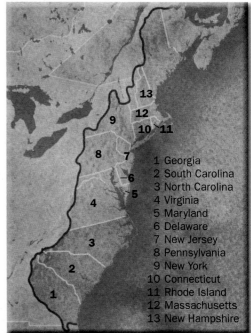

1 Georgia
2 South Carolina
3 North Carolina
4 Virginia
5 Maryland
6 Delaware
7 New Jersey
8 Pennsylvania
9 New York
10 Connecticut
11 Rhode Island
12 Massachusetts
13 New Hampshire

▶ *Gerardus Mercator was a mapmaker from Flanders (in modern Belgium). In 1569 he drew Earth's surface onto a flat sheet of paper. It was easier for sailors to navigate by this kind of map or chart.*

What is a projection?

Because the earth is round, mapmakers have a difficult job representing it on a flat map. The earth has to be stretched and distorted to make it appear flat on a page. The way in which the earth is stretched is called a map projection, and each projection stretches the image of the earth in a different way. There are several different types of projection, and the ones shown below are most commonly used. Some projections show the shape of the land accurately but their size is incorrect. With others, the opposite is true. However, no projection is completely accurate, and all distort to some extent.

Cylinder shaped

Imagine wrapping a sheet of paper around a lit-up globe of the world and projecting the lines of latitude and longitude (page 13) onto the paper. Unwrap the paper and spread it flat to produce the kind of flat map often used by sailors.

Cone shaped

Imagine placing a paper cone over a lit-up globe, and projecting the lines of latitude and longitude onto the cone. Unwrap and flatten the paper to produce the kind of map that often shows wide areas of land such as the United States or Russian Federation.

Plane shaped

Imagine holding a sheet of paper so that it touches one place on a lit-up globe. Project the lines of latitude and longitude onto the paper and then lay it on a flat surface. This kind of map is often used to show the world's polar regions.

Boundaries in Europe

A political map shows the boundaries of different states and countries. The maps below show the same area of land, but the boundaries are very different. The map on the left shows Europe in 1980. The one on the right shows the same area in 1999. By this time Czechoslovakia and Yugoslavia had broken up, but East and West Germany had united to form the new Germany.

1980

1999

1 West Germany
2 East Germany
3 Poland
4 USSR
5 Czechoslovakia
6 Hungary
7 Romania
8 Yugoslavia
9 Bulgaria
10 Albania

1 Germany
2 Poland
3 Kaliningrad
4 Lithuania
5 Latvia
6 Belarus
7 Russian Federation
8 Ukraine
9 Czech Republic
10 Slovakia

11 Hungary
12 Romania
13 Moldova
14 Slovenia
15 Croatia
16 Bosnia-Herzegovina
17 Yugoslavia
18 Bulgaria
19 Albania
20 Macedonia

Using Maps

A MAP IS A PICTURE OF AN AREA ON EARTH'S
surface. It uses lines, colors, and symbols to give
you information about that area. It may be a picture
of the whole world or of a small area in a city or
town. Maps tell you many different things—the
location of countries, cities, and towns; the features
of the landscape, the distribution of the population,
or the climate of a particular region.

Different maps

People choose a type of map that best suits how
they are going to use it. A hiker, for example, needs
a different kind of map from one that is needed by
someone driving a car. The hiker needs a physical
map showing the height and shape of the land, the
course of rivers and streams, where bridges are, the
route of footpaths, and so on. The driver, on the
other hand, needs a road map which shows
highways and other main roads, scenic routes,
parks, and nature preserves, as well as the location
of highway services and intersections.

All about scale

The area shown on a map is, of course, much bigger
than it appears on the printed page—this is because
the map is drawn to scale. A map of the world
shows us only a small amount of detail—we call it a
small-scale map. A street map may show details of
every building—it is called a large-scale map.

How to use a map scale

1 To measure the distance
between two cities, first mark
the positions of the city dots
onto the edge of a small piece
of paper.

2 Place the paper along the
map's scale, with the left-hand
mark against the 0. If the scale
is shorter than the distance you
want to measure, mark where
the scale ends, say 200 miles
(320 km). Note the distance
already measured. Place this
new mark against the 0.

3 Repeat this last step until you
have reached the mark for the
second city. Then add up each
of the distances. This will give
you the correct total of the
number of miles between the
two cities.

Street map
You use a street map to find your way around a city. This street map shows, in detail, an area of the city of San Francisco, California.

Road map
Here is a road map showing the main U.S. highways, intersections, four-lane roads, scenic routes, and some minor roads in California.

Political map
This political map shows the state and county boundaries of California, its neighboring states, the state capital, and the names and locations of major cities and towns.

Physical map
The natural features of California are shown in this physical map—the highland and lowland areas, deserts, lakes, rivers, and the shape of the coastline.

Satellite image
This shows the area of Earth's surface that makes up the state of California.

The Earth in space
Satellite photographs can be taken from space. They show sections of Earth's surface.

Finding the location of a place
Maps are marked with a system of lines to help you describe and find the location of a certain place. The horizontal lines are called lines of latitude, and the vertical ones are lines of longitude. Latitude and longitude are measured in degrees (°).

Lines of latitude
These are imaginary lines that circle the world in an east–west direction. They tell you how far north or south a place is from the Equator, a line drawn at 0° latitude. They are drawn parallel to the Equator. Two special lines of latitude are the Tropic of Cancer and the Tropic of Capricorn. The Tropic of Cancer marks the northern boundary of the tropics. The Tropic of Capricorn marks the southern boundary. Because these regions lie close to the Equator, it is very hot, as the Sun shines directly overhead.

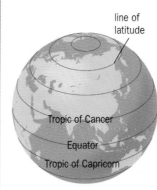

line of latitude

Tropic of Cancer

Equator

Tropic of Capricorn

Lines of longitude
These are imaginary lines that run across Earth's surface in a north–south direction, from the North Pole to the South Pole. We start counting lines of longitude to the east and the west of the Greenwich Meridian, the 0° line of longitude that passes through the borough of Greenwich in London, England.

line of longitude

Hemispheres

Western Hemisphere

180° Meridian

Eastern Hemisphere

The Greenwich Meridian and the 180° Meridian divide the world into two halves called the Eastern Hemisphere and the Western Hemisphere— each hemisphere has 180 degrees of longitude.

Northern Hemisphere

Equator

Southern Hemisphere

The Equator divides the world into two halves called the Northern Hemisphere and the Southern Hemisphere— each hemisphere has 90 degrees of latitude.

On a map you can find any place on Earth's surface if you know its latitude and its longitude. For example, the exact location of the city of Philadelphia (Pennsylvania) is as follows: 40°N, 75°W. In other words, Philadelphia lies on the line of latitude which is 40 degrees north of the Equator, and on the line of longitude 75 degrees west of the Greenwich Meridian.

The Earth in Space

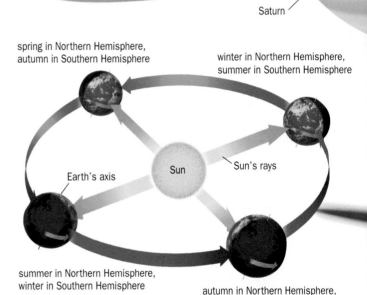

EARTH IS PART OF A FAMILY OF PLANETS, moons, comets, asteroids, and other space material traveling around the Sun. We call this family the Solar System (after the Latin word *sol*, which means the Sun). The Sun is a small star, one of millions in an enormous star group called the Milky Way. We belong to this galaxy, which is just one of millions of others in the vast Universe.

Each of the nine known planets moving around the Sun travels along an oval-shaped path called an orbit. The planets take different amounts of time to make a complete orbit around the Sun. Earth takes 365 $^1/_4$ days, or one year. Mercury, the planet closest to the Sun, takes just 88 days to orbit it. Pluto, which is usually the planet farthest from the Sun, takes almost 248 years to complete its orbit.

The moving Earth

Earth turns around on its axis like a spinning top. This axis is an imaginary line between the North and South poles. It takes 24 hours for Earth to spin all the way around, giving us day and night. As Earth spins, it is daytime in places facing the Sun, and nighttime in places facing away from the Sun. At the same time, Earth is also moving around the Sun. The axis of the moving Earth is not in an upright position—it tilts by 23 $^1/_2$° away from the vertical. It is this tilt which gives us our seasons. In summer, for example, a place may have more hours of daylight, and in winter, it may have less.

Pluto

Neptune

Uranus

Saturn

spring in Northern Hemisphere, autumn in Southern Hemisphere

winter in Northern Hemisphere, summer in Southern Hemisphere

Earth's axis

Sun

Sun's rays

summer in Northern Hemisphere, winter in Southern Hemisphere

autumn in Northern Hemisphere, spring in Southern Hemisphere

Earth's axis

day

Sun

night

Earth revolving on its axis

Night and day
Earth spins around on its axis once every 24 hours, which gives us day and night. Each day begins when the Sun rises in the east, and night begins when the Sun sets in the west. Noon is when the Sun is at its highest point in the sky.

Earth's orbit
The tilted angle of Earth's axis and Earth's orbit around the Sun give us our seasons. From March to September, Earth's Northern Hemisphere is tilted toward the Sun. Places in the Northern Hemisphere have spring, followed by summer. At the same time, places in the Southern Hemisphere have fall, followed by winter. From September to March the Southern Hemisphere is tilted toward the Sun. Places in the south have spring and summer, while those in the north have fall and winter.

▶ *This dramatic photo was taken by the Hubble Space Telescope (HST). It shows the clouds of gas around a dying star. First launched into space in 1990, the HST has produced the clearest, most detailed pictures of space ever seen. Every few years astronauts from the space shuttle repair and maintain the telescope.*

International Date Line   Greenwich Meridian

1 2 3 4 5 6 7 8 9 10 11 12 1 2 3 4 5 6 7 8 9 10 11 12
A.M.   TIME   P.M.

Time zones

To make it easier for travelers, the world is divided into 24 time zones. The zones are numbered from the Greenwich Meridian, the line of longitude at 0°, and each zone measures about 15° of longitude. There are 23 full time zones, and two half zones, one on each side of the International Date Line. This is an imaginary line at 180°, exactly halfway around the world from the Greenwich Meridian. Each time zone is one hour ahead of its neighboring zone to the west, and one hour behind its neighboring zone to the east.

So if you travel east across two time zones, you have to put your watch forward two hours. If you travel west across one time zone, you put your watch back one hour.

Jupiter

Mars

Sun

Venus

Earth

Mercury

The planets

Some of the planets, such as Earth and Mars, are made mainly of rock. Others are made of gas and are much bigger than our planet Earth. We sometimes call them the gas giants. Pluto, the smallest planet, is a mixture of ice and rock. Earth is the only one of the nine planets on which we know for sure that life exists.

Our Planet Earth

A DESERT COVERING ALMOST ONE-THIRD OF THE huge African continent, a waterfall with a drop of over 3,000 feet (914 m)—that's almost three times the height of the Empire State Building—and an underground cave system stretching around 345 miles (555 km). These are just three of the natural features that you can find on our amazing, and totally unique, planet Earth.

About 73 percent of our planet is covered with water. The Pacific Ocean, the largest body of water, covers almost one-third of Earth's surface. The remaining land is divided up into today's seven great continents—from largest to smallest: Asia, Africa, North America, South America, Antarctica, Europe, and Oceania. The landscape is dotted with a huge variety of wonderful natural features: towering mountains and hot, dry deserts, fast-flowing rivers and large lakes, majestic volcanoes and steep-sided valleys, caves and caverns many miles underground, huge rivers of ice called glaciers, and vast ice sheets.

There are now more than six billion people living on Earth, and we inhabit almost every corner of the globe. We share this natural world with more than two million species of living things, ranging in size from giant sequoia trees and huge blue whales to tiny organisms that you can see only with the help of a powerful microscope.

Country populations

Around half the world's population is concentrated in just five countries: China, India, the United States, Indonesia, and Brazil.

1	China	1,250,066,000
2	India	1,000,848,550
3	United States	275,306,000
4	Indonesia	216,108,345
5	Brazil	171,853,126
6	Russian Federation	146,393,569
7	Pakistan	138,123,359
8	Bangladesh	127,117,967
9	Japan	126,182,077
10	Nigeria	113,828,587

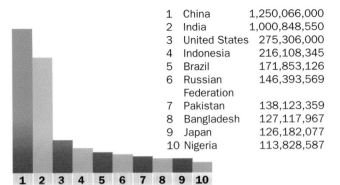

```
1  2  3  4  5  6  7  8  9  10
```

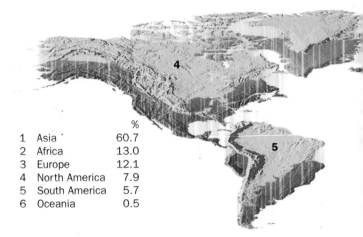

		%
1	Asia	60.7
2	Africa	13.0
3	Europe	12.1
4	North America	7.9
5	South America	5.7
6	Oceania	0.5

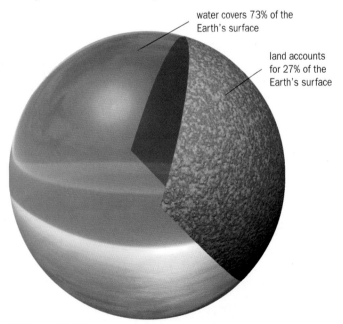

water covers 73% of the Earth's surface

land accounts for 27% of the Earth's surface

Water on Earth
The oceans and seas contain 97 percent of all the water on Earth. The remaining 3 percent is either frozen in ice caps and glaciers or in lakes, rivers, and under the ground.

◀ *Highest mountain*
Mount Everest is on the border of Nepal and China. Scientists have recently discovered that it's even bigger than they previously thought! In November 1999 the mountain's official height was changed to 29,028 ft (8,848 m)— that's 7 ft (2 m) more than its previous official height.

▶ *Lowest place*
The Dead Sea makes up part of the border between Israel and Jordan. It lies at 1,312 ft (400 m) below sea level. It is called the Dead Sea because no fish and only a few kinds of plants can survive in its very salty waters.

◀ *Largest desert*
The Sahara Desert covers almost one-third of the huge continent of Africa. Its surface measures 1.35 million sq mi (3.5 million sq km). Only 30% is sand and sand dunes; the rest of the desert consists of broad flat areas of small rocks and gravel.

Highest population

The diagram below shows the populated continents of the world peeled back from Earth's surface in layers. Asia, the most heavily populated continent, is shown as the highest layer.

Population explosion

The world's population is on average growing by 212,000 people every day. However, the population is not evenly distributed as some larger countries have small populations.

Area and population

Australia covers almost 3 million square miles (7.8 million sq km). Yet it has a population of just 18.8 million. The Netherlands is just 16,033 square miles (41,525 sq km), yet its population is almost as big as that of Australia—15.8 million.

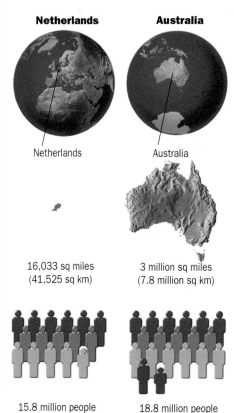

Netherlands   **Australia**

Netherlands   Australia

16,033 sq miles   3 million sq miles
(41,525 sq km)   (7.8 million sq km)

15.8 million people   18.8 million people

Population density

Few people live in the huge desert areas and dry plains of Australia's interior; most of the population lives on or near the cooler coastal regions where there is more rainfall. On average, this sparsely populated country has no more than 6 people living in every square mile (2.3 per sq km). The tiny Netherlands, on the other hand, has 985 people in every square mile (380 per sq km). Bangladesh, in southern Asia, is one of the most densely populated countries with an average of 2,286 people living in every square mile (883 per sq km).

Netherlands   **Australia**

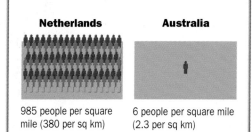

985 people per square   6 people per square mile
mile (380 per sq km)   (2.3 per sq km)

◀ *Largest ocean*
The Pacific Ocean is almost double the size of the Atlantic, covering 64,186,300 sq mi (1,662,425,000 sq km).

▶ *Largest island*
Greenland is more than four times the size of the second-largest island, Papua New Guinea. The ice-cold land of Greenland covers an area of 840,000 sq mi (2,175,600 sq km). It is a province of Denmark and is about 50 times bigger than Denmark itself.

◀ *Largest lake*
Asia's Caspian Sea covers an area of 152,239 sq mi (394,299 sq km). Although it is landlocked, which means it is surrounded by land on all sides, the Romans called it a "sea" because its waters are salty. The largest freshwater lake is Lake Superior, one of North America's five Great Lakes.

▶ *Longest river*
Africa's mighty Nile River flows for 4,145 mi (6,670 km) from its source near Lake Victoria northward to the Mediterranean Sea. By contrast, the world's shortest recorded river is the Roe in the state of Montana—it's just 201 ft (64 m) long!

The Moving Earth

EARTH IS A HUGE ROCKY BALL. LARGE CHUNKS of land called continents and vast expanses of ocean cover its surface. They are part of the hard "skin," or crust, that surrounds the whole Earth. This rocky outer layer is thicker under the continents, where it is up to 25 miles (40 km) thick, than under the oceans, where it is about 5 miles (8 km) thick.

Beneath this crust are layers of hot rocks and metals, some of them solid and some liquid. Immediately below the crust is a layer of hard rock reaching down about 1,800 miles (2,900 km). We call this layer the mantle. Its rocks are made up of different materials: silicon, aluminum, magnesium, iron, and oxygen. Below the mantle is the next layer, called the outer core. Here it is so hot that the rocks of iron and nickel have melted and become liquid. The temperature in the outer core can be as hot as 9,000° F (5,000° C)—that's 500 times hotter than boiling water!

Farther down still, at the very center of Earth, lies a ball of solid iron and nickel—the inner core. Its center is about 4,000 miles (6,400 km) from the surface. Scientists learn about Earth's interior by studying how earthquake waves travel.

crust

mantle

outer core of molten metal

solid metal inner core

Inside the Earth
The part of Earth's crust that lies beneath the continents is known as continental crust. Oceanic crust lies beneath the oceans and seas. As you move down through the thick, rocky mantle the temperature increases. We can only imagine what the outer and inner cores are like. Scientists have never seen them, nor obtained any samples from them, but guess that the outer core may be made from liquid iron and nickel, while the inner core may be solid metal.

A moving jigsaw
Earth's crust is divided into 16 huge pieces, called plates. Each one is made up of rock and a section of the upper mantle. The plates float on the hot liquid rocks below them, while the currents in these rocks keep the plates moving all the time. You cannot feel the land beneath your feet shifting because the plates move very slowly— between about ½ and 4 inches (1.25 and 10 cm) a year. There is more likely to be volcanic and earthquake activity where the plates meet.

▲ major volcanoes
● major earthquake sites
〰 plate boundaries

Plates
1 North American
2 Eurasian
3 Arabian
4 Iranian
5 Philippine
6 Caroline
7 Fiji
8 Indo-Australian
9 Antarctic
10 African
11 South American
12 Scotia
13 Nazca
14 Cocos
15 Caribbean
16 Pacific

Plate movement

The plates that make up Earth's crust sometimes move away from each other, and sometimes toward each other. They also slide past each other. When two plates collide, one plate may pile up against the other to form a great mountain range, such as the Andes in South America. This mountain building does not happen quickly, though—it takes millions of years. After a collision, one plate might be forced down below the other to form a deep trench on the ocean floor.

The boundary between two sliding plates is called a fault line. Where plates slide past each other, this movement often strains the rocks on each side of the fault line. If the strain becomes too great, the rocks snap and jerk, and an earthquake happens.

fault line

sliding motion causes rocks to strain

◀ *A devastating earthquake in 1999 destroyed the homes of thousands of Turkish people.*

Fiery volcanoes

When one plate is pushed below another, the hard rocks of the crust melt in the hot mantle. Sometimes this melted rock forces its way back upward and bursts through the surface, forming a volcano.

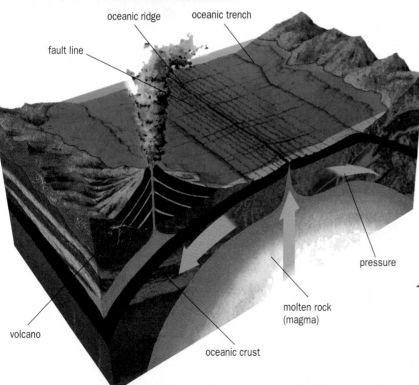

oceanic ridge

oceanic trench

fault line

pressure

volcano

molten rock (magma)

oceanic crust

The changing Earth

200 million years ago

The world consisted of a huge single land mass, Pangaea, which began to break apart slowly. The very biggest dinosaurs roamed the land, and the first birds appeared. Shelled squid, snails, and many kinds of fish lived in the warm seas.

120 million years ago

The breakup of the supercontinent Pangaea produced two smaller landmasses—Laurasia to the north and Gondwanaland to the south. The first flowering plants appeared on the land, and dinosaurs developed spiky horns and body armor.

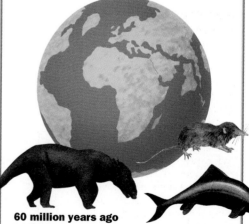

60 million years ago

Laurasia and Gondwanaland eventually broke up to form the seven continents we know today. By this time the last dinosaurs had died out and warm-blooded mammals were becoming common.

Oceans and Seas

SALT WATER COVERS MORE THAN TWO-THIRDS OF Earth's surface. It is contained in the four great oceans (the Pacific, the Atlantic, the Indian, and the Arctic) and in smaller areas of water called seas, as well as in many gulfs and bays.

Teeming with life
The oceans are teeming with life. The huge variety of creatures living in them ranges from the microscopic plankton that float on the water's surface to the mighty blue whale, the largest creature alive today: An adult male can grow up to 100 feet (30 m) long. Most marine life lives near the surface where food supplies are plentiful—only a few creatures survive in the cold, dark depths and on the ocean floor itself.

A moving ocean floor
Oceanographers are scientists who study the sea. They have found that the ocean floor is actually on the move. It is slowly shifting by between $^1/2$ and 4 inches (1.25 and 10 cm) a year. This movement happens because the huge plates that form Earth's crust are constantly on the move, carrying the ocean floor with them. Sometimes the plates drift slowly apart, and new ocean floor forms between them. The floor of the Atlantic Ocean, for instance, is growing wider by about 1 inch (2.5 cm) every year. Something different is happening in the Pacific Ocean—it's shrinking a little each year as two plates collide and one is forced under the other.

▲ Strange-looking giant tube worms cluster around hydrothermal vents on the ocean floor. Hot, black water heated by the hot rocks below the ocean floor pours out of these chimney-like vents on the ocean floor.

continental shelf is the underwater land close to the edge of the continents

What are tides?
When the sea rises up the beach, it is called high tide; when it falls back down the beach, it is known as low tide. In most places there are two high tides and two low tides in every 24-hour period. Tides are caused by the Moon's gravity pulling on Earth and its oceans and seas. This gravity pulls the water upward at places directly below the Moon to create a bulge. At the same time a second bulge forms on the opposite side of Earth. High tide occurs at these two bulges, while at the same time, places in between the bulges have low tide. These two bulges always stay in the same place, one under the Moon and the other on the opposite side of Earth. As Earth is constantly rotating, these tides occur at different places at different times of the day.

Moon

Earth

gravitational pull

tidal bulge (high tide)

low tide

Sun

▲ In warm tropical seas a coral reef is packed with brightly colored coral formations in a mass of different shapes and sizes. The reef itself is formed from the skeletons of the tiny coral animals.

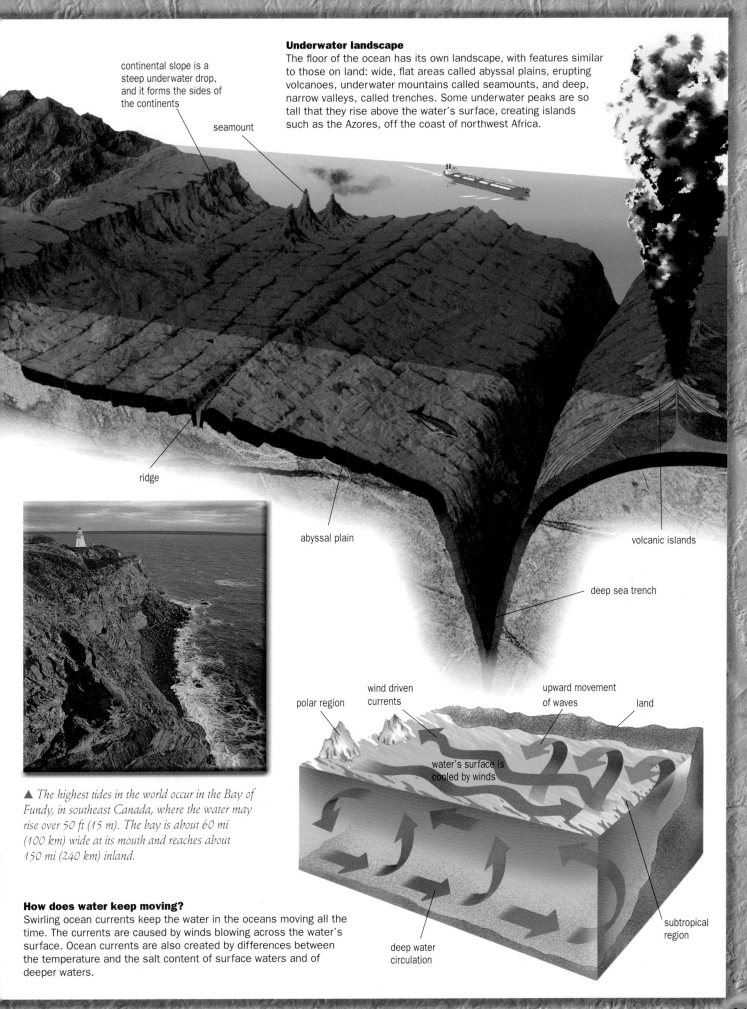

Underwater landscape
The floor of the ocean has its own landscape, with features similar to those on land: wide, flat areas called abyssal plains, erupting volcanoes, underwater mountains called seamounts, and deep, narrow valleys, called trenches. Some underwater peaks are so tall that they rise above the water's surface, creating islands such as the Azores, off the coast of northwest Africa.

continental slope is a steep underwater drop, and it forms the sides of the continents

seamount

ridge

abyssal plain

volcanic islands

deep sea trench

polar region

wind driven currents

upward movement of waves

land

water's surface is cooled by winds

subtropical region

deep water circulation

▲ *The highest tides in the world occur in the Bay of Fundy, in southeast Canada, where the water may rise over 50 ft (15 m). The bay is about 60 mi (100 km) wide at its mouth and reaches about 150 mi (240 km) inland.*

How does water keep moving?
Swirling ocean currents keep the water in the oceans moving all the time. The currents are caused by winds blowing across the water's surface. Ocean currents are also created by differences between the temperature and the salt content of surface waters and of deeper waters.

Weather and Climate

WILL IT RAIN AT TOMORROW'S BASEBALL GAME?
How hot will it be at the beach? Will there be
enough wind to fly a kite this afternoon? All these
are questions about the weather, such as the
rain, sunshine, snow, wind, and storms that
can affect our lives from day to day. The place
we live in usually has the same pattern of
weather over a longer period of time.
However, it may have hot, dry weather in
summer and warm, wet weather in winter.
This usual, or average, pattern of weather
over a longer period of time is called climate.

Climates of the world

What's the climate like where you live? If you live
near the Equator, your climate will be warm or hot.
If you live in the far north of the world, you will
have a cold climate. The position of a place north or
south of the Equator—its latitude—affects its
climate. The height of a place above sea level—its
altitude—and its distance from the ocean also affect
its climate.

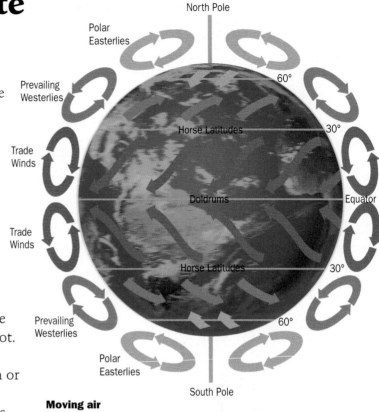

Moving air
The Sun heats the ground unevenly. The air above heated areas
rises, and cooler air flows in to replace the rising hot air. This
movement, or circulation, of air produces winds. Six main belts of
winds blow over large areas of Earth's surface. However there are
areas where there is very little or no wind at all. The doldrums is an
area around the Equator where air only rises instead of moving
across Earth. At 30 degrees north and south of the Equator lie other
areas of very little wind movement. These are the horse latitudes,
so called because many horses died on board sailing ships that
were stalled by lack of wind.

How rain forms
Warm, moist air rises
from the oceans and
seas. When it cools down,
the water vapor condenses into
droplets of water and forms clouds.
The water droplets fall back down to the
ground as rain, sleet, or snow.

Different types of climate
Every place on Earth has its
own climate. Sometimes places
with the same kind of climate
are far away from each other.
For instance, you can find
places where it is hot and rainy
all year round in Brazil, in
central Africa, and in southeast
Asia. Scientists have given
names to the different types of
climate found across the world.
The main types are: polar, wet
temperate, dry temperate,
desert, tropical, and mountain.

- polar
- wet temperate
- dry temperate
- desert
- tropical
- mountain

Heat from the Sun

Because the Earth is curved, different places receive different intensities of heat from the Sun. In tropical places near the Equator, the Sun's rays shine down almost directly overhead, providing lots of heat. As Earth curves round to the north or south, the Sun's rays have to travel farther, and the intensity of heat is reduced. This is why the farther from the Equator you go, the colder it becomes.

Arctic zone
The Sun's rays are weaker when they reach this region in the far north.

Temperate zone
At this angle of Earth's curve, the Sun's rays are more direct.

Tropical zone
The Sun shines almost directly overhead all year round.

▲ Lightning, a giant spark of electricity, flashes across a dark sky during a thunderstorm.

◄ The violent, twisting winds of a tornado can uproot trees, destroy buildings, and suck up large objects such as automobiles, carrying them for hundreds of feet.

The atmosphere

The atmosphere is the layer of gases that surrounds Earth. It contains the gases nitrogen and oxygen, which make up about 99 percent of the atmosphere. The other one percent consists of tiny amounts of argon, carbon dioxide, water vapor, hydrogen, and other gases. The atmosphere protects us from the Sun's harmful rays. At the same time it helps to keep us warm by trapping some of the Sun's heat. Scientists divide the atmosphere into four layers: the troposphere, the stratosphere, the mesosphere, and the thermosphere.

Auroras are flashes of light that occur hundreds of miles above the Earth's surface.

The thermosphere is the upper layer of the atmosphere. Beyond it lies the beginning of space.

The mesosphere reaches about 50 miles (80 km) above Earth's surface. You can see the trails left by meteors, or shooting stars, in this layer.

Within the stratosphere is the ozone layer, which absorbs the Sun's dangerous ultraviolet rays.

The stratosphere reaches about 30 miles (48 km) above the ground. Jet planes fly in this layer to avoid the weather in the troposphere below.

The troposphere is the layer closest to Earth. Most of our weather happens here.

Shaping the Land

THE LANDSCAPE AROUND US IS CONTINUALLY changing—but so slowly that we do not notice. All the time new mountains are being formed, existing ones are changing shape, rocks are being worn away, and new valleys are taking shape.

Making mountains

The giant slow-moving plates of Earth's crust sometimes collide, pushing a section of crust up to form a mountain range. At other times, the crust is squeezed into folds of land thousands of feet high. Many mountain ranges were made hundreds of millions of years ago. The Appalachian Mountains in the United States first formed over 400 million years ago—before the first dinosaurs appeared. The European Alps, in contrast, are young mountains which were still forming just 15 million years ago.

Changing shape

The shape and size of a mountain depend on its age and how it was formed. The shape also depends on how much of it is being worn away.

The land is continually reshaped as rocks are broken up by water, ice, and chemicals in water. This is "weathering." The pieces of rock are then carried from place to place by wind, water, or glaciers. As this material moves, it wears away mountain slopes, changes the shape of rock formations, widens river valleys, and carves out new ones. Rivers and streams carry rock pieces over long distances, wearing away rocks as they flow. In the Grand Canyon, the Colorado River has cut through layers of rocks over millions of years to create a valley which is over one mile (1.6 km) deep in places.

active volcano

vent

layers of lava and ash

Volcanic mountains form when hot molten rock from deep inside Earth bursts through the surface. It cools and becomes solid rock, eventually forming a mountain. Two very famous examples of volcanic mountains are Mount Kilimanjaro in Tanzania and Mount Fuji in Japan.

Fold mountains are created when two plates of Earth's crust collide. The rocky layers crumple and wrinkle, creating wave-like folds of mountains. The Himalayas and the Rocky Mountains were formed in this way.

compression

layers of rock buckle

compression

Glaciers are found in the world's polar regions and in high, mountainous areas. A glacier is a huge mass of compacted ice and snow. Eventually the glacier becomes so thick that it moves under the pressure of its own weight. A glacier collects small rocks while moving downhill, and then deposits them as the ice melts. As it moves, the bottom of the glacier carves the valley into a u-shape. Most glaciers advance about 12 inches (30 cm) a day, but some cover 50 inches (130 cm).

u-shaped valley

snout

crevasses

meltwater

◄ *Sand blown by the wind has eroded this soft rock in Namibia, Africa to create this strange-looking rock shape.*

Block mountains

form when a large block-like area of crust is forced upward along a fault line or between two separate fault lines. This is how California's Sierra Nevada was formed.

fault

tension
block forced up
block forced down

Dome mountains

are made when a section of Earth's crust is pushed up into a dome-shaped bulge. The Black Hills in South Dakota are a good example of dome mountains.

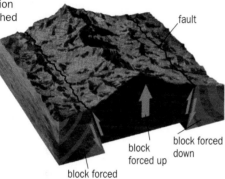

fault

block forced down
block forced up
block forced down

▲ *Young mountains, such as the Alps in central Europe, have towering, jagged peaks, not yet showing signs of erosion.*

▲ *Old mountains usually are more rounded in shape, with gentler and lower slopes. They have been worn down by millions of years of erosion.*

Rock types

Three kinds of rock make up Earth's hard outer layer: igneous rock, sedimentary rock, and metamorphic rock. Although all three kinds are made from the same basic materials, they were formed in different ways.

Igneous

Liquid rock from deep inside Earth slowly cools and hardens to form igneous rock. Sometimes the melted rock bursts onto Earth's surface as lava during a volcanic eruption, before cooling and hardening in the same way.

Granite is an igneous rock made of lots of coarse, colorful grains. Some forms are a pinkish color. Granite is a very strong rock and is often used in buildings—the large number of rosy-pink granite buildings in the Scottish city of Aberdeen have earned it the nickname "Granite City."

granite

Dark-colored basalt is the most common igneous rock on the Earth. It's even found on the flat parts of the Moon's surface!

basalt

Sedimentary

Sedimentary rocks form from the remains of plants and animals that lived on the ocean floor long ago, or from the sand and mud remains of ancient rocks. These remains build up in layers and eventually harden to form solid rock.

Chalky limestone is a sedimentary rock. It is common in seaside cliffs. You can often see the fossilized skeletons and shells of tiny sea creatures in its rocky layers.

limestone

Shale is a fine-grained sedimentary rock formed when mud and clay are squeezed together. We break up shale and use it to make cement and bricks.

shale

Metamorphic

Metamorphic rocks are igneous and sedimentary rocks that have been changed by heat, pressure, or heat and pressure together inside Earth's crust.

Slate is a metamorphic rock formed from shale. It can be split into smooth, thin sheets and used for roof tiles.

slate

Marble is a metamorphic rock formed from limestone. It has many beautiful color variations and is a prized material for buildings, sculptures, monuments, and decorative ornaments.

marble

Water on the Move

RIVERS CONTAIN LESS THAN ONE PERCENT OF ALL the water on Earth's surface, and yet they are an important natural feature. Since ancient times, rivers have supplied us with water for drinking and washing, and watering our crops. They have also provided vital transportation routes, by linking coasts and inland areas. Many towns and cities grew up where bridges had been built to cross the local river. A fast-flowing river can also be used to generate electricity.

Rivers are a powerful force shaping our landscape. During its journey a river erodes the rocks over which it flows, changing the shape of valleys and cutting deep gorges in the land.

From beginning to end

Most rivers have their source, or beginning, in mountains or hills where rain and melted snows collect. Sometimes a number of small streams come together to form a river. Other rivers start where natural underground springs bubble up to the surface, or where the thick ice of a glacier melts. At the beginning, the river is quite shallow, and it may have several steep waterfalls and fast-flowing rapids. The water flows at its fastest speed here, continuously eroding and cutting out a V-shaped valley with steep sides.

Further from the source, the river flows more slowly across a fairly flat area called the floodplain. It snakes from one side of the plain to the other in wide curves called meanders. As the river reaches the sea, it becomes wider and its waters flow even more slowly. Where it joins the sea, huge quantities of transported material are deposited to form a delta, such as the Mississippi Delta.

◀ Huge dams of stone, concrete, or earth are constructed to create artificial lakes, such as Egypt's Lake Nasser. Water from Lake Nasser is used to irrigate farmland and generate electricity.

▲ Tons of silt and sand are carried along by the Colorado River on its 1,450-mi (2,333-km) long course from the Rocky Mountains of Colorado to the Gulf of California.

upper course

middle course

rapids

meander

floodplain

lower course

delta

mouth

◀ A powerful tugboat pushes huge barges on the Mississippi River. These barges carry agricultural products, coal, petroleum, and steel goods.

The river's journey

A river makes a journey, or course, from its source to its mouth, where it finally joins the sea, a lake, or a larger river. The river is fast flowing in the upper course, but it flows more slowly and smoothly during the middle and lower courses.

glacier

stream

The Great Lakes

The biggest group of freshwater lakes in the world—the Great Lakes—make up part of the border between Canada and the United States. The group consists of five lakes. Lake Superior is the world's largest freshwater lake.

Depth of lakes
Superior 1,330 ft (405 m)
Michigan 923 ft (281 m)
Ontario   802 ft (244 m)
Huron   750 ft (229 m)
Erie   210 ft (64 m)

Area of lakes
1 Superior 31,700 sq mi (82,420 sq km)
2 Huron   23,050 sq mi (59,930 sq km)
3 Michigan 22,300 sq mi (57,980 sq km)
4 Erie   9,910 sq mi (25,766 sq km)
5 Ontario   7,550 sq mi (19,630 sq km)

Superior   Michigan   Huron   Erie   Ontario

sinkhole

stalactite

stalagmite

underground stream

Limestone caves

Caves form in areas where the rock is made mostly of limestone. Over thousands of years, water makes its way through cracks in the rock and slowly dissolves the limestone. Underground streams also eat away at the limestone until eventually a hollow cave is created. Stalactites are formations of crystals that hang from the roof of a cave. Stalagmites are pillars of crystallized material that rise up from a cave floor.

▶ *Venezuela's spectacular Angel Falls, flows into the Churún River. It has the longest unbroken drop in the world—a staggering 3,212 ft (979 m).*

What kind of delta?

The Nile Delta forms where the Nile River joins the Mediterranean Sea. (The name comes from the triangle-shaped Greek letter, Δ delta.)

the Nile Delta is shaped like a triangle

At the end of its course the Mississippi River joins the Gulf of Mexico. It divides into several smaller channels, forming a delta shaped like a bird's foot.

the Mississippi Delta is shaped like a bird's foot

Islands and Coastlines

ISLANDS COME IN MANY DIFFERENT SIZES, FROM THE huge ice-capped island of Greenland to tiny uninhabited fragments of rock dotted around the oceans. Although Australia is an island, we usually refer to it as a country, because it is so big. Some countries, such as the Philippines and Indonesia, are made up of thousands of separate islands. Every island is a piece of land surrounded by water.

An island is born

Many islands were formed thousands or even millions of years ago. Some were joined onto a larger piece of land but became separated when the sea level rose—this is how the British Isles were cut off from continental Europe more than 10,000 years ago. Some islands are fragments of land that broke off from continents. Some were formed when the land connecting the island to a continent was worn away—either by waves or by rivers and streams.

Other islands appeared much more recently— and new ones are still made from time to time. In 1963, a new island appeared off the coast of Iceland. The island, called Surtsey, is made of the cooled, hardened lava from a volcano erupting on the seabed. The lava built up in layers until eventually it rose above the water and formed an island.

The changing coast

Around the edges of every piece of land, whether a huge continent or a small island, the action of the sea is constantly changing and reshaping the coastline. Waves cut away rocks that line the shore to form cliffs. In places, so much rock is worn away at the base of a sea cliff that a cave forms. Besides being destructive, the sea can also create. Waves carry broken rocks and sand and deposit them to form ridges of shingle, or small pebbles, called spits.

▲ *When the volcanic eruptions that created Surtsey finally stopped, the island's tip reached more than 644 ft (170 m) above the sea. Surtsey is named after an Icelandic god of fire.*

▲ *More than 40% of the Netherlands was at one time covered by the sea. The Dutch have pumped out the water to "reclaim" the land.*

Continental island
A continental island, such as Greenland, was at some time joined onto a continent.

Volcanic island
A volcanic island is built up from layers of lava deposited on the ocean floor. A curving row of these islands, such as Japan, is known as an island arc.

sand bar   sand dune   shingle spit

stack (rock eroded on either side)   arch through eroded cliff   cave

How an atoll is formed

In warm seas, coral islands are made from the limestone skeletons of millions of tiny coral animals. The skeletons are packed together to form a coral reef. Sometimes a reef grows around the rim of a sinking volcano. Eventually the reef is a complete ring, called an atoll, surrounding an area of water known as a lagoon. Over time, soil collects on parts of the coral reef and plants begin to grow there. The atoll gradually breaks up into small coral islands.

a coral reef grows around the rim of a sinking volcanic land

the reef forms a complete ring called an atoll

the atoll breaks up into small islands of coral

◀ *Some coral islands of the Maldives, in the Indian Ocean, are less than 6 ft (1.8 m) above sea level. If the sea levels around the world were to rise slightly, most of these islands would disappear beneath the ocean.*

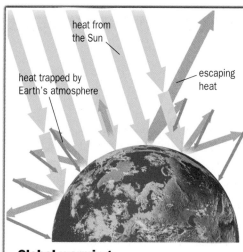

heat from the Sun

heat trapped by Earth's atmosphere

escaping heat

Global warming

Scientists who study Earth's climate have observed that temperatures around the world are gradually increasing. During the 21st century, the temperature of Earth may rise by between 1.8° and 7°F (1°and 3.5°C) above average. Why is this happening?

The gases in the atmosphere help to keep Earth warm by trapping some of the Sun's heat. However, human activities such as burning fossil fuels—coal, oil, and gas—have increased the levels of these gases. The increased gas levels are trapping too much heat, causing Earth's temperature to rise. A hotter planet might cause areas of farmland to turn to desert, and the ice caps around the poles might melt, making sea levels rise—this would flood some islands and low-lying coastal areas.

Coastal features

The continuous action of the oceans—their waves, tides, and currents—reshapes and rebuilds every coastline around the world. In some places material is added, while in others it is worn away. The ocean erodes rocks to form cliffs and caves, and in other places builds up reefs and shingle spits.

salt marsh

cliffs

bay

crest

trough

breaking wave

shore

underwater circulation

Moving waves

The wind causes most of the ocean's waves. Out at sea, the waves break after reaching their biggest height. The longer, smoother waves race towards the shore. The waves break once again towards the shoreline.

Natural Regions

ALL THE PLANTS AND ANIMALS FOUND ON EARTH make up our living world. We already know about more than two million different kinds, or species, of animals and plants—and there may be millions more that we have not yet discovered! The land can be divided into a series of natural regions. Each type of region has its own particular landscape and climate, and the plants and animals found there are typical of that region.

The animals and plants of a particular region have adapted over many, many thousands of years to suit their surroundings. In hot deserts, for example, plants such as the cactus grow thick, fleshy stems that can store water. On cold mountaintops, the thick, hairy coats and sure-footed hooves of wild goats help them to survive in harsh, rugged conditions.

Key to the world's natural regions

mountain	desert	coniferous forest
polar	grassland	tropical forest
tundra	temperate forest	ocean

◀ Mountain
The higher you climb a mountain, the colder it becomes. Above a certain height, which is called the tree line, it becomes too cold even for trees to grow. Many mountain animals have thick fur coats to protect their bodies from the cold surroundings.

▼ Polar
These regions are bitterly cold all year round. Very few animals live in these areas, but those that do are perfectly adapted to their environment.

▶ Tundra
These are very cold areas where the summers are short. Few land animals live here, where the land stays frozen for much of the year. No trees grow, but some mosses, low shrubs, and small wildflowers survive.

▶ Ocean

The ocean is home to more than 13,000 different kinds of fishes, as well as many other animals, from tiny shrimps to large sea mammals, such as seals and whales. Marine plants, which include seaweed, live in the sunlit waters near the surface.

◀ Tropical forest

In tropical rain forests, tall trees grow so close together that little sunlight reaches the forest floor. More kinds of plants and animals live here than in any other kind of natural region.

▼ Coniferous forest

These are made up of evergreen trees, which keep their leaves all year round. In the cold winter months some animals hibernate, which means they sleep much of the winter.

▶ Temperate forest

Most of the trees in a temperate forest are deciduous, which means they lose their leaves in places with cold winters. Some animals hibernate and some survive on stored food during the cold winters, while others travel to warmer places to find food.

▼ Grassland

These are large, open areas where different kinds of grasses grow, providing food for grazing animals. Many grassland areas are now used for growing crops.

▲ Desert

Deserts are usually very hot, dry areas where animals have to find shade to escape from the extreme daytime heat.

The Earth's Resources

THE EARTH PROVIDES US WITH EVERYTHING WE NEED to live on this planet. It gives us fresh water for drinking and washing, and for watering our crops. It provides plants for us to eat and feed for our animals. It gives us materials such as timber and cotton as well as animals to give us milk, meat, wool, and other products. All these are natural resources that should never run out if we look after them carefully—they are renewable. The Earth provides us with other natural resources, too, such as coal, oil, and gas fuels; metals; and precious stones such as diamonds and emeralds. These resources are non-renewable—they do not regrow or reappear, and one day supplies of them will be used up.

The world's energy

Energy resources are some of our most important natural resources. Without them we could not heat and light our homes, travel by train, plane, ship, or automobile, operate machines, have plastic products, and so on. Most of the world's energy comes from coal, oil, and gas. We call these fossil fuels, because they are made from the remains of plants and animals that lived millions of years ago.

Supplies of fossil fuels will run out one day and burning fossil fuels causes serious pollution and contributes to global warming (see page 29). So, people are looking for ways to obtain energy from renewable resources such as solar power, wind power, and hydroelectric power—the energy obtained from flowing water. As supplies of fossil fuels run out, these renewable and less polluting resources will become more and more important.

coal 27%

gas 23%

oil 40%

nuclear 7%

hydroelectric/alternative sources 3%

World energy
Fossil fuels such as oil, coal, and gas will eventually run out. Alternative energy sources are constantly being tested. The pie chart above shows how much of our energy still comes from fossil fuels, and how little is supplied by other sources.

Energy distribution
The map below shows the distribution of fossil fuels around the world.

forestry

grazing for animals

growing crops

meat

quarrying

▲ *Some natural resources, such as salt, are obtained from the sea. Salt mining is a cost-effective way of making use of the sea.*

▲ *Panels of solar cells on the roof of this house turn sunlight into electricity for use in the home and to provide hot water.*

▲ *Large numbers of tall wind turbines, which drive the generators that produce electricity, combine to create a "wind farm."*

▲ *The fertile soils of the prairies of North America have been used to create rich farmland for grazing animals and for growing crops.*

How coal is formed

Dead plant remains collect on the floor of swampy areas. They slowly build up and harden into a thick layer of peat.

The peat layers are buried under deposits of sand and minerals. These sediments press down on the peat.

As more and more layers compress the peat, some of the sediments turn into rock called lignite. The extra pressure from the rocky layers eventually turns the peat into coal.

swamp

peat

lignite

coal

Using the land

The land provides us with a wealth of different natural resources. We should take care to preserve the resources available to us for as long as we can.

mining

wind farms

fishing

World in a Day

ONE WHOLE DAY AND ONE WHOLE NIGHT LAST FOR a total of 24 hours. What happens to you during that time? You get out of bed each morning, go to school, eat your meals, come home and play or watch TV, and then finally go to bed and sleep—all in one 24-hour period. But what is happening in the world around you at the same time? Some truly amazing things can take place on the planet Earth in 24 hours—here are just a few of the things that happen in the world in a day.

▲ **360,187 babies are born and 148,348 people die.**
At least another 25 babies will be born while you are reading this sentence.

◀ **The world's population increases by 211,839.**
The world's population is growing all the time—it has more than doubled in the past 50 years.

▼ **8.5 million tons (7.7 million t) of water evaporate from the Dead Sea, on the border between Israel and Jordan.**
The Dead Sea, the lowest place on the earth's surface, is in fact a lake. This girl, floating in the Dead Sea, is unable to sink because the water is at least nine times more salty than seawater, making it very buoyant.

▲ **1,000 very minor earthquakes occur.**
A "very minor earthquake" measures between 2 and 3 on the scale used to describe the strength of earthquakes, but a "major earthquake" may measure between 7 and 8 and be up to 60 times more powerful.

▶ **45,000 thunderstorms occur, and lightning strikes the earth's surface about 518,400,000 times.**
During a thunderstorm, bright flashes of lightning usually appear in the sky—they are really giant sparks of electricity. Although thunderstorms occur all over the world, they are most frequent in tropical areas.

◀ **102,240 million gallons (464,790 million l) flow over the Victoria Falls.**
Water drops 343 ft (105 m) at the center of the spectacular falls on the Zambezi River, between Zambia and Zimbabwe, southern Africa.

▼ **A bamboo plant can grow 18 in (46 cm).**
Bamboo, much loved by pandas, is a kind of giant grass with strong, hollow stems. In tropical countries it is used to make houses, furniture, mats, and rafts.

▼ **More than 2,000 planes land and take off at Chicago's O'Hare International Airport, one of the busiest in the world, and more than 54,200 Americans travel abroad.**
Passengers can fly from New York to London, for example, in about seven hours—just 60 years ago the same journey took about 24 hours!

▼ **About 2,000 lb (900 kg) of space dust and debris fall onto the earth's surface.**
The dust and debris are probably tiny leftover pieces of the material that originally formed the Moon and the planets.

▼ **6 tons (5.4 t) of meteorites hit the earth.**
A meteorite, a piece of rocky or metallic material from space, has created this giant meteor crater.

▲ **The average person watches four hours of television.**
Americans own more than 220 million TV sets. In our homes, the television is switched on for an average of seven hours each day.

Countries of the World

KEY

1 ALBANIA
2 ANDORRA
3 BOSNIA-HERZEGOVINA
4 CROATIA
5 LIECHTENSTEIN
6 LUXEMBOURG
7 MACEDONIA
8 MOLDOVA
9 MONACO
10 NETHERLANDS
11 SAN MARINO
12 VATICAN CITY
13 SLOVENIA
14 SWITZERLAND
15 YUGOSLAVIA
16 ARMENIA
17 AZERBAIJAN
18 UNITED ARAB EMIRATES
19 KALININGRAD
   (RUSSIAN FEDERATION)

DISCOVER MORE

• *Political maps show the borders of countries, states, or counties. They show capital cities and major centers of population. They may show transportation networks as well. On political maps, coloring may be used to separate one country or region from another.*

World facts

Number of countries	Number of dependencies	Largest country by area sq mi (sq km)	Largest country by population
194	64	Russian Federation 6,592,735 (17,075,184)	China 1,250,066,000

This map of the world is a cylindrical projection

The Physical World

QUEEN ELIZABETH IS

Ellesmere I.

Greenland

BEAUFORT SEA

Baffin Bay

Victoria I.

Baffin I.

BROOKS RANGE

Great Bear L.

Back

Davis Strait

Denma

Mackenzie

Great Slave L.

Yukon

Hudson Bay

Gulf of Alaska

R O C K Y M O U N T A I N S

L. Winnipeg

CANADIAN SHIELD

Newfoundland

ALEUTIAN IS

G r e a t P l a i n

The Great Lakes

Missouri

Mississippi

MID - ATLANTIC

NORTH AMERICA

NORTH ATLANTIC OCEAN

SIERRA MADRE

Rio Grande

Gulf of Mexico

WEST INDIES

HAWAII

MID-AMERICA TRENCH

CARIBBEAN SEA

GALAPAGOS IS

LLANOS

Orinoco

GUIANA HIGHLANDS

MID - A

PACIFIC OCEAN

A N D E S

Amazon

Amazon Basin

SOUTH AMERICA

Selvas

PERU-CHILE TRENCH

BRAZILIAN HIGHLANDS

GRAN CHACO

Pampas

FALKLAND IS

Cape Horn

Antarctic Peninsula

DISCOVER MORE

- *Physical maps can include many details. They show the relief of the land—its height above or below sea level. They show mountain ranges, with the altitude of the highest peaks. They show plains and the courses of rivers. They show coastlines, lakes, islands, and oceans. Coloring may help to indicate the nature of the landscape, with deserts in yellow, or rain forests in dark green.*

World facts			
Circumference of Earth mi (km)	Area of water sq mi (sq km)	Area of land sq mi (sq km)	Largest continent sq mi (sq km)
24,902 (40,075)	139,782,000 (362,033,000)	57,151,000 (148,021,000)	Asia 17,400,000 (45,066,000)

This map of the world is a cylindrical projection

ARCTIC OCEAN

SVALBARD

FRANZ JOSEF LAND

SEVERNAYA ZEMLYA

NOVAYA ZEMLYA

LAPTEV SEA

NEW SIBERIAN IS

EAST SIBERIAN SEA

KARA SEA

BARENTS SEA

NORWEGIAN SEA

Lappland

NORTH SEA

BALTIC SEA

EUROPEAN PLAIN

EUROPE

Drina

Dnieper

Volga

CARPATHIAN MTS

ALPS

Danube

BLACK SEA

MEDITERRANEAN SEA

ATLAS MTS

ARY

Ural

URAL MOUNTAINS

Ob

Irtysh

CASPIAN SEA

ARAL SEA

Turanian Plateau

Siberian Lowland

Ob

Yenisey

Yenisey

Siberian

Central Siberian Plateau

Nizhnyaya Tunguska

Angara

Lena

Lena

Aldan

SEA OF OKHOTSK

BERING SEA

ASIA

SAYAN MTS.

L. Baykal

Gobi Desert

L. Balkhash

TIEN MTS

KUNLAN MTS

Huang

KURIL TRENCH

SEA OF JAPAN

HINDU KUSH

ZAGROS MTS

Euphrates

Tigris

Indus

Tibetan Plateau

HIMALAYA

Ganges

Chang Jiang

EAST CHINA SEA

PACIFIC OCEAN

Sahara Desert

Nubian Desert

Nile

RED SEA

Arabian Peninsula

ARABIAN SEA

DECCAN

Brahmaputra

Bay of Bengal

Irrawaddy

Mekong

SOUTH CHINA SEA

MICRONESIA

PHILIPPINE SEA

Gulf of Aden

AFRICA

Niger

Gulf of Guinea

ETHIOPIAN HIGHLANDS

Uele

Congo

CONGO BASIN

Kasai

GREAT RIFT VALLEY

L. Victoria

MID-INDIAN RIDGE

CELEBES SEA

EAST INDIES

MELANESIA

JAVA TRENCH

OCEANIA

CORAL SEA

SOUTH ATLANTIC OCEAN

Madagascar

INDIAN OCEAN

WALVIS RIDGE

Kalahari Desert

Orange

Great Sandy Desert

Great Victorian Desert

Great Australian Bight

GREAT DIVIDING RANGE

TASMAN SEA

Cape of Good Hope

SOUTHWEST INDIAN RIDGE

SOUTHEAST INDIAN RIDGE

ANTARCTICA

A

B

C

D

E

F

G

ARCTIC

North America

ONE SIGN OF SPRING IN THE UNITED STATES IS THE HONKING of Canada geese flying northward toward the Arctic Circle in wedge-shaped formations. There, in their breeding grounds on the treeless tundra of the far north, the snow and ice are beginning to melt after the long, bitter winter. The flight paths of many migrating birds cross over this continent from the hot, humid Gulf of Mexico to the glaciers of Greenland.

The world's third largest continent includes Canada, the United States of America (with the separate state of Alaska in the northwest), Mexico, and the seven small nations of Central America. It also includes the Danish territory of Greenland (the world's biggest island), and the minuscule French islands of St. Pierre and Miquelon.

From Pacific shore to Atlantic shore, west to east, the land surface crumples. First, there are coastal mountain ranges—Coast, Cascade, Sierra Nevada. Then there is the Great Basin, a strange land of salt lakes and eroded rocks, with deserts extending into Mexico. The massive ranges of the Rockies drop to the Great Plains and the Mississippi–Missouri river system.

Mountains continue southward, with Mexico's Sierra Madre range converging to join the rocky spine that runs through Central America. Northern deserts give way to a natural rain forest zone, which in many areas has been cleared by farmers and ranchers.

BEAUFORT SEA

Alaska (U.S.A.)

Aleutian Is

Kodiak I.

Gulf of Alaska Juneau

Queen Charlotte Is

C   A

PACIFIC OCEAN

UNITED

Gulf of California

Hawaii (U.S.A.)

DISCOVER MORE

• Lake Superior, between Canada and the United States, is the largest body of fresh water in the world. About 200 rivers drain into the lake, and it covers an area of 32,483 sq mi (84,131 sq km).

• The lowest point in North America is Badwater, in Death Valley, California. It lies at 282 ft (86 m) below sea level.

The rocks of the Grand Canyon, in Arizona, have been eroded for a billion years. The world's biggest gorge has been carved out by the Colorado River.

Continent facts

	Area sq mi (sq km)	% of Earth's area	Population	Largest country by area sq mi (sq km)	Largest country by population
North America	9,400,000 (24,346,000)	16.2	475,815,000	Canada 3,851,800 (9,976,162)	U.S.A. 281,421,906

OCEAN

Ellesmere I.

**Greenland
(DENMARK)**

*Baffin
Bay*

Victoria I.

Baffin I.

*LABRADOR
SEA*

*Hudson
Bay*

Belcher Is

C A N A D A

Newfoundland

Where in the world?

Washington, DC to Juneau
2,830 mi (4,554 km)
✈ 5 hr 25 min

3 A.M.   7 A.M.
Juneau   Washington, DC

Search and find

Antigua & Barbuda F10	Jamaica F8
Aruba F9	Juneau C5
Bahamas E8	Martinique F10
Barbados F10	Mexico F6
Belize F7	Montserrat F9
Bermuda E9	Netherlands
Canada C6	Antilles F9
Costa Rica G8	Nicaragua F8
Cuba F8	Panama G8
Dominica F10	Puerto Rico F9
Dominican	St. Kitts & Nevis .F9
Republic F9	St. Lucia F9
El Salvador F7	St. Vincent & the
Greenland A8	Grenadines ...F9
Grenada F9	Trinidad &
Guadeloupe ...F10	Tobago F10
Guatemala F7	U.S.A. D5
Haiti F9	Virgin Islands ...E9
Honduras F8	Washington, DC .D8

*ATLANTIC
OCEAN*

✪ **Washington, DC**

U N I T E D   S T A T E S   O F   A M E R I C A

Bermuda
(U.K.)

1,500 miles

2,000 km

N W E S

*Gulf of
Mexico*

BAHAMAS

CUBA

Virgin Is
(U.K. & U.S.A.)

**ANTIGUA &
BARBUDA**

**DOMINICAN
REPUBLIC**

Puerto
Rico
(U.S.A.)

**ST. KITTS
& NEVIS**
Montserrat
(U.K.)

Guadeloupe
(FRANCE)

DOMINICA

HAITI

Martinique
(FRANCE)

ST. LUCIA

BARBADOS

JAMAICA

**ST. VINCENT &
THE GRENADINES**

GRENADA

MEXICO

*CARIBBEAN
SEA*

Aruba
(NETH.)

Netherlands
Antilles

**TRINIDAD
& TOBAGO**

BELIZE

GUATEMALA

HONDURAS

NICARAGUA

EL SALVADOR

COSTA RICA

PANAMA

*The Canadian national ice hockey
team battles for possession during
the 1998 Winter Olympics.*

United States of America

THE UNITED STATES OF AMERICA is a country that is on the move. Departure boards in airports and bus stations display the names of American towns and cities across six time zones.

The endless traffic flows through the great cities of the east before spreading out along the interstate highway network. Here are the huge green-and-yellow patchwork fields of Nebraska, under a thundery sky. Drivers draw up at a truck stop for a doughnut and a pot of coffee. There are the hills of Wyoming in pale moonlight and the shimmering desert highways of Arizona. And here on the West Coast, traffic crosses San Francisco's Golden Gate Bridge and the freeways of Los Angeles.

Although the United States is the most populous country in the Americas, it still has many areas of wilderness. It is bordered to the east by the Atlantic Ocean and to the west by the Pacific Ocean. To the south, its border with Mexico follows the Rio Grande, whereas most of the northern border with Canada is a straight line ruled straight across the map, rather than a natural feature. Alaska, in the northwest, forms an Arctic outpost, while the volcanic islands of Hawaii lie far to the west in the Pacific Ocean.

The 50 states are home to many different peoples. There are Inuits, Native Americans, and many people with African, European, Asian, or Polynesian roots. English is the first language, but Spanish is widely spoken, and other languages may also be heard.

The Caribbean island of Puerto Rico is self-governing but has especially close links with the United States and is called a Commonwealth Territory.

DISCOVER MORE

• *A road trip across the United States, from the coast of New York to the coast of California, is approximately 3,000 mi (4,828 km).*

• *Nearly one-third of land in the U.S. is protected by the government, including national parks, forests, seashores, and wildlife refuges.*

Country facts

	Area sq mi (sq km)	Population	Language	Religion	Currency
United States	3,717,796 (9,629,092)	281,421,906	English	Protestant/Catholic	Dollar

United States of America

The impressive dome of the Capitol towers over Washington, DC. On its base are inscribed the Latin words E Pluribus Unum—*which means "Out of the Many, One."*

Where in the world?

Washington, DC lies on
38° 54'N latitude
77° 01'W longitude

7 A.M.
Washington, DC

noon
GMT

Life facts

How long do people live?
U.S.A.

76 years

How many people in 100 own cars?

48

MAINE

MINNESOTA

MICHIGAN

VERMONT

WISCONSIN

NEW HAMPSHIRE

NEW YORK

MASSACHUSETTS
RHODE ISLAND
CONNECTICUT

PENNSYLVANIA

Mississippi

IOWA

OHIO

NEW JERSEY

Missouri

INDIANA

Washington, DC

DELAWARE

ILLINOIS

WEST VIRGINIA

MARYLAND

VIRGINIA

MISSOURI

KENTUCKY

ATLANTIC OCEAN

NORTH CAROLINA

ARKANSAS

TENNESSEE

SOUTH CAROLINA

ALABAMA

GEORGIA

MISSISSIPPI

Cape Canaveral

LOUISIANA

FLORIDA

Gulf of Mexico

Florida Keys

1,000 miles

1,500 km

Since 1886 the Statue of Liberty, a gift to the United States from France, has held her torch high above New York City's harbor. Inside, steps allow visitors to climb up to the head.

Search and find

U.S.A.		Missouri	. . . . . .D7
Capital:		Montana	. . . . . .C5
Washington, DC	.C8	Nebraska	. . . . . .C6
Alabama	. . . . . .D7	Nevada	. . . . . .D4
Alaska	. . . . . . .A5	New Hampshire	.C9
Arizona	. . . . . .D4	New Jersey	. . . .C8
Arkansas	. . . . . .D7	New Mexico	. . . .D5
California	. . . . .D4	New York	. . . . . .C8
Colorado	. . . . . .D4	North Carolina	. .D8
Connecticut	. . . .C9	North Dakota	. . .C6
Delaware	. . . . . .C8	Ohio	. . . . .C8
Florida	. . . . .E8	Oklahoma	. . . . .D6
Georgia	. . . . . . .E8	Oregon	. . . . . . .C4
Hawaii	. . . . .F4	Pennsylvania	. . .C8
Idaho	. . . . .C4	Rhode Island	. . .C9
Illinois	. . . . . . .D7	South Carolina	. .D8
Indiana	. . . . . . .C7	South Dakota	. . .C6
Iowa	. . . . .C7	Tennessee	. . . . .D7
Kansas	. . . . . .D6	Texas	. . . . .E6
Kentucky	. . . . . .D7	Utah	. . . . .D4
Louisana	. . . . . .E7	Vermont	. . . . . .C8
Maine	. . . . .B9	Virginia	. . . . . .D8
Maryland	. . . . . .D8	Washington	. . . .C4
Massachusetts	.C9	West Virginia	. . .D8
Michigan	. . . . . .C7	Wisconsin	. . . . .C7
Minnesota	. . . . .C6	Wyoming	. . . . . .C5
Mississippi	. . . .E7		

United States: The Northeast

New York, Maine, Vermont, New Hampshire, Massachusetts, Connecticut, Rhode Island

Soaring skyscrapers have dominated Manhattan for over a hundred years. This island forms the center of New York City.

New York City has more skyscrapers than any other city in the world. Their sheer walls divide the island of Manhattan, flanked by the East River and the Hudson River, into canyons of glass and steel. Here is Wall Street, the financial center of the United States, and also the theater lights of Broadway. In winter the streets may be filled with swirling snow, in summer they may swelter in a heat wave. New York City is home to 7.4 million people. To the west lies the rolling green farmland of New York State, bordered to the west by two of the Great Lakes, Ontario and Erie.

The northeastern states take in the Allegheny Mountains, one of the Appalachian ranges, and the rocky coasts of the North Atlantic Ocean. Large areas are covered with birch and maple forests, which are spectacular in the fall as the leaves turn to red and gold. The six most northeasterly states are often referred to as New England. They extend from the forests and tidal pools of Maine to the trim wooden houses and white churches of historical Massachusetts and the city of Boston, to the shores of Rhode Island and Connecticut.

New Hampshire and Vermont sit between these states, and are both known for their scenic beauty. Their snow-covered mountains attract thousands of skiers during the winter months.

DISCOVER MORE

• *Each day in the United States begins in Maine. As the easternmost American state, it is always the first to see the sunrise.*

• *Approximately 202,000 cu ft (5,720 cu m) per second of water is harnessed to generate electricity at the American and the Horseshoe falls on the Niagara River in Canada.*

New York

Maine

Vermont

New Hampshire

Massachusetts

Connecticut

Rhode Island

State facts

	Area sq mi (sq km)	Population	Flower	Tree	Bird
New York	53,989 (139,832)	18,976,457	Rose	Sugar maple	Bluebird
Maine	33,741 (87,389)	1,274,923	White pinecone/tassel	Eastern white pine	Chickadee
Vermont	9,615 (24,903)	608,827	Red clover	Sugar maple	Hermit thrush
New Hampshire	9,283 (24,043)	1,235,786	Purple lilac	White birch	Purple finch
Massachusetts	9,241 (23,934)	6,349,097	Mayflower	American elm	Chickadee
Connecticut	5,544 (14,359)	3,405,565	Mountain laurel	White oak	Robin
Rhode Island	1,231 (3,188)	1,048,319	Violet	Red maple	Rhode Island red

A

B

C

D

E

F

G

Many lighthouses were built to guide shipping through shoals off Cape Cod, Massachusetts.

Where in the world?

7 A.M. Washington, DC 7 A.M. Augusta noon GMT

Washington, DC to Augusta
531 mi (855 km)
1 hr

Augusta lies on
44° 20'N latitude
69° 44'W longitude

Presque Isle

MAINE

Penobscot

Bangor

Mt Washington
6,288 ft
(1,917 m)

Augusta

Lewiston

Portland

NEW
HAMPSHIRE

NORTH
ATLANTIC
OCEAN

200 miles

300 km

Concord

Portsmouth

Manchester

Nashua

Salem

Boston

Cape Cod

Worcester

Springfield

MASSACHUSETTS

Providence

Hartford

RHODE ISLAND

New
Haven

CONNECTICUT

Bridgeport

Long I.

New York City

The lush New England landscape of Vermont is the perfect environment for cattle farming. Cattle are kept for meat and milk.

Acadia National Park lies on the Atlantic coast of Maine. This is a wild land of forests, lakes, and tidal pools.

Life facts

What percentage of people?	How many people per sq mi (sq km)?
U.S.A. 71.4 12.8 11.8 4.1 0.9	75 (29)
New York 64.1 18.2 15.4 5.7 0.4	384 (148)
Maine 97.6 0.4 0.6 0.7 0.5	41 (16)
Vermont 97.2 0.3 1.0 1.0 0.3	64 (26)
New Hampshire 96.7 0.7 0.5 1.1 0.2	136 (53)
Massachusetts 83.6 6.7 7.0 4.0 0.2	791 (305)
Connecticut 79.8 9.8 8.7 2.4 0.2	678 (262)
Rhode Island 85.3 5.4 7.6 2.8 0.4	955 (369)

White Black Hispanic Asian Other/American Indian

Search and find

New York
State Capital:
Albany D6
Buffalo D4
New York City . . .E6
Niagara Falls . . .D4
Rochester D4
Schenectady . . .D6
Syracuse D5
Troy D6
Utica D5
Watertown D5

Maine
State Capital:
Augusta C7
Bangor C7
Lewiston C7
Portland C7
Presque Isle . . .B7

Vermont
State Capital:
Montpelier . . .C6
Burlington C6

New Hampshire
State Capital:
Concord D7
Manchester D7
Nashua D7
Portsmouth D7

Massachusetts
State Capital:
Boston D7
Salem D7
Springfield D6
Worcester D7

Connecticut
State Capital:
Hartford D6
Bridgeport E6
New Haven D6

Rhode Island
State Capital:
Providence D7

United States: Mid-Atlantic

PENNSYLVANIA, MARYLAND, NEW JERSEY, DELAWARE, WASHINGTON, DC

SOUTH OF NEW YORK STATE, the New Jersey coastline is surrounded by sand dunes and wetlands. The eastern part is densely populated, with major cities such as Trenton and Newark.

The coastal plain rises, continuing into neighboring Pennsylvania, beyond the Delaware River. This land of woods and waterways became one of the first industrial states, a great center of coal mining and steel manufacturing. Its chief cities are the industrial center of Pittsburgh and historic Philadelphia, the great seaport where the original thirteen colonies declared their independence from Britain in 1776.

On the Atlantic seaboard, Maryland is a small state bordering the Chesapeake Bay, which bites deep into the coastal plain, creating the long Delmarva peninsula (shared by the small states of Delaware, Maryland, and Virginia). This coast is famous for its clams and crabs. Its chief port is Baltimore.

The federal capital, Washington, occupies its own territory on the Potomac River, the District of Columbia (DC). It is dominated by the great dome of the Capitol building, the meeting place for Congress. Here, too, is the White House, the official residence of the President.

A Pittsburgh welder sets the sparks flying. In the 1800s, Pittsburgh was the world's biggest steel-producing city. It remains a major industrial center, but many of its mills and chimneys have been replaced by modern skyscrapers and green parkland.

The Amish live in Pennsylvania and the Midwest where they farm land in the traditional way and use no modern machinery.

Pennsylvania

Maryland

New Jersey   Delaware   Washington, DC

DISCOVER MORE

• *Maryland has one of the most irregular state borders in the whole country. It runs across a peninsula, around headlands and coastal inlets, and follows the course of winding rivers.*

• *The world's biggest library is in Washington, DC. The Library of Congress has more than 95 million books.*

State facts

	Area sq mi (sq km)	Population	Flower	Tree	Bird
Pennsylvania	46,058 (119,290)	12,281,054	Mountain laurel	Hemlock	Ruffed grouse
Maryland	12,297 (31,849)	5,296,486	Black-eyed Susan	White oak	Baltimore oriole
New Jersey	8,215 (21,277)	8,414,350	Purple violet	Red oak	Eastern goldfinch
Delaware	2,396 (6,206)	783,600	Peach blossom	American holly	Blue hen chicken
Washington, DC	70 (181)	572,059	Western rhododendron	Western hemlock	Willow goldfinch

100 miles

150 km

W N E W   Y O R K
P E N N S Y L V A N I A
Scranton
Paterson
Newark
Jersey City
Allentown
Trenton
Reading
NEW JERSEY
Harrisburg
Philadelphia
Wilmington
Vineland Atlantic City
Baltimore
Dover Delaware Bay
MARYLAND
Annapolis DELAWARE
★ DC
Washington
VIRGINIA
Chesapeake Bay
Potomac
Susquehanna
Delaware
APPALACHIAN MTS
VIRGINIA

Where in the world?

7 A.M. Washington, DC
7 A.M. Philadelphia
noon GMT

Washington, DC to Philadelphia
126 mi (203 km)
15 min

Philadelphia lies on
40° 00′N latitude
75° 08′W longitude

Life facts

What percentage of people?	How many people per sq mi (sq km)?
U.S.A.	
71.4 12.8 11.8 4.1 0.9	75 (29)
Pennsylvania	
85.7 10.0 2.7 1.8 0.1	272 (105)
Maryland	
63.9 28.2 4.1 4.2 0.2	540 (208)
New Jersey	
68.0 15.2 12.8 5.8 0.2	1,102 (426)
Delaware	
75.8 19.1 3.3 2.0 0.3	388 (150)
Washington, DC	
29.1 61.4 7.6 2.9 0	8,574 (3,289)

White Black Hispanic Asian Other/American Indian

The lights of Baltimore's skyline and inner harbor seen at dusk. It is one of the country's busiest ports.

The Delaware River winds through a wooded valley in Pennsylvania and mountains in New Jersey. The Delaware Water Gap is a popular recreation area.

Search and find

Pennsylvania
State Capital:
Harrisburg . . .C7
Allentown C8
Erie B5
Philadelphia . . .C8
Pittsburgh C6
Reading C8
Scranton B8

Maryland
State Capital:
Annapolis D8
Baltimore D8

New Jersey
State Capital:
Trenton C9
Atlantic City C9
Jersey City B9
Newark B9
Paterson B9
Vineland C9

Delaware
State Capital:
Dover D8
Wilmington C8

District of Columbia
Capital:
Washington . .D8

United States: The South

FLORIDA, GEORGIA, ARKANSAS, NORTH CAROLINA, ALABAMA, LOUISIANA, MISSISSIPPI, VIRGINIA, TENNESSEE, KENTUCKY, SOUTH CAROLINA, WEST VIRGINIA

SOUTH OF THE CHESAPEAKE Bay, the pounding of Atlantic breakers has created a long chain of sandy beaches, flanked by offshore islands and lagoons, that extend from Virginia to the Florida Keys. Coastal plains and plateaus rise to form the ranges of the Appalachian Mountains.

The estuaries of four rivers cut through the state of Virginia, which has large industrial centers in Richmond and Norfolk. Beyond the mountains lies West Virginia, a land of whitewater rivers and forests.

Farther south, the Atlantic coast passes through the humid lands of North and South Carolina, and Georgia. Hills, waterways, and woodlands stretch west through Tennessee and Kentucky. The fertile farmland of the South produces peanuts, tobacco, and cotton. Atlanta, Georgia, is a major business center.

The sunny, palm-fringed state of Florida stretches south to Key West, attracting tourists from all over the world. Alligators and snakes are among the creatures that live in the wetlands of The Everglades.

The southernmost states line the oil-rich Gulf of Mexico. This thundery coastline is indented by creeks, bayous, and the maze of the Mississippi Delta. New Orleans, Louisiana, lies on the east bank of the Mississippi River, shielded from floodwater by high walls, called levees. About half of the land in Louisiana is covered by forests.

Florida

Georgia

Arkansas

North Carolina

Alabama

Louisiana

Mississippi

Virginia

Tennessee

Kentucky

South Carolina

West Virginia

DISCOVER MORE

• *Giant dunes and huge waves are a feature of the Outer Banks, a long spit of sand on the North Carolina coast. This part of the coast has seen so many shipwrecks that it is sometimes called "the Graveyard of the Atlantic."*

State facts

	Area sq mi (sq km)	Population	Flower	Tree	Bird
Florida	59,928 (155,214)	15,982,378	Orange blossom	Sabal palmetto palm	Mockingbird
Georgia	58,977 (152,750)	8,186,453	Cherokee rose	Live oak	Brown thrasher
Arkansas	53,182 (137,741)	2,673,400	Apple blossom	Pine	Mockingbird
North Carolina	52,672 (136,420)	8,049,313	Dogwood	Pine	Cardinal
Alabama	52,237 (135,294)	4,447,100	Camellia	Southern longleaf pine	Yellowhammer
Louisiana	49,651 (128,596)	4,468,976	Magnolia	Cypress	Eastern brown pelican
Mississippi	48,286 (125,061)	2,844,658	Magnolia	Magnolia	Mockingbird
Virginia	42,326 (109,624)	7,078,515	Dogwood	Dogwood	Cardinal
Tennessee	42,146 (109,158)	5,689,283	Iris	Tulip poplar	Mockingbird
Kentucky	40,411 (104,664)	4,041,769	Goldenrod	Tulip poplar	Cardinal
South Carolina	31,189 (80,780)	4,012,012	Yellow jessamine	Palmetto	Carolina wren
West Virginia	24,231 (62,758)	1,808,344	Big rhododendron	Sugar maple	Cardinal

A
B
C
D
E
F
G

NSYLVANIA

MARYLAND

Morgantown

Richmond

VIRGINIA • Norfolk

Roanoke

ensboro • Durham

Raleigh

Outer Banks

Cape Hatteras

Winston-Salem

NORTH CAROLINA

Charlotte • Wilmington

Columbia Cape Fear

OUTH CAROLINA

Charleston

Savannah

ATLANTIC OCEAN

Jacksonville

St. Augustine

Daytona Beach

rlando Cape Canaveral

FLORIDA

Tampa

Petersburg L. Okeechobee

West Palm Beach

Fort Myers Fort Lauderdale

Naples • Miami

The Everglades

ey West Florida Keys

raits of Florida

200 miles

300 km

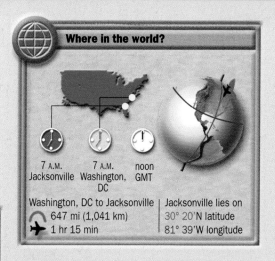

Where in the world?

7 A.M.
Jacksonville

7 A.M.
Washington, DC

noon
GMT

Washington, DC to Jacksonville
647 mi (1,041 km)
1 hr 15 min

Jacksonville lies on
30° 20'N latitude
81° 39'W longitude

A space shuttle is attached to the rocket's side as it takes off from John F. Kennedy Space Center, on Florida's Cape Canaveral.

Search and find

Florida
State Capital:
Tallahassee . . .C6
Clearwater D6
Daytona Beach . .D6
Fort Lauderdale .D7
Fort Myers D6
Jacksonville C6
Key West E7
Miami D7
Naples D6
Orlando D6
Pensacola D5
St. Augustine . . .C6
St. Petersburg . .D6
Tampa D6
West Palm
  Beach D7

Georgia
State Capital:
Atlanta C5
Albany C5
Augusta C6
Columbus C5
Macon C6
Savannah C6

Arkansas
State Capital:
Little Rock . . .C4
El Dorado C4
Fort Smith B3
Hot Springs C3
Pine Bluff C4

North Carolina
State Capital:
Raleigh B7
Charlotte B6
Durham B7
Greensboro B6
Wilmington B7
Winston-Salem . .B6

Alabama
State Capital:
Montgomery . .C5
Birmingham C5
Huntsville B5
Mobile D5

Louisiana
State Capital:
Baton Rouge . .D4
Alexandria C4
Lafayette D4
Lake Charles . . .D3
New Orleans . . .D4
Shreveport C3

Mississippi
State Capital:
Jackson C4
Biloxi D4
Greenville C4
Hattiesburg C4
Meridian C4
Natchez C4

Virginia
State Capital:
Richmond A7
Norfolk A7
Roanoke A6

Tennessee
State Capital:
Nashville B5
Chattanooga . . .B5
Clarksville B5
Johnson City . . .B6
Knoxville B5
Memphis B4

Kentucky
State Capital:
Frankfort A5
Lexington B5
Louisville B5
Owensboro B5
Paducah B4

South Carolina
State Capital:
Columbia B6
Charleston C6
Greenville B6

West Virginia
State Capital:
Charleston . . .C6
Huntington A6
Morgantown A6
Wheeling A6

Life facts

What percentage of people?   **How many people per sq mi (sq km)?**

U.S.A.
71.4   12.8   11.8   4.1   0.9   75 (29)

Florida
68.3   15.3   15.7   1.8   0.3   282 (109)

Georgia
66.9   28.9   2.4   1.8   0.2   134 (52)

Arkansas
81.9   15.5   1.3   0.7   0.6   50 (19)

North Carolina
73.9   22.3   1.6   1.2   1.2   160 (62)

Alabama
72.5   25.5   0.8   0.8   0.4   88 (34)

Louisiana
63.1   32.7   2.7   1.4   0.5   102 (39)

Mississippi
62.3   35.9   0.7   0.7   0.3   59 (23)

Virginia
72.3   20.2   3.8   3.8   0.3   177 (68)

Tennessee
81.4   16.4   1.0   1.0   0.2   137 (53)

Kentucky
93.6   7.2   0.8   0.7   0.2   67 (26)

South Carolina
68.0   30.0   1.1   0.9   0.2   128 (50)

West Virginia
95.4   3.2   0.6   0.6   0.1   76 (29)

White   Black   Hispanic   Asian   Other/American Indian

United States: The Southwest

TEXAS, NEW MEXICO, ARIZONA, OKLAHOMA

TEXAS IS THE BIGGEST AMERICAN state after Alaska. It borders the steamy Gulf of Mexico, the Rio Grande, and the hot, dusty, short-grass plain, which extends into New Mexico. Some Texans have become wealthy through the production of oil and by running cattle ranches. Many Texans wear traditional cowboy boots, belt, and a broad-brimmed Stetson hat, even though they may live in a large, modern city such as San Antonio, Houston, or Dallas.

North across the Red River lies Oklahoma, another state that built its economy on cattle and oil. Most of its population work as farmers, and wheat is the chief crop.

Neighboring New Mexico is a sunny state with deserts of glistening white sand in the south and mountains in the north. Many people work in the mining industry.

Westward again, the climate becomes hotter and drier, but dams and irrigation systems make it possible to grow cotton, grains, and fruit in some areas. Southern Arizona is a land covered in thorny scrub and saguaro, the world's biggest cactus. Ancient rock dwellings may still be seen across this land. They were once inhabited by a Native American people known as the Anasazi. South of Phoenix, in Arizona, desert stretches over the Mexican border.

The southwestern states are home to many people of Mexican origin and to Native American peoples such as the Apache and the Navajo.

Much of the Arizona landscape is arid. Annual rainfall at Yuma is just 3 in (7.5 cm) compared to Hawaii which receives as much as 200 in (508 cm) on the mountaintops and 25 in (64 cm) on the lowlands.

DISCOVER MORE

• *The Carlsbad Caverns in New Mexico are home to millions of bats. At sundown they swarm out of Bat Cave, forming a great, dark cloud.*

• *The Grand Canyon is the world's largest gorge, eroded from the plateau lands of northern Arizona by the Colorado River. It is 217 mi (349 km) long, between 3 and 15 mi (8 and 25 km) wide, and in places drops 6,230 ft (1,900 m).*

Texas · New Mexico · Arizona · Oklahoma

State facts

	Area sq mi (sq km)	Population	Flower	Tree	Bird
Texas	267,277 (692,247)	20,851,820	Bluebonnet	Pecan	Mockingbird
New Mexico	121,598 (314,939)	1,819,046	Yucca	Piñon	Roadrunner
Arizona	114,006 (295,276)	5,130,632	Blossom of the saguaro cactus	Paloverde	Cactus wren
Oklahoma	69,903 (181,049)	3,450,654	Mistletoe	Redbud	Scissor-tailed flycatcher

COLORADO · KANSAS · MISSOURI · ARKANSAS · LOUISIANA

North Canadian · Cimarron

Santa Fe · Enid · Ponca City · Tulsa

Elk City · Oklahoma City · Muskogee

Amarillo · OKLAHOMA

NEW MEXICO · Lawton · Norman · Durant

Clovis · Lubbock · Wichita Falls · Red

Roswell · Dallas · Longview

Hobbs · Fort Worth · Tyler · Sabine

Carlsbad · Midland · T E X A S · Trinity

Guadalupe Peak 8,751 ft (2,667 m) · Odessa · Abilene · Waco · Leon

Pecos · San Angelo · Brazos · Beaumont

Edwards Plateau · Colorado · Port Arthur

Rio Grande · Austin · Houston

Del Rio · San Antonio · Galveston

Laredo · Corpus Christi · Gulf of Mexico

Brownsville

Where in the world?

6 A.M. Houston | 7 A.M. Washington, DC | noon GMT

Washington, DC to Houston
🔄 1,221 mi (1,965 km)
✈ 2 hr 20 min

Houston lies on
29° 46'N latitude
95° 23'W longitude

200 miles

300 km

Search and find

Texas
State Capital:
  Austin C8
Abilene C8
Amarillo B7
Beaumont C9
Brownsville E8
Corpus Christi ..D8
Dallas C8
Del Rio D7
El Paso C6
Fort Worth C8
Galveston D9
Houston C9
Laredo D8
Longview C9
Lubbock B7
Midland C7
Odessa C7
Pecos C7
Port Arthur C9
San Angelo C7
San Antonio D8
Tyler C9
Waco C8
Wichita Falls ...B8

New Mexico
State Capital:
  Santa Fe B6
Albuquerque ...B6
Carlsbad C6

Clovis B7
Deming C5
Farmington ...A5
Gallup B5
Hobbs C7
Las Cruces C6
Los Alamos B6
Roswell B6
Silver City C5

Arizona
State Capital:
  Phoenix B4
Douglas C5
Flagstaff B5
Mesa B4
Prescott B4
Tucson C5
Winslow B5
Yuma B4

Oklahoma
State Capital:
  Oklahoma City B8
Durant B8
Elk City B8
Enid B8
Lawton B8
Muskogee B9
Norman B8
Ponca City B8
Tulsa B8

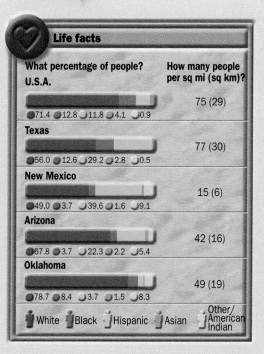

Life facts

What percentage of people? | **How many people per sq mi (sq km)?**

U.S.A.
71.4 · 12.8 · 11.8 · 4.1 · 0.9 | 75 (29)

Texas
56.0 · 12.6 · 29.2 · 2.8 · 0.5 | 77 (30)

New Mexico
49.0 · 3.7 · 39.6 · 1.6 · 9.1 | 15 (6)

Arizona
67.8 · 3.7 · 22.3 · 2.2 · 5.4 | 42 (16)

Oklahoma
78.7 · 8.4 · 3.7 · 1.5 · 8.3 | 49 (19)

White · Black · Hispanic · Asian · Other/American Indian

Texas has become rich producing more oil than any other state in the United States.

United States: The Midwest

MINNESOTA, KANSAS, NEBRASKA, SOUTH DAKOTA,
NORTH DAKOTA, MISSOURI, IOWA

Alaska

United States

Hawaii

A PICKUP TRUCK BOUNCES along a farm track, crossing wide, flat fields planted with soybeans and corn. The farmer eyes the sky anxiously, for it is early summer, and the radio forecasts twisters. These tornadoes are dark, funnel-like whirlwinds that can lift the roof off a barn. Summers are hot but stormy. Winters can be very cold, with heavy snowfalls.

From the Mississippi River west to Wyoming and Montana is a vast, sloping plateau called the Great Plains. Short grasses are the natural vegetation of the dry west, but longer grasses have always grown in the east, where the rainfall is higher. The grasslands, which form part of the North American prairies, extend northward across Canada and have become one of the world's "breadbaskets," or key grain-producing regions. The prairie is rich with wildlife, such as the North American bison (or buffalo) and burrowing rodents called prairie dogs.

In St. Louis, Missouri, is the Midwest's most famous landmark, a graceful 630-feet (192-m) high arc of steel called the Gateway Arch. Westward lie the agricultural states of Iowa, Kansas, and Nebraska.

Minnesota, on the shores of Lake Superior, is known for its dairy farms and is one of the country's main milk-producers. On the sparsely populated prairies of North and South Dakota, cattle are raised.

CANADA

Williston   Minot   Grand Forks   *Red Lake*

L. Sakakawea   MINNE

NORTH DAKOTA

MONTANA

Bismarck   Jamestown   Fargo   Moorhead

Aberdeen

SOUTH DAKOTA

Rapid City

Watertown

Mount Rushmore   Cheyenne   Pierre

White   Sioux Falls

WYOMING

Minneapoli

Minnesota

IO

Missouri

Sioux City   Des Moin

NEBRASKA

North Platte   North Platte   Grand Island   Omaha   Council Bluffs

Platte   Lincoln

COLORADO   Republican   St. Joseph

Kansas   Kansa City

Hays   Salina   Topeka

KANSAS   Arkansas   Hutchinson

Cimarron   Dodge City   Wichita

OKLAHOMA

DISCOVER MORE

• *In most years, the United States can expect over 900 tornadoes, or "twisters." They are created by warm air from the Gulf of Mexico meeting cool air from the Rocky Mountains over the Great Plains. Front-line states in "Tornado Alley" include Kansas, Nebraska, Iowa, Missouri, and many in the South and Southwest.*

St. Louis's Gateway Arch rises above the lights of the city reflected in the water at night.

Mount Rushmore, in South Dakota, has been carved into gigantic rock face portraits of U.S. presidents— George Washington, Thomas Jefferson, Theodore Roosevelt, and Abraham Lincoln.

WISCONSIN

Duluth

St. Paul

Rochester

IOWA

Waterloo

Cedar Rapids

Davenport

Des Moines

ILLINOIS

Columbia

St. Louis

Jefferson City

MISSOURI

Cape Girardeau

Springfield

ARKANSAS

Life facts

What percentage of people? | **How many people per sq mi (sq km)?**

U.S.A.
71.4 · 12.8 · 11.8 · 4.1 · 0.9 — 75 (29)

Minnesota
90.8 · 3.3 · 2.0 · 2.9 · 1.3 — 61 (23)

Kansas
85.9 · 6.4 · 5.2 · 1.9 · 1.0 — 33 (13)

Nebraska
90.3 · 4.2 · 3.6 · 1.3 · 0.9 — 22 (9)

South Dakota
89.8 · 0.6 · 1.0 · 0.6 · 7.7 — 10 (4)

North Dakota
92.3 · 0.8 · 0.9 · 0.9 · 4.8 — 10 (4)

Missouri
85.6 · 11.3 · 1.6 · 1.1 · 0.4 — 80 (31)

Iowa
94.4 · 2.1 · 1.9 · 1.4 · 0.3 — 52 (20)

White · Black · Hispanic · Asian · Other/American Indian

Where in the world?

6 A.M. Minneapolis | 7 A.M. Washington, DC | noon GMT

Washington, DC to Minneapolis
934 mi (1,503 km)
1 hr 50 min

Minneapolis lies on
44° 58'N latitude
93° 16'W longitude

Search and find

Minnesota
State Capital:
St. Paul B6
Duluth B6
Minneapolis B6
Moorhead B5
Rochester C6

Kansas
State Capital:
Topeka D6
Dodge City E4
Hays D5
Hutchinson E5
Salina D5
Wichita E5

Nebraska
State Capital:
Lincoln D5
Grand Island . . .D5
North Platte D4
Omaha D5

South Dakota
State Capital:
Pierre C4
Aberdeen B5
Rapid City C4
Sioux Falls C5

Watertown C5

North Dakota
State Capital:
Bismarck B4
Fargo B5
Grand Forks B5
Jamestown B5
Minot B4
Williston B4

Missouri
State Capital:
Jefferson City .D7
Cape Girardeau .E7
Columbia D7
Kansas City D6
Springfield E6
St. Joseph D6
St. Louis D7

Iowa
State Capital:
Des Moines . .D6
Cedar Rapids . . .C7
Council Bluffs . .D7
Davenport C7
Sioux City C5
Waterloo C6

200 miles

300 km

 Minnesota
 Kansas
 Nebraska
 South Dakota
 North Dakota
 Missouri
 Iowa

State facts

	Area sq mi (sq km)	Population	Flower	Tree	Bird
Minnesota	86,943 (225,182)	4,919,479	Pink and white lady's slipper	Red pine	Common loon
Kansas	82,282 (213,110)	2,688,418	Native sunflower	Cottonwood	Western meadowlark
Nebraska	77,358 (200,357)	1,711,263	Goldenrod	Cottonwood	Western meadowlark
South Dakota	77,121 (199,743)	754,844	Pasqueflower	Black Hills spruce	Chinese red-necked pheasant
North Dakota	70,704 (183,123)	642,200	Wild prairie rose	American elm	Western meadowlark
Missouri	69,709 (180,546)	5,959,211	Hawthorn	Dogwood	Bluebird
Iowa	56,276 (145,755)	2,926,324	Wild rose	Oak	Eastern goldfinch

United States: Great Lakes

MICHIGAN, WISCONSIN, ILLINOIS, OHIO, INDIANA

CHICAGO IS CALLED "THE Windy City" because strong winds blowing off Lake Michigan are funneled around its gigantic skyscrapers. The Great Lakes form a body of water about 98,185 square miles (245,300 sq km) in area. They were scooped out of the continent by movements of ice in prehistoric times. Michigan is the only lake lying entirely within the United States. Superior, Huron, Erie, and Ontario all form part of the U.S.-Canadian border.

The shores of the Great Lakes include bluffs topped by sand dunes, weathered rocks, forest, and farmland. Here, too, are large industrial cities such as Detroit, nicknamed "Motor City" for being the center of the U.S. automobile industry, and the port of Cleveland.

Ohio has long been a center of manufacturing, but the western part of the state consists largely of wooded countryside and farmland. In Indiana there are steel mills along the shores of Lake Michigan, wide fields of corn, and rolling hills on the Kentucky border. Wisconsin is crossed by rivers and streams and dotted with thousands of small lakes. It is a major center of dairy farming, producing milk, butter, and cheese.

The Great Lakes region has been the center of the U.S. car industry since its early days. It was in the factories of Detroit that production-line methods of manufacturing were first developed.

200 miles

300 km

DISCOVER MORE

• Winds in Illinois can change temperatures by as much as 20°F (11°C) in an hour.

• Isle Royale is the largest island in Lake Superior, and the wildest spot in the region, home to timber wolves, moose, and beaver.

State facts

	Area sq mi (sq km)	Population	Flower	Tree	Bird
Michigan	96,705 (250,465)	9,938,444	Apple blossom	White pine	Robin
Wisconsin	65,499 (169,642)	5,363,675	Wood violet	Sugar maple	Robin
Illinois	57,918 (150,007)	12,419,293	Native violet	White oak	Cardinal
Ohio	44,828 (116,104)	11,353,140	Scarlet carnation	Buckeye	Cardinal
Indiana	36,420 (94,327)	6,080,485	Peony	Tulip poplar	Cardinal

A

B

C

D

E

F

G

The Chicago River, an inlet of Lake Michigan, runs through the heart of the city. It is crossed by a series of bridges and tunnels. It divides Chicago into a North Side, a West Side, and a South Side.

Where in the world?

7 A.M. Detroit

7 A.M. Washington, DC

noon GMT

Washington, DC to Detroit
400 mi (643 km)
✈ 45 min

Detroit lies on
42° 23'N latitude
83° 06'W longitude

Huron
Saginaw
Port Huron
Flint
Detroit
Ann Arbor
Toledo   Cleveland   Akron
PENNSYLVANIA
L. Erie
O H I O
Columbus
Dayton
Cincinnati
Ohio
WEST VIRGINIA

The Ohio River forms the southern borders of Ohio, Indiana, and Illinois, and the northern borders of West Virginia and Kentucky.

Michigan

Wisconsin

Illinois

Ohio

Indiana

Life facts

What percentage of people?	How many people per sq mi (sq km)?
U.S.A.	75 (29)
71.4 12.8 11.8 4.1 0.9	
Michigan	167 (64)
80.4 14.8 2.7 1.7 0.6	
Wisconsin	95 (37)
88.8 6.1 2.6 1.8 0.9	
Illinois	217 (84)
71.0 15.4 10.5 3.5 0.2	
Ohio	276 (107)
85.4 11.7 1.6 1.2 0.2	
Indiana	169 (65)
88.3 8.3 2.3 1.0 0.3	

White   Black   Hispanic   Asian   Other/American Indian

Search and find

Michigan
State Capital:
  Lansing C6
Ann Arbor C6
Detroit C6
Flint C6
Grand Rapids . . .C6
Marquette B5
Port Huron C7
Saginaw C6

Wisconsin
State Capital:
  Madison C5
Appleton C5
Eau Claire B4
Green Bay B5
Milwaukee C5
Oshkosh C5

Illinois
State Capital:
  Springfield . . .D5

Chicago C5
Decatur D5
East St. Louis . .E5
Peoria D5
Rockford C5

Ohio
State Capital:
  Columbus D7
Akron C7
Cincinnati D6
Cleveland C7
Dayton D6
Toledo C6

Indiana
State Capital:
  Indianapolis . .D6
Evansville E5
Fort Wayne D6
Gary D5
South Bend C5

United States: Mountain

MONTANA, NEVADA, COLORADO, WYOMING, UTAH, IDAHO

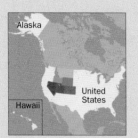

BENEATH BLUE SKIES AND WHITE clouds, jagged peaks of granite streaked with snow tower over dark pines and aspens that shiver in the wind. The massive Rocky Mountains, home of bighorn sheep, goats, deer, and grizzly bears, run north to south in the western part of the region, from the Canadian border to New Mexico. The Rockies include a series of mountain chains.

This dramatic scenery attracts many backpackers and tourists to national parks such as Yellowstone, and Colorado is a center for winter sports. The mountains are rich in minerals. They are flanked to the east by the short grass prairie of the Great Plains, well known as cattle-ranching country.

To the west of the Rockies lies the Great Basin, a vast inland area drained by westward-flowing rivers. Here are vast salt lakes, deserts, mesas, buttes, and canyons, rocks that have been eroded by wind and water into arches and pinnacles. Large cities have grown up around these extraordinary landscapes, such as Salt Lake City, heart of the Mormon faith, and Las Vegas, a neon-lighted sprawl of casinos, gambling arcades, theaters, and hotels in the Nevada desert.

DISCOVER MORE

• *The world's tallest active geyser is the Steamboat, in Yellowstone National Park, Wyoming. Geysers are jets of water heated by volcanic activity deep beneath the Earth. Steamboat sends up jets between 195 to 375 ft (60 to 115 m) high.*

• *Empty, flat wildernesses, such as Bonneville Salt Flats in Utah, are ideal places for trying to break land speed records.*

200 miles

300 km

State facts

	Area sq mi (sq km)	Population	Flower	Tree	Bird
Montana	147,046 (380,849)	902,195	Bitterroot	Ponderosa pine	Western meadowlark
Nevada	110,567 (286,369)	1,711,263	Sagebrush	Single-leaf piñon and Bristle-cone pine	Mountain bluebird
Colorado	104,100 (269,619)	4,301,261	Rocky Mountain columbine	Colorado blue spruce	Lark bunting
Wyoming	97,818 (253,349)	493,782	Indian paintbrush	Plains cottonwood	Western meadowlark
Utah	84,904 (219,901)	2,233,169	Sego lily	Blue spruce	Seagull
Idaho	83,574 (216,457)	1,293,953	Syringa	White pine	Mountain bluebird

A

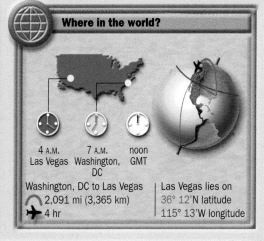

Where in the world?

4 A.M. Las Vegas	7 A.M. Washington, DC	noon GMT

Washington, DC to Las Vegas
2,091 mi (3,365 km)
4 hr

Las Vegas lies on
36° 12'N latitude
115° 13'W longitude

B

Bighorn sheep live wild in the dry hill and mountain regions of the western states. Both rams and ewes use their horns in head-butting contests.

C

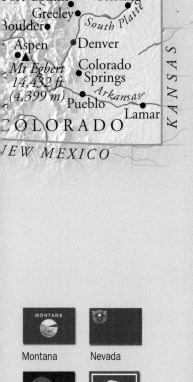

Many people travel to ski on the spectacular snow-covered mountains in Colorado.

D

Life facts

What percentage of people?	How many people per sq mi (sq km)?
U.S.A. 71.4 12.8 11.8 4.1 0.9	75 (29)
Montana 90.6 0.3 2.1 0.7 6.4	7 (3)
Nevada 73.0 7.4 14.8 4.5 1.7	17 (7)
Colorado 78.4 4.7 14.3 2.6 1.0	40 (16)
Wyoming 89.3 1.1 6.7 1.3 2.4	5 (2)
Utah 88.9 1.0 6.3 2.8 1.6	27 (10)
Idaho 89.9 0.6 7.1 1.3 1.6	16 (6)

White   Black   Hispanic   Asian   Other/American Indian

Search and find

Montana
State Capital:
  Helena B5
Billings B6
Bozeman B5
Butte B5
Great Falls B5
Miles City B7
Missoula B5

Nevada
State Capital:
  Carson City . . .D3
Elko D4
Las Vegas E4
Reno D3
Tonopah D4
Winnemucca . . .C4

Colorado
State Capital:
  Denver D7
Aspen D6
Boulder D7
Colorado
  Springs D7
Durango E6
Fort Collins D7
Grand Junction . .D6

Greeley D7
Lamar E7
Pueblo E7

Wyoming
State Capital:
  Cheyenne D7
Casper C6
Cody C6
Gillette C7
Jackson C5
Laramie D7
Rock Springs . . .D6

Utah
State Capital:
  Salt Lake City .D5
Brigham City . . .D5
Cedar City E5
Ogden D5
Provo D5

Idaho
State Capital:
  Boise C4
Idaho Falls C5
Lewiston B4
Pocatello C5
Twin Falls C5

E

Montana   Nevada

Colorado   Wyoming

Utah   Idaho

F

G

United States: West Coast

CALIFORNIA, OREGON, WASHINGTON

Water plunges for 2,424 ft (739 m) over Yosemite Falls, swollen by melting snow in the spring. Situated in Yosemite National Park, it is the world's second-highest waterfall.

SAN FRANCISCO, CALIFORNIA, is one of North America's most beautiful cities. Its steep streets, lined with fine old frame houses, look out over a wide bay, sparkling blue on a fresh spring morning, or shrouded in a white sea mist. Downtown are high-rise office buildings, old waterfronts, and the bustling streets of Chinatown.

South of San Francisco, the climate is dry and warm. Ocean spray crashes over sea lions as they emerge onto sun-baked rocks offshore. Warm sunshine fills the air with the scent of pines. Moving south, highways converge on Los Angeles, the second most populated city and the largest in area in the United States. Freeways cut through sprawling suburbs, often dense with smog, to palm-lined avenues, theme parks, and the film and television studios of Hollywood.

Eastern California takes in the Sierra Nevada mountains, the rock faces of Yosemite, and forests of gigantic sequoia trees. To the southeast lie the arid wildernesses of Death Valley and the Mojave Desert.

To the north of California are the states of Oregon and Washington, with major ports at Portland and Seattle. The economy here depends on technology, fruit and vegetable crops, timber, and fishing. Winds from the Pacific Ocean shed heavy rain and snow on the windward slopes of the Cascade Range. Foggy forests fringe the slopes of snowy peaks, some of them active volcanoes. The whole Pacific coast is a danger zone for earthquakes and volcanic activity.

Mount Rainier towers over Washington, to a height of 14,409 ft (4,392 m) above sea level. It is a volcano that experiences heavy snowfalls.

DISCOVER MORE

• *The highest temperature ever recorded in the United States—134°F (57°C)—was measured in Death Valley in California on July 10, 1913.*

• *Washington's nickname, the "Evergreen State," comes from the many evergreen trees that grow in the state. It has large areas of thick forests.*

Life facts

What percentage of people? U.S.A.	How many people per sq mi (sq km)?
● 71.4 ● 12.8 ● 11.8 ● 4.1 ● 0.9	75 (29)
California	
● 47.9 ● 7.4 ● 32.7 ● 13.2 ● 0.9	209 (81)
Oregon	
● 88.0 ● 1.9 ● 5.7 ● 3.4 ● 1.5	35 (14)
Washington	
● 83.3 ● 3.3 ● 6.1 ● 6.1 ● 1.8	88 (34)

White   Black   Hispanic   Asian   Other/American Indian

California

Oregon

Washington

State facts

	Area sq mi (sq km)	Population	Flower	Tree	Bird
California	158,869 (411,471)	33,871,648	Golden poppy	California redwood	California valley quail
Oregon	97,132 (251,572)	3,421,399	Oregon grape	Douglas fir	Western meadowlark
Washington	70,637 (182,949)	5,894,121	Western rhododendron	Western hemlock	Willow goldfinch

Strait of Juan de Fuca

Cape Flattery

C A N A D A

Bellingham
Skagit

W A S H I N G T O N

Seattle
Tacoma

Olympia ▲ *Mt Rainier*
14,409 ft (4,392 m)

Mt St Helens
8,364 ft (2,549 m) ▲

Yakima
Yakima

Spokane

Vancouver

Snake

Portland

Salem

Pendleton

Corvallis

La Grande

Eugene

Deschutes

O R E G O N

C A S C A D E R A N G E

Snake

Cape Blanco

Upper
Klamath L.

L. Albert

Malheur L.

Medford

Klamath Falls

Owyhee

Goose L.

Upper L.

Eureka
Cape
Mendocino

Redding

Eel

C O A S T R A N G E S

Sacramento

S I E R R A

Santa Rosa
Sacramento
Oakland
San Francisco
Palo Alto
Stockton
San Jose
San Joaquin
Monterey Bay
Monterey Salinas
Point Sur

L. Tahoe

Mono L.

Yosemite
National
Park

N E V A D A

Death Valley

Fresno

▲ *Mt Whitney*
14,449 ft (4,418 m)

C A L I F O R N I A

Bakersfield

Point Arguello

Santa Barbara
Oxnard

SAN RAFAEL MTS

Mojave Desert

Pomona
Los Angeles
Long Beach Anaheim

San Bernardino
Riverside

Colorado

*Salton
Sea*

A R I Z O N A

PACIFIC
OCEAN

Gulf of
Santa
Catalina

San Diego

M E X I C O

I D A H O

200 miles

300 km

A
B
C
D
E
F
G

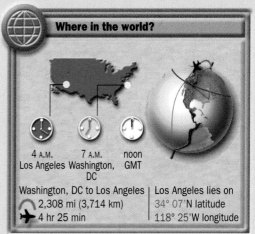

Where in the world?

4 A.M.
Los Angeles

7 A.M.
Washington,
DC

noon
GMT

Washington, DC to Los Angeles
2,308 mi (3,714 km)
✈ 4 hr 25 min

Los Angeles lies on
34° 07'N latitude
118° 25'W longitude

The blue skies of Oregon are reflected in Crater Lake,
the deepest inland body of water in the United States,
situated in the Cascade Mountains of Oregon. It was
formed nearly 7,000 years ago, when a volcano
collapsed inward after a massive eruption.

Search and find

California
State Capital:
  Sacramento . . E7
Anaheim G8
Bakersfield F8
Eureka D7
Fresno E8
Long Beach G8
Los Angeles F8
Monterey E7
Oakland E7
Oxnard F8
Palo Alto E7
Pomona F8
Redding D7
Riverside G8
Salinas E7
San Bernardino . G8
San Diego G8
San Francisco . . E7
San Jose E7
Santa Barbara . . F7
Santa Rosa E7

Stockton E7

Oregon
State Capital:
  Salem B7
Corvallis C7
Eugene C7
Klamath Falls . . . C7
La Grande C9
Medford C7
Pendleton B8
Portland B7

Washington
State Capital:
  Olympia B8
Bellingham A8
Seattle B8
Spokane B9
Tacoma B8
Vancouver B8
Yakima B8

United States: Pacific States

ALASKA, HAWAII

EAST MEETS WEST AT THE Bering Strait, where the coastline of Alaska is just 55 mi (90 km) from Asia and the Russian Federation. To the south, the Aleutian Islands emerge from the Pacific Ocean. Alaska has coasts on both the Pacific and Arctic oceans, each full of countless islands, sounds and straits, deltas and bays. Glaciers descend to foggy waters cruised by great whales. Most Alaskans live in the milder south, in cities such as Anchorage. The state's interior is largely a wilderness of snowy forests, icy mountains, and bare tundra, stretching far into the arctic. It is roamed by caribou, wolves, and bears. The far north is home to isolated Inuit communities and the oil workers of Point Barrow. Oil is piped south across the tundra.

The Hawaiian Islands lie in the ocean swell of the mid-Pacific Ocean. Small wonder that surfing was invented here. There are eight major islands. Their original inhabitants are the Hawaiians, a Polynesian people. Today, Hawaii's busy state capital, Honolulu, on the island of Oahu, has been settled by many people from Asia and the mainland United States. Honolulu is a popular tourist destination. The islands are lush and green, surrounded by deep-blue seas. There are brilliantly colored flowers, cascading waterfalls, and palm trees. Sugar cane is Hawaii's most important crop, and pineapples are also grown.

Oil and natural gas provide the state of Alaska with 80 percent of its wealth. A pipeline carries oil across the state from Prudhoe Bay, in the far north, to the southern tanker terminal at Valdez, on Port William Sound.

### Map labels

ARCTIC

CHUKCHI SEA

Point Hope

RUSSIAN FEDERATION

Bering Strait

Pe

Nome

Gambell • Norton

St. Lawrence I. Alakanu

Alakanu

BERING SEA

Hooper Bay

St. Matthew I.

Nunivak I.

Cape Neu

St. Paul I.

St. George I.

Unimak

Near Is

Fox Is

ALEUTIAN IS

Dutch Harbo

Rat Is

Andreanof Is

Kauai

Mt Kawaikini 5,243 ft ▲ • Kapaa

(1,598 m)

Puuwai • Lihue

Niihau

Kauai Channel

Oah

Waialua

Wahiawa

Waipahu

Honolul

H

A

N

Alaska

Hawaii

Kilauea Crater on Hawaii Island belches out red-hot lava and smoke. The volcanic activity that created the Hawaiian Islands is still shaping them today.

State facts					
	Area sq mi (sq km)	Population	Flower	Tree	Bird
Alaska	615,230 (1,593,446)	626,932	Forget-me-not	Sitka spruce	Willow ptarmigan
Hawaii	6,459 (16,729)	1,211,537	Yellow hibiscus	Kukui (candlenut)	Hawaiian goose

OCEAN

Point Barrow
●Barrow
●Wainwright

BEAUFORT SEA

ARCTIC COASTAL PLAIN

Colville

atak

BROOK RANGE

Kobuk

Koyukuk

Yukon

Fort Yukon ●

Tanana ●   Fairbanks ●

A L A S K A

Yukon

Mt McKinley ▲
20,320 ft
(6,194 m)

ALASKA RANGE

Anchorage ●

Cordova ●

Yakutat ●

Juneau ●

CANADA

ethel

Kenai ●

Sitka ●

Kwethluk

Iliamna L.

Seward ●
Homer ●

Gulf of Alaska

ALEXANDER ARCHIPELAGO

Ketchikan ●

illingham

Bristol
Bay

Kodiak ●
Kodiak I.

Alaska Peninsula

500 miles

800 km

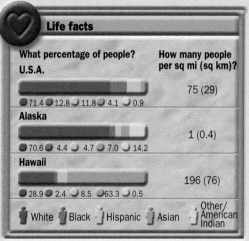

Life facts

What percentage of people?
U.S.A.

71.4   12.8   11.8   4.1   0.9

Alaska

70.6   4.4   4.7   7.0   14.2

Hawaii

28.9   2.4   8.5   63.3   0.5

How many people
per sq mi (sq km)?

75 (29)

1 (0.4)

196 (76)

White   Black   Hispanic   Asian   Other/
American
Indian

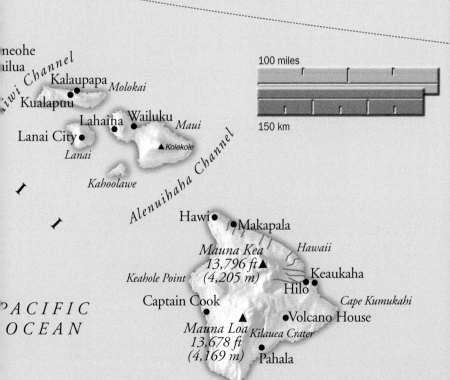

neohe
ailua

Kiwi Channel

Kalaupapa ●
Kualapuu ●

Molokai

Lahaina ●
Lanai City ●

Wailuku ●

Maui

Lanai

▲Kolekole

Kahoolawe

Alenuihaha Channel

Hawi ●
●Makapala

100 miles

150 km

Mauna Kea
13,796 ft ▲
(4,205 m)

Keahole Point

Hawaii

Captain Cook ●

Hilo ●

Keaukaha ●

Cape Kumukahi

▲

●Volcano House

Mauna Loa
13,678 ft
(4,169 m)

Kilauea Crater

Pahala ●

Ka Lea

P A C I F I C
O C E A N

Search and find

Alaska		Hawaii	
State Capital:		*State Capital:*	
Juneau	C9	Honolulu	E6
Alakanuk	B6	Captain Cook	G8
Anchorage	B7	Hawi	F8
Barrow	A7	Hilo	G8
Bethel	C7	Kailua	E6
Cordova	C7	Kalaupapa	E7
Dillingham	C7	Kaneohe	E6
Dutch Harbor	D6	Kapaa	D5
Fairbanks	B7	Keaukaha	G8
Fort Yukon	A7	Kualapuu	E7
Gambell	B6	Lahaina	F7
Homer	C7	Lanai City	F7
Hooper Bay	B6	Lihue	E5
Kenai	C7	Makapala	F8
Ketchikan	C9	Pahala	G8
Kodiak	C7	Puuwai	E4
Kwethluk	C6	Volcano House	G8
Nome	B6	Wahiawa	E6
Point Hope	A6	Waialua	E6
Seward	C7	Wailuku	F7
Sitka	C8	Waipahu	E6
Tanana	B7		
Wainwright	A6		
Yakutat	C8		

A
B
C
D
E
F
G

Canada

Canada

CANADA STRETCHES NORTH from the Great Lakes to the Arctic Ocean, taking in broad bands of treeless tundra, forests of spruce and birch, and in the milder south, sugar maple. It is a land of lakes and rivers, big skies, and empty spaces. The west rises to a series of high mountain ranges, including the northern limits of the Rockies. In the east, ice has carved out the sweep of Hudson Bay.

Canada is the world's second-largest country, but its population is only 11 percent of that of the United States, its neighbor to the south and west. Because of the icy northern climate, about three-quarters of all Canadians live in towns and cities near the southern border. The close ties between Canada and the United States stretch back to their shared history.

Canadians, however, are an independent-minded people with a strong sense of their own identity. That identity varies greatly from one part of Canada to another, from English-speaking Toronto to French-speaking Montreal, from the fishing villages of Newfoundland on the east coast to the central prairies, and from the city streets of Vancouver in the west to the Inuit settlements of the Arctic north.

1,000 miles
1,500 km

ARCTIC OCEAN

BEAUFORT SEA   Banks I.

Prince Rupert I.
Melville I.   Bathurst I.
Victoria I.   Prince of Wales I.

As Heibe

ALASKA (U.S.A.)
• Dawson
YUKON TERRITORY
Mt Logan 19,524 ft (5,951 m)   • Whitehorse

Great Bear L.
NORTHWEST TERRITORIES
• Yellowknife   Dubawnt

Mackenzie
Liard   Great Slave L.

BRITISH COLUMBIA   C   A   N
Prince Rupert •   • Prince George
Queen Charlotte Is
PACIFIC OCEAN
COAST MTS   Fraser   Peace
ROCKY MTS
L. Athabasca
Reindeer L.
ALBERTA   MA
• Edmonton
• Calgary   • Saskatoon   L. Winnipegosis
SASKATCHEWAN
Vancouver I. • Vancouver   • Medicine Hat   • Regina   L. Manito
Victoria •   Winnip

UNITED STATES OF AME

DISCOVER MORE

• At 1,820 ft (555 m), Toronto's CN Tower, on the shores of Lake Ontario, is the world's tallest telecommunications tower.

• Compass needles do not point due north, but spin toward a point called the Magnetic North Pole, which is located in the Canadian Arctic. Its precise position varies from year to year, reflecting changes in the earth's magnetic field.

The Royal Canadian Mounted Police force has a history dating back to 1873. Mounties still wear their traditional uniform for ceremonial occasions.

Country facts					
	Area sq mi (sq km)	**Population**	**Language**	**Religion**	**Currency**
Canada	3,851,800 (9,976,162)	31,006,347	English/French	Catholic/Protestant	Dollar

Canada

Ellesmere I.

Greenland (DENMARK)

Devon I.

Baffin Bay

Baffin I.

Davis Strait

A

N A V U T

Foxe Basin

Iqaluit

Southampton I.

Hudson Strait

LABRADOR SEA

Coats I.

Mansel I.

Ungava Peninsula

A   **D**   **A**

Labrador

Hudson Bay

Churchill

NEWFOUNDLAND AND LABRADOR

Gander

Belcher Is.

Newfoundland St. John's

OBA

James Bay

Severn

Q U E B E C

Albany

Fort Albany

nnipeg

O N T A R I O

PRINCE EDWARD I.

NEW BRUNSWICK

Charlottetown

NOVA SCOTIA

L. Nipigon

Quebec

Thunder Bay

L. Superior

Fredericton

Halifax

CA

Montreal

ATLANTIC OCEAN

L. Huron

Ottawa

Toronto

L. Ontario

L. Erie

The Canadian national parliament meets in Ottawa, a city in Ontario with about 314,000 inhabitants. The parliament buildings tower above the Ottawa River.

Where in the world?

7 A.M. Washington, DC   7 A.M. Ottawa   noon GMT

Washington, DC to Ottawa
455 mi (732 km)
55 min

Ottawa lies on
45° 25'N latitude
75° 40'W longitude

Life facts

How long do people live?

U.S.A.
76 years

Canada
79 years

How many people in 100 own cars?

48

43

Dense fur, covered by long hair, keeps the musk ox warm in the Canadian Arctic. It is not a true ox, but a relative of sheep and goats. However, at 1,100 lb (500 kg), it is no lightweight.

The Canadian Rockies form some of the most spectacular mountain scenery in the world. The jagged rocks and snowcapped peaks attract many climbers.

Search and find

Canada
Capital: Ottawa .E8
Calgary E5
Charlottetown . .E9
Churchill D6
Dawson C4
Edmonton D5
Fort Albany E7
Fredericton E9
Gander D10
Halifax E9
Iqaluit C8
Medicine Hat . . .E5
Montreal E8

Prince George . .D4
Prince Rupert . .D3
Quebec E8
Regina E5
Saskatoon E5
St. John's D10
Thunder Bay . . .E6
Toronto F8
Vancouver E4
Victoria E4
Whitehorse C4
Winnipeg E6
Yellowknife C5

Canada: The East

QUEBEC, ONTARIO, NEWFOUNDLAND AND LABRADOR,
NEW BRUNSWICK, NOVA SCOTIA, PRINCE EDWARD ISLAND

A
B
C
D
E

Canada

500 miles

800 km

IT'S WINTER IN SNOWY OTTAWA.
Skaters link arms on the frozen waters of the Rideau Canal, their breath turning to mist in the cold air. Some stop to warm themselves with a cup of hot chocolate. On the skyline are the towers of the parliament buildings, for Ottawa is the capital of Canada.

The biggest city is Toronto, in Ontario. A center of business, it bristles with skyscrapers, rising from the shores of Lake Ontario. Montreal is a historic city on the St. Lawrence River. It is in the province of Quebec, which extends northward along Hudson Bay. Most Canadians live in the southeast of the country.

Parts of the St. Lawrence have been turned into canals to form a seaway that links the Great Lakes with the Atlantic Ocean. The seaway passes through farmland and woods of maple and birch, meeting the sea opposite the foggy island of Newfoundland. Labrador, on the mainland, is a region of bogs, lakes, and forests. Southward lie three small provinces of farms and forests, known as the Maritimes—Nova Scotia, New Brunswick, and Prince Edward Island.

Canada's eastern provinces are populated by First Peoples such as the Innu and Mohawk, and by people of Asian, African, and European descent. The Europeans are divided between English speakers, including many of Scottish and Irish descent, and French speakers. Most French Canadians live in Quebec and parts of New Brunswick.

Hudso
Ungava Peninsul

Hudson Bay

Hudson Bay Lowlands

James Bay

MANITOBA

Severn

Canadian Shield

Albany

Fort Albany

ONTARIO

L. Nipigon

Lake of the Woods

Thunder Bay

L. Superior

UNITED STATES OF AMERICA

Geo
L. H

Windso

DISCOVER MORE

• The largest of Canada's provinces is Quebec, which is slightly bigger than Alaska. The smallest is Prince Edward Island, which is about the size of Delaware.

• The Bay of Fundy between New Brunswick and Nova Scotia experiences the highest tides in the world. The record stands at 54 ft (16.6 m).

Quebec

Ontario

Newfoundland and Labrador

New Brunswick

Nova Scotia

Prince Edward Island

Province facts	Area sq mi (sq km)	Population	Flower
Quebec	594,860 (1,540,687)	7,138,795	White garden lily
Ontario	412,581 (1,068,585)	10,753,573	White trillium
Newfoundland and Labrador	156,649 (405,721)	551,792	Pitcher plant
New Brunswick	28,355 (73,439)	738,133	Violet
Nova Scotia	21,425 (55,490)	909,282	Trailing arbutus
Prince Edward Island	2,185 (5,659)	134,557	Lady's slipper

F
G

LABRADOR SEA

Feuilles

Labrador Peninsula

Nairn

La Grande Rivière

Canadian Shield

Goose Bay

Smallwood Reservoir

NEWFOUNDLAND AND LABRADOR

QUEBEC

Gander

Newfoundland

St. John's

Péribonca

Anticosti I.

Gulf of St. Lawrence

PRINCE EDWARD ISLAND

Charlottetown

Chicoutimi

NEW BRUNSWICK

NOVA SCOTIA

ATLANTIC OCEAN

Quebec

Fredericton   St. John

St. Lawrence

Trois-Rivières

Halifax

Sherbrooke

Montreal

Bay of Fundy

udbury

Ottawa

Bay

Oshawa

L. Ontario

Toronto

Niagara Falls

ener

Hamilton

London

. Erie

Where in the world?

7 A.M. Washington, DC   7 A.M. Ottawa   noon GMT

Washington, DC to Ottawa
455 mi (732 km)
55 min

Ottawa lies on
45° 25'N latitude
75° 40'W longitude

Search and find

Quebec
Province Capital:
  Quebec D8
Chicoutimi D8
Montreal D7
Sherbrooke . . .D8
Trois-Rivières . . .D8

Ontario
Province Capital:
  Toronto E7
Fort Albany C6
Hamilton E7
Kitchener E6
London E6
Oshawa E7
Ottawa E7
Sudbury E6
Thunder Bay . . .D5
Windsor F6

Newfoundland and Labrador
Province Capital:
  St. John's . . .C10
Gander C10
Goose Bay B8
Nairn B8

New Brunswick
Province Capital:
  Fredericton . . .D8
St. John D8

Nova Scotia
Province Capital:
  Halifax D9

Prince Edward Island
Province Capital:
  Charlottetown .D9

Toronto's name comes from a Native American word meaning "meeting place."

Life facts

What percentage of people?   **How many people per sq mi (sq km)?**

U.S.A.
71   13   12   4   Less than 1   75 (29)

Canada
84.6   1.6   0.4   6.9   6.5   8 (3)

Quebec
91.5   1.5   0.6   2.4   4   12 (5)

Ontario
81.9   2.7   0.5   9.3   5.6   26 (10)

Newfoundland and Labrador
97.8   0   0   0.4   1.7   3 (1)

New Brunswick
98   0.1   0   0.4   1.5   26 (10)

Nova Scotia
95.9   0.5   0   0.8   2.8   42 (16)

Prince Edward Island
98.5   0   0   0.4   1.1   66 (25)

White   Black   Hispanic   Asian   Other/American Indian

A   B   C   D   E   F   G

Canada: The North and West

NUNAVUT, NORTHWEST TERRITORIES, BRITISH COLUMBIA, ALBERTA, SASKATCHEWAN, MANITOBA, YUKON TERRITORY

Canada

A SEA OF WHEAT RIPPLING IN THE wind awaits the line of harvesters. Storage elevators line the railroad track. These are Canada's prairie provinces—Manitoba, Saskatchewan, and Alberta—and they help to feed the world. Cattle graze grasslands, and large cities have grown up based on farming, food processing, and the oil wealth of Alberta. Towering over the Alberta landscape are the Canadian Rockies, a breathtaking panorama of high peaks and ridges.

British Columbia is a land of misty forests and mountains, bordering the Pacific Ocean. The province's biggest city is Vancouver, a major seaport and industrial center.

Northern Canada is a sparsely populated land of snowy mountains and dark conifer forests, where beavers build dams and loons call across lonely lakes. In the far north, beyond the frozen tundra, thousands of islands are locked in permanent ice. The wilderness is divided into territories instead of provinces. They are the Yukon, in the western mountains, Northwest Territories, around Great Slave Lake, and Nunavut, an Inuit homeland that stretches from Coppermine to Ellesmere and Baffin islands.

First Peoples of the region include the Inuit of Nunavut, the Déné of the northern forests, the Kwakiutl of British Columbia, and the Cree and Ojibway of the prairies. Vancouver has many people of British descent and is home to a large Asian population, while many farmers on the prairies are of Ukrainian, German, or Scandinavian descent.

DISCOVER MORE

• *Nunavut territory occupies one-fifth of all Canada, yet it is home to just 26,000 people—and quite a few polar bears.*

• *The Saskatchewan River takes its name from the Cree language. Kis-is-ska-tche-wan means "swift-flowing." Saskatchewan is now the name of the whole province.*

Province facts

	Area sq mi (sq km)	Population	Flower
Nunavut	818,959 (2,121,104)	26,000	Arctic poppy
Northwest Territories	503,951 (1,305,233)	39,672	Mountain avens
British Columbia	365,948 (947,805)	3,724,500	Pacific dogwood
Alberta	255,287 (661,193)	2,696,826	Wild rose
Saskatchewan	251,866 (652,333)	990,237	Prairie lily
Manitoba	250,947 (649,953)	1,113,898	Pasqueflower
Yukon Territory	186,661 (483,452)	30,766	Fireweed

ARCTIC OCEAN

BEAUFORT SEA

Prince Rupert I.

Melvi

Banks I.

Victoria I

ALASKA (U.S.A.)

Inuvik

Norman Wells

Kugluktuk (Coppermine

Great Bear L.

Dawson

YUKON TERRITORY

MACKENZIE MTS

Mackenzie

NORTHWEST TERRITORIES

▲ Mt Logan 19,524 ft (5,951 m)

Whitehorse

Liard

R O C K Y

Yellowknife

Great Slave L.

Fort Resolution

Fort Smi

Peace

L. Athabas

Hazelton

ALBERTA

Prince Rupert

BRITISH COLUMBIA

Peace River

Grande Prairie

Queen Charlotte Is

COAST MTS

Prince George

Fraser

Edmonton

N. Saskatchewan

Prince Albert

PACIFIC OCEAN

Kamloops

M T S

Calgary

Vancouver I.

Vancouver

Medicine Hat

S. Saskatchewan

Saskatoon

Moos Jaw

Victoria

Lethbridge

SASKATC

UNITED STATES OI

Nunavut

Northwest Territories

British Columbia

A

B

C

D

E

F

G

Ellesmere I.

Axel
Heiberg I.

Bathurst
I.

Devon I.

Prince of
Wales I.

Baffin
Bay

Baffin I.

Davis Strait

Cambridge Bay
(Iqaluktuutiak)

N U N A V U T

Foxe
Basin

Iqaluit

Southampton
I.

Coral Harbour
(Salliq)

Hudson Strait

Dubawnt
L.

Rankin Inlet
(Kangiqtiniq)

Coats
I.

Mansel I.

Arviat

Hudson Bay

Shield

Churchill

Churchill

Nelson

...deer L.

MANITOBA

ONTARIO

L.
Winnipegosis

L.
Winnipeg

...gina

L.
Manitoba

...AN Brandon

Winnipeg

...MERICA

500 miles

1,000 km

Where in the world?

7 A.M.
Washington,
DC

4 A.M.
Vancouver

noon
GMT

Washington, DC to Vancouver
2,361 mi (3,799 km)
4 hr 30 min

Vancouver lies on
49° 15'N latitude
123° 05'W longitude

The skyscrapers of downtown Vancouver rise from a
narrow strip of land.

Life facts

What percentage of people?	How many people per sq mi (sq km)?
U.S.A.	75 (29)
71 13 12 4 Less than 1	
Canada	8 (3)
84.6 1.6 0.4 6.9 6.5	
British Columbia	10 (4)
76.9 0.3 0.3 14.7 7.8	
Alberta	11 (4)
82.1 0.6 0.4 6.8 10.1	
Saskatchewan	4 (2)
81.7 0.2 0.1 1.7 16.3	
Manitoba	4 (2)
78.8 0.7 0.3 4.6 15.6	
Yukon Territory	0.2 (0.06)
80.4 0.1 0.1 1.8 17.6	

White Black Hispanic Asian Other/ American Indian

Nunavut and Northwest Territories—not available

Alberta

Saskatchewan

Manitoba

Yukon Territory

Search and find

Mexico

A B C D E F G

Mexico

A COUNTRY BUS strains its way up a rough mountain road, its windshield bordered with colored lights. Lightning forks across the dark sky, and heavy rain drums on the roof. The bus pulls into a small town square, in front of an ornate, twin-towered church and dripping palm trees. The next morning, the sun shines brightly in a clear blue sky and the intense heat returns. This is market day. There are crates of oranges for sale, heaps of onions and fiery chili peppers, brightly colored bottled drinks, and tasty snacks wrapped in pancakes called *tortillas*.

Mexico's national flag shows an eagle on a cactus grasping a snake, a suitable emblem for this land of deserts and volcanoes. The flag recalls an old myth of the Aztec people, who believed that this sight was a sign from their gods to start building the city of Tenochtitlán. In 1521 the Spanish invaded and destroyed the Aztec civilization. Today, most Mexicans are of Spanish, indigenous, or mixed descent. Tenochtitlán has become the vast sprawl of Mexico City, one of the world's biggest, liveliest, and most polluted cities—which is not surprising, since the city has more than 130,000 factories. Mexico's industry is based on oil, mining, machinery, textiles, and foods.

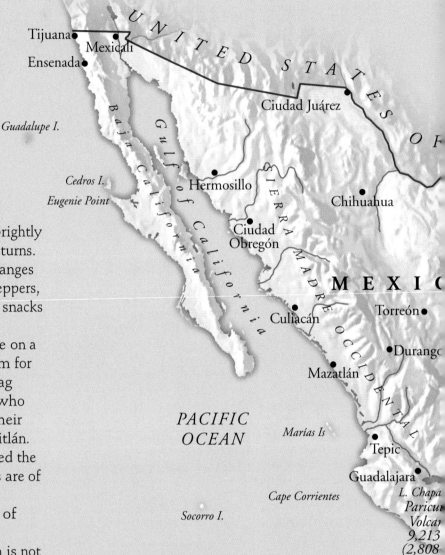

UNITED STATES OF

Tijuana
Mexicali
Ensenada

Guadalupe I.

Ciudad Juárez

Cedros I.

Eugenie Point

Hermosillo

Chihuahua

Ciudad Obregón

M E X I C

Culiacán

Torreón

Durango

Mazatlán

PACIFIC OCEAN

Marías Is

Tepic

Cape Corrientes

Guadalajara

Socorro I.

L. Chapa
Paricu
Volcar
9,213
(2,808

Baja California

Gulf of California

SIERRA MADRE OCCIDENTAL

DISCOVER MORE

• In 1943, a new volcano suddenly appeared in Mexico. It was given the name Paricutín. Red-hot lava continued to pour out of the ground on this spot. Within a year the volcano had risen to more than 980 ft (300 m) high.

Flowers add color to a market in southern Mexico. The sellers are Zapotecs, a people who live by farming the slopes and valleys of the Southern Sierra Madre Mountains.

A B

Many tourists visit the sites of Mexico's ancient civilizations. This sacred platform is at Chichén Itzá, which was a center of the Mayan culture, known for its extensive cities, about 1,000 years ago.

Where in the world?

7 A.M.   noon   6 A.M.
Washington, DC   GMT   Mexico City

Washington, DC to Mexico City
1,882 mi (3,029 km)
3 hr 35 min

Mexico City lies on
19° 28'N latitude
99° 09'W longitude

Life facts

How long do people live?

U.S.A. 76 years

Mexico 72 years

How many people in 100 own cars?

48

8

300 miles

500 km

Search and find

Mexico
Capital:
  Mexico City E7
Acapulco E7
Aguascalientes .D6
Cancún D9
Chihuahua C5
Ciudad Juárez . .B5
Ciudad Obregón .C4
Coatzacoalcos . .E8
Culiacán C5
Durango D5
Ensenada B3
Guadalajara E6
Hermosillo C4
León D6
Matamoros C7

Mazatlán D5
Mérida D9
Mexicali B3
Monterrey C6
Morelia E6
Nuevo Laredo . .C7
Oaxaca E7
Puebla E7
Saltillo D6
San Luis
  Potosí D6
Tampico D7
Tepic D5
Tijuana B3
Torreón D6
Veracruz E7
Villahermosa . . .E8

### Map labels

A M E R I C A

SIERRA MADRE ORIENTAL

Nuevo Laredo
Monterrey
Matamoros
tillo
San Luis Potosí
uascalientes
León
Tampico
Morelia
Orizaba 18,701 ft (5,700 m)
Mexico City
Puebla
Veracruz
Coatzacoalcos
Oaxaca
Acapulco

SIERRA MADRE DEL SUR

GULF OF MEXICO

Bay of Campeche

Términos Lagoon

Villahermosa

Gulf of Tehuantepec

Cancún
Mérida
Chichén Itzá
Cozumel I.
Yucatán Peninsula

GUATEMALA
BELIZE

Mexico

Country facts

	Area sq mi (sq km)	Population	Language	Religion	Currency
Mexico	756,066 (1,958,211)	100,294,036	Spanish	Catholic	New Peso

C D E F G

Central America

NICARAGUA, HONDURAS, GUATEMALA, PANAMA, COSTA RICA, BELIZE, EL SALVADOR

A MAYAN WOMAN, HER black, shiny hair tied in a single braid, kneels in front of a tree. A strap tied around her waist is joined to a loom, lengths of thread attached by a bar to a tree branch. In and out of the threads she passes a wooden shuttle, weaving patterns of brilliant scarlet and blue stripes. She is making a loose shirt called a *huipil*, to wear in the Holy Week procession before Easter. Each Guatemalan village has its own traditional weaving patterns.

The seven small countries of Central America are lands of rugged mountains, lakes, tropical forests, and steamy coastal plains, producing coffee, bananas, and sugarcane. Central America lies in an earthquake zone, and its eastern shores are regularly battered by hurricanes. The region's inhabitants are mostly descended from indigenous peoples and from the Spanish, who conquered these lands in the 1500s. There are also people of African descent. Spanish is the most common language.

DISCOVER MORE

• *The Panama Canal is one of the world's engineering marvels. It is 40 mi (64 km) long and cuts through the continent at its narrowest part. Opened in 1914, it soon became one of the world's most important shipping routes, linking the Atlantic and Pacific oceans.*

• *Where can you see the Pacific and Atlantic oceans at the same time? One such spot—when the clouds permit—is the volcanic crater of Irazú, in Costa Rica, 11,260 ft (3,432 m) above sea level.*

*Map labels:*
ME X I C O
Belize City
◉ Belmopan
BELIZE
Gulf of Honduras
Bahía Is
• La Ceiba
• San Pedro Sula
Volcán Tajmulco 13,845 ft (4,220 m)
GUATEMALA
HONDURAS
Patuca
▲ Chichicastenango
Motagua
Quetzaltenango •
◉ Guatemala City
Tegucigalpa ◉
Santa Ana
EL SALVADOR
NICA
◉ San Salvador
San Miguel
Chinandega
León
L. Managua
Managua ◉
L. Nicaragua
PACIFIC OCEAN
CO

The great cinder cone of the Santa Ana volcano towers over the landscape of western El Salvador.

300 miles

500 km

 Nicaragua   Honduras   Guatemala   Panama   Costa Rica   Belize   El Salvador

A

B

Where in the world?

7 A.M.   noon   6 A.M.
Washington, DC   GMT   Managua

Washington, DC to Managua
1,927 mi (3,100 km)
3 hr 40 min

Managua lies on
12° 10'N latitude
86° 16'W longitude

A Mayan weaver passes her shuttle through the stretched threads of a backstrap loom in the market town of Chichicastenango, north of Guatemala City.

Mosquito Coast

AGUA

Rio Grande

Mosquito Coast

CARIBBEAN
SEA

TA RICA

Alajuela   Limón

★ San José

Colón
Panama Canal
★ Panama City

P A N A M A

• David

Gulf of
Panama

*Azuero
Peninsula*

Coiba I.

COLOMBIA

Life facts

How long do people live?		How many people in 100 own cars?
U.S.A.	76 years	48
Nicaragua	67 years	2
Honduras	65 years	1
Guatemala	66 years	1
Panama	75 years	5
Costa Rica	76 years	1
Belize	69 years	1
El Salvador	70 years	1

C

D

E

Search and find

Nicaragua
Capital: Managua D5
Chinandega C5
León D5

Honduras
Capital:
   Tegucigalpa . . C5
La Ceiba B5
San Pedro Sula . B5

Guatemala
Capital:
   Guatemala City C4
Chichicastenango C3
Quetzaltenango . C3

Panama
Capital: Panama City . E8

Colón D8
David E7

Costa Rica
Capital:
   San José D6
Alajuela D6
Limón D7

Belize
Capital:
   Belmopan B4
Belize City A4

El Salvador
Capital:
   San Salvador . C4
San Miguel C5
Santa Ana C4

F

G

Country facts

	Area sq mi (sq km)	Population	Language	Religion	Currency
Nicaragua	50,893 (131,813)	4,717,132	Spanish	Catholic	Córdoba
Honduras	43,278 (112,090)	5,997,327	Spanish	Catholic	Lempira
Guatemala	42,042 (108,889)	11,800,000	Spanish	Catholic	Quetzal
Panama	30,193 (78,200)	2,778,526	Spanish	Catholic	Balboa/US Dollar
Costa Rica	19,730 (51,101)	3,674,490	Spanish	Catholic	Colón
Belize	8,865 (22,960)	235,789	English/Creole	Catholic	Dollar
El Salvador	8,124 (21,041)	5,839,079	Spanish	Catholic	Colón

Caribbean Islands

CUBA, DOMINICAN REP., HAITI, BAHAMAS, JAMAICA, TRINIDAD & TOBAGO, DOMINICA, ST. LUCIA, ANTIGUA & BARBUDA, BARBADOS, ST. VINCENT & THE GRENADINES, GRENADA, ST. KITTS & NEVIS

Caribbean Islands

THE CARIBBEAN SEA IS A western arm of the Atlantic Ocean, cradling chains of coral reefs and palm-fringed tropical islands; some are steep volcanoes blanketed in lush, green vegetation. The region is a mixture of peoples and cultures. Some islands have a predominantly Hispanic heritage, while others have African heritage. There are Asian and European minorities. Languages include Spanish and dialects of English, French, and Dutch.

Cuba is the largest island. Cubans love Latin dance music, such as salsa, and sports such as baseball. On Jamaica, the main sports are soccer and cricket, and the music is a thumping reggae. On Trinidad, Carnival is the biggest event of the year—featuring colorful costumes and dancing to the lilting music of steel drums.

Many Caribbean islands, such as Haiti, are desperately poor, and their plight is often made worse by the hurricanes that sweep the region causing destruction in late summer and fall.

Cuba   Dominican Rep.   Haiti   Bahamas

Jamaica   Trinidad & Tobago   Dominica   St. Lucia

Antigua & Barbuda   Barbados   St. Vincent & the Grenadines   Grenada   St. Kitts & Nevis

Great Abaco

Grand Bahama

Nassau ⊛   BAHAMAS

Andros I.   Turks & Caicos I (U.K.)

Havana ⊛   Santa Clara   Great Inagua

Pinar del Rio   Cienfuegos   C U B A   Holguín   Cap Haïtien

Camagüey   Guantánamo

Isle of Youth   G   Santiago de Cuba   HAITI

R   Port-au-Prince ⊛

Cayman Is (U.K.)   E   A   T   E   R   A   N

Montego Bay ⊛   Kingston

JAMAICA

DISCOVER MORE

- One of the strangest sights in the Caribbean is Trinidad's Pitch Lake. This lake does not contain water. In fact, it is sometimes possible to walk over it. It contains hot, sticky, black tar, which covers about 140 acres (57 hectares), to a depth of 135 ft (41 m).

- The Caribbean Sea is famous for beaches of white sand, but on the island of Montserrat they are gray, brown, or black. The grains of sand are formed from volcanic rock.

Country facts

	Area sq mi (sq km)	Population	Language	Religion	Currency
Cuba	42,803 (110,860)	11,096,395	Spanish	NR*	Cuban Peso
Dominican Rep.	18,815 (48,731)	8,129,734	Spanish	Catholic	Peso
Haiti	10,714 (27,749)	6,884,264	Haitian Creole	Catholic/Voodoo	Gourde
Bahamas	5,382 (13,939)	283,705	English	Baptist/NR/C**	Dollar
Jamaica	4,243 (10,989)	2,652,443	English	Pentecostal/NR/C**	Dollar
Trinidad & Tobago	1,981 (5,131)	1,102,096	English	Catholic/Hindu	Dollar
Dominica	290 (751)	64,881	FC***/English	Catholic	East Caribbean Dollar
St. Lucia	239 (619)	154,020	English/FC***	Catholic	East Caribbean Dollar
Antigua & Barbuda	170 (440)	64,246	English	Anglican	East Caribbean Dollar
Barbados	166 (430)	259,191	English	Anglican/Pentecostal	Dollar
St. Vin. & Gren.	150 (389)	120,519	English	NR/Anglican	East Caribbean Dollar
Grenada	131 (339)	97,008	English	Catholic	East Caribbean Dollar
St. Kitts & Nevis	104 (269)	42,838	English	Anglican/Methodist	East Caribbean Dollar

*Non-religious **Non-religious/Catholic ***French Creole

1   2   3   4   5

Dunn's River Falls are a major attraction on the island of Jamaica. The waterfall has a drop of 600 ft (181 m) and rushes over rocky terraces on its way to the sea.

Search and find

Cuba
Capital: Havana D3
Camagüey D4
Cienfuegos D4
Guantánamo . . .D5
Holguín D5
Pinar del Rio . . .D3
Santa Clara D4
Santiago de Cuba E5

Dominican Republic
Capital:
   Santo Domingo E6
Santiago D6

Haiti
Capital:
   Port-au-Prince .E6
Cap Haïtien D6

Bahamas
Capital: Nassau .C4

Jamaica
Capital:
   Kingston E5
Montego Bay . . .E4

Trinidad & Tobago
Capital:
Port of Spain . . .F9

Dominica
Capital: Roseau .E8

St. Lucia
Capital: Castries E9

Antigua & Barbuda
Capital:
   St. John's D8

Barbados
Capital: Bridgetown E9

St. Vincent & the Grenadines
Capital: Kingstown E9

Grenada
Capital:
   St. George's . .F9

St. Kitts & Nevis
Capital:
   Basseterre . . .D8

Where in the world?

7 A.M. noon 8 A.M.
Washington, DC GMT Santo Domingo

Washington, DC to Santo Domingo	Santo Domingo lies on
1,477 mi (2,377 km)	18° 26'N latitude
2 hr 50 min	69° 40'W longitude

Life facts

How long do people live? | How many people in 100 own cars?

U.S.A. 76 years | 48
Cuba 76 years | 0.2
Dominican Republic 70 years | 1
Haiti 51 years | 0.5
Bahamas 74 years | 25
Jamaica 75 years | 2
Trinidad & Tobago 71 years | 11
Dominica 70 years | 1
St. Lucia 72 years | 7
Antigua & Barbuda 71 years | 21
Barbados 75 years | 17
St. Vin. & Gren. 74 years | 4
Grenada 71 years | n.a.
St. Kitts & Nevis 68 years | n.a.

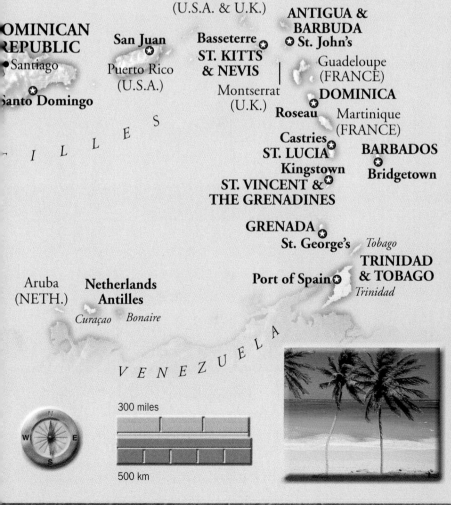

Virgin Is
(U.S.A. & U.K.)

DOMINICAN REPUBLIC
Santiago
San Juan
Santo Domingo
Puerto Rico
(U.S.A.)

ANTIGUA & BARBUDA
✪ St. John's

Basseterre ✪
ST. KITTS & NEVIS
Montserrat
(U.K.)

Guadeloupe
(FRANCE)

DOMINICA
Roseau

Martinique
(FRANCE)

Castries ✪
ST. LUCIA
Kingstown ✪
ST. VINCENT & THE GRENADINES

BARBADOS
✪ Bridgetown

GRENADA ✪
St. George's

Tobago

TRINIDAD & TOBAGO
Port of Spain ✪
Trinidad

N T I L L E S

Aruba
(NETH.)
Netherlands Antilles
Curaçao Bonaire

V E N E Z U E L A

300 miles

500 km

White sands, blue seas, and palm trees attract tourists to the island of Barbados.

South America

STRETCHING FROM THE WARM CARIBBEAN SEA TOWARD cold Antarctic waters, South America is the world's fourth-largest continent. It is attached to Central America by the Isthmus of Panama, a narrow strip of land. To the west of South America is the South Pacific Ocean and to the east is the South Atlantic Ocean.

Stresses and strains within the earth's crust have pushed up the massive ridges and plateaus of the Andes Mountains, which run from the north to the south down the western side of the continent. To the west of the mountains is a narrow coastal plain, partly fertile, partly barren desert. To the east is the Amazon rain forest, the largest tropical rain forest on earth, which drains into the surging, muddy flow of the Amazon River on its way to the Atlantic Ocean.

South of the rain forest, scrub, swamp, and grasslands called the pampas give way to the bleak valleys of Patagonia. Beyond the Strait of Magellan, the southern island of Tierra del Fuego has been shaped by ice, wind, and rain.

The indigenous peoples of South America developed ancient civilizations in the Andes and Pacific regions. Today's South Americans are of European, African, and Asian, as well as indigenous, descent.

The chief European languages of the continent are Spanish and Portuguese (spoken in Brazil). Indigenous languages are still spoken in many regions. The great majority of South Americans are Roman Catholics, but there are a growing number of Protestants, too. South America is a meeting point for many different peoples and cultures.

DISCOVER MORE

• The widest point of South America is between Pariñas Point in Peru and Coqueiros Point in Brazil, a distance of 3,180 mi (5,120 km).

• The largest freshwater island on earth is Marajó in the Amazon River's estuary, in northeastern Brazil. It covers an area of about 15,500 sq mi (40,150 sq km).

These parrots, called macaws, live in the canopy, or treetops, of the Amazon rain forest. Their powerful beaks are used for eating wild fruits and berries. Their brilliantly colored plumage is used to make headdresses by some of the forest peoples.

CARIBBEAN SEA

Lesser Antille

Isthmus of Panama

VENEZUEL

COLOMBIA

ECUADOR

PERU

BOLIVI

SOUTH PACIFIC OCEAN

CHILE

ARGENTIN

1,000 miles

1,500 km

Chiloé I.

Gu.

Tierra del Fuego

A

B

GUYANA

SURINAME

FRENCH GUIANA

*NORTH
ATLANTIC
OCEAN*

*Fernando de
Noronha I.*

B R A Z I L

PARAGUAY

● Rio de Janeiro

*SOUTH
ATLANTIC
OCEAN*

URUGUAY

f San Matías

an Jorge

*Falkland Is
(U.K.)*

*South Georgia
(U.K.)*

SCOTIA SEA

C

D

E

F

G

Where in the world?

Washington, DC
to Rio de Janeiro

4,769 mi (7,675 km)
9 hr 10 min

7 A.M.
Washington,
DC

9 A.M.
Rio de
Janeiro

Search and find

Argentina E6
Bolivia D6
Brazil C7
Chile E5
Colombia B5
Ecuador B4
French Guiana . .B7
Guyana B6
Paraguay D6
Peru C4
Rio de Janeiro . .D8
Suriname B6
Uruguay E6
Venezuela A5

In the dense forests of southeastern Venezuela, the Carrao River, a tributary of the
Caroní, plunges over a sheer cliff to form the world's highest waterfall. Known locally
as Cherun-Meru, its international name is Angel Falls. This name comes from a U.S.
pilot named Jimmy Angel, who sighted the falls in 1933.

Continent facts

	Area sq mi (sq km)	% of Earth's area	Population	Largest country by area sq mi (sq km)	Largest country by population
South America	6,900,000 (17,871,000)	11.9	343,294,000	Brazil 3,286,485 (8,511,957)	Brazil 171,853,126

Colombia and Venezuela

THE ANDES MOUNTAINS FORM A long spine down the western South American continent. The northern end of this range splits into three chains; the eastern chain reaches into northwest Venezuela. These mountains drop to fertile valleys, hot and humid coastal plains, the cattle country of Venezuela's Llanos grasslands, and vast tracts of rain forest. Through this winds the Orinoco River, dividing into a delta on the east coast.

Colombia produces some of the world's finest coffee and is rich in emeralds and gold. In Venezuela, oil derricks rise from the shallow waters of Lake Maracaibo. Colombians and Venezuelans are descended mainly from indigenous peoples, Spanish colonists, and African slaves.

The soaring towers of Bogotá, the Colombian capital, rise from a plain against a backdrop of hills and mountains. The city's modern business districts and wealthy suburbs give way to shantytowns of poor shacks. Far from the bustle of the big city, Colombia's southern highlands present a different scene. Sheep graze on green pastures in the cool mountain air. A family of the Guambiano people walk to market, dressed in cloaks, called ponchos, and round felt hats, the women in long blue skirts.

In Venezuela, most people live in the towns and cities. Poor workers from other parts of Latin America have joined local people to seek employment in the factories of the busy capital, Caracas. Rural populations include llaneros (cowboys of the Llanos) and native peoples such as the Yanomami, who live in the remote rain forests.

CARIBBEAN S

Point Gallinas

Barranquilla
Pico Cristóbal Colón ▲
Cartagena ● 18,947 ft
(5,775 m)

Gulf of Venezuela

Maracaibo ●
L. Maracaibo

Pico Bolívar ▲
16,411 ft
(5,001 m)

ANDES MTS

Cauca
Magdalena

● Medellín

Cape Corrientes

● Manizales
Pereira ●

⊕ Bogotá

Meta
L.

Armenia ●   ● Ibagué

Cali ●

C O L O M B I A

▲ Nevado del Huila
18,865ft (5,749 m)

E C U A D O R

Vaupés

Apaporis
Caquetá

P E R U

Putumay

DISCOVER MORE

• A lake in the Colombian Andes is believed to contain priceless gold and emeralds thrown into its waters long ago by the Chibcha people. Legends of their ruler, the fabulous "golden man" or El Dorado, lured Spanish invaders to the region in the 16th century.

Caracas, capital of Venezuela, stretches for more than 9 mi (15 km) along the floor of a basin.

A

LESSER ANTILLES

Caracas ★

Valencia

Barcelona

Barquisimeto

Orinoco
Delta

Orinoco

Ciudad
Bolivar

Ciudad
Guayana

VENEZUELA

GUYANA

Angel
Falls

Gauviare

Orinoco

BRAZIL

300 miles

500 km

Colombia   Venezuela

Where in the world?

7 A.M.
Washington, DC

noon
GMT

7 A.M.
Bogotá

Washington, DC to Bogotá
2,365 mi (3,807 km)
4 hr 30 min

Bogotá lies on
04° 38'N latitude
74° 06'W longitude

Life facts

How long do people live?   How many people in
                             100 own cars?
U.S.A.
                76 years   48
Colombia
                70 years   3
Venezuela
                73 years   7

Linked by interweaving scarves,
men and women dance through
the streets of Medellín,
Colombia. They are celebrating
the Festival of Flowers, which is
held in the city each August. The
city exports flowers and is
famous for its orchids.

Search and find

Colombia   **Venezuela**
Capital: Bogotá .C5   *Capital*:
Armenia . . . . . .C4   Caracas B7
Barranquilla . . . .B5   Barcelona B8
Cali . . . . .D4   Barquisimeto . . .B6
Cartagena . . . . .B4   Ciudad Bolivar . .B8
Ibagué . . . . .C4   Ciudad
Manizales . . . . .C4   Guayana B8
Medellín . . . . . .C4   Maracaibo B5
Pereira . . . . . . .C4   Valencia B7

Country facts

	Area sq mi (sq km)	Population	Language	Religion	Currency
Colombia	440,762 (1,141,574)	39,309,422	Spanish	Catholic	Peso
Venezuela	352,143 (912,054)	23,203,466	Spanish	Catholic	Bolivar

B

C

D

E

F

G

The Guianas

GUYANA, SURINAME, FRENCH GUIANA

THE GUIANA HIGHLANDS RUN across the northeast of the South American continent, their mountain ridges clad in dense, tropical rain forest. Rivers drain the northern slopes, plunging down as spectacular waterfalls before crossing a hot, humid coastal plain. From here they flow into the Atlantic Ocean.

Most people live in the coastal region. The streets of Paramaribo, capital of Suriname, are lined with white wooden houses with balconies and porches, buildings in the old Dutch style, mosques, churches, and Hindu temples. Such contrasts are common in the region, for these three lands are inhabited by a mixture of peoples, partly of indigenous origin, partly descended from Africans, the British, Dutch, French, Portuguese, Chinese, Indians, and Southeast Asians. The result is one of the most exciting blends of cultures and languages in the Americas.

Lowland regions are fertile and enjoy a high rainfall. Many people work in sugarcane plantations, or farm rice and other tropical crops. Others work in mines, for the Guianas are rich in bauxite, the ore used to make aluminum.

In the remote forests of the interior, communities still live by hunting, fishing in the rivers, or growing crops such as cassava. This root produces a flour, which is made into starchy pancakes.

ATLANTIC
OCEAN

VENEZUELA

Charity

Cuyuni

Georgetown

New
Amsterdam

Linden

Corriverton

GUYANA

PAKARAIMA MTS

Mt Roraima
9,094 ft
(2,772 m)

S

Apoteri

Essequibo

KANUKU
MOUNTAINS

B

DISCOVER MORE

• *Red-hot cayenne peppers are named after the capital of French Guiana.*

• *The name Guiana or Guyana means "land of many waters." Many rivers flow across these lands.*

A statue of Queen Victoria (1819–1901) looks out over Georgetown, capital of Guyana. The country was ruled by Britain from 1831 to 1966. Today it is an independent republic.

A fisherman hauls in a heavyweight catch from muddy waters in the forests of French Guiana.

Where in the world?

7 A.M.   noon   8.00 A.M.
Washington, DC GMT Georgetown

Washington, DC to Georgetown
2,520 mi (4,056 km)
4 hr 50 min

Georgetown lies on
06° 29'N latitude
58° 16'W longitude

Life facts

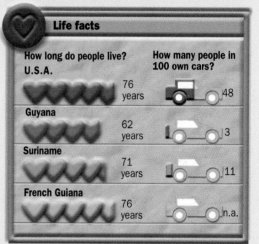

How long do people live?   How many people in 100 own cars?

U.S.A.
76 years   48

Guyana
62 years   3

Suriname
71 years   11

French Guiana
76 years   n.a.

Search and find

Guyana
Capital:
    Georgetown . . .C5
Apoteri D5
Charity B5
Corriverton C6
Linden C5
New Amsterdam .C6

Suriname
Capital:
    Paramaribo . . .C7

Albina C8
Nieuw Nickerie .C6
Totness C7

French Guiana
Capital:
    Cayenne D9
Kourou D9
Mana C8
Sainte-Elie D8
Saint Laurent
    du Maroni C8

Guyana

Suriname

French Guiana

Paramaribo

Nieuw Nickerie • Totness

• Mana
Albina • Saint Laurent du Maroni

Devil's I.

Kourou

SURINAME

W.J. van Blommestein L.

WILHELMINA MOUNTAINS

Juliana Top
4,200 ft
1,280 m)

Suriname

Maroni

Sainte-Elie   Cayenne

FRENCH GUIANA

ORANJE MOUNTAINS

B R A Z I L

100 miles

100 km

Country facts

	Area sq mi (sq km)	Population	Language	Religion	Currency
Guyana	83,000 (214,970)	705,156	English/Creole	Hindu/Protestant	Dollar
Suriname	63,039 (163,271)	431,156	Dutch/Sranan/Hindu	Hindu/Catholic/Sunni Muslim	Suriname Guilder
French Guiana	33,399 (86,503)	167,982	French	Catholic	Euro

Brazil

A LIGHT AIRCRAFT BUMPS ONTO a red-dirt landing strip, cleared from remote rain forest near Brazil's border with Venezuela. This is the territory of the Yanomami people. Inside large, circular, palm-thatched huts, children play on floors of beaten earth. Several families live in the same building, each with their own hearth, where they cook fish or a starchy root called cassava. Hunters rest on hammocks slung between the hut's timbers.

Tens of thousands of streams feed the broad, muddy Amazon River as it winds eastward to the Atlantic Ocean. On the coast, large, modern cities such as Rio de Janeiro and São Paulo rise behind long, sandy beaches. The downtown skyscrapers and rich suburbs are fringed by *favelas* (slums). Most Brazilians, whether rich or poor, whether of African, Portuguese, or mixed descent, love sport (especially soccer), music, and dance, especially the samba. Rio's five days of carnival must be seen to be believed.

The great rain forests of Brazil take up one-third of the country. The northeast is mostly a dry land of woodland and scrub.

Brazil

DISCOVER MORE

• *Do you like your coffee sweet? Brazil produces more sugarcane and more coffee than any other country in the world.*

• *Brazil has won soccer's World Cup four times, more than any other country.*

• *The Amazon is the world's second longest river and drains an area of more than 2.7 million sq mi (7 million sq km).*

200 miles

300 km

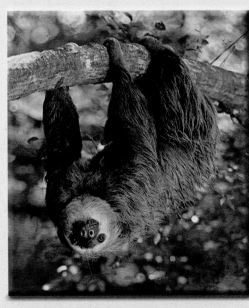

The sloth, a slow-moving creature of the Amazon rain forest, hangs upside down from the branches of trees.

**Map labels:**
COLOMBIA, VENEZUELA, GUYANA, SURINAME, FRENCH, Branco, Negro, Neblina Peak 9,988 ft (3,013 m), Manaus, Amazon, Japurá, SELVAS, Madeira, Tapajós, Juruá, Purus, Aripuanã, PERU, Jiparaná, Arinos, SERRA DOS PARECIS, Guaporé, BOLIVIA, MAT P, Cuiabá, Campo Gran, PARAGUAY, Par, Ita Rese, Iguaç Falls, ARGENTINA, Uruguay, Sant Mari, URUGUAY, Mir L

1   2   3   4   5

The city of São Paulo has the largest population in South America—more than 17 million. It lies on the rim of a rich agricultural and industrial region, whose inhabitants are known as Paulistas.

Where in the world?

7 A.M.
Washington, DC

noon
GMT

9 A.M.
Brasília

Washington, DC to Brasília
4,212 mi (6,778 km)
✈ 8 hr 6 min

Brasília lies on
15° 52'N latitude
47° 55'W longitude

Life facts

How long do people live?

U.S.A.
76 years

Brazil
65 years

How many people in 100 own cars?

48

8

Marajó Bay

Marajó I.

•Belém

Tocantins

São Marcos Bay
•São Luís

•Fortaleza

Fernando de Noronha I.

•Teresina

Cape São Roque

•Natal

S E R T Ã O

•Recife

Araguaia

Parnaíba

Sobradinho Reservoir

São Francisco

•Maceió

A Z I L

•Salvador

R O S S O
E A U

BRAZILIAN HIGHLANDS

⊙Brasília

ATLANTIC OCEAN

•Goiânia

•Uberlândia

•Belo Horizonte

•Campos• *Cape São Tomé*

•São Paulo
•Rio de Janeiro
•Santos

SERRA DO MAR

•Curitiba

•Florianópolis

•Pôrto Alegre
tos Lagoon

A canoe is paddled out from a village hut on the shores of the Amazon River. This broad, muddy river flows through the world's largest rain forest. Its waters are inhabited by fierce, flesh-eating piranha fish.

Longest rivers

Nile   4,145 mi (6,670 km)

Amazon   4,000 mi (6,437 km)

Mississippi   3,741 mi (6,020 km)

Brazil

Search and find

Brazil	
Capital: Brasília .D7	Manaus B5
Belém B7	Natal C9
Belo Horizonte . .E7	Pôrto Alegre F6
Campo Grande . .E6	Recife C9
Campos E8	Rio de Janeiro . .E7
Cuiabá D5	Salvador D8
Curitiba F6	Santa Maria F6
Florianópolis . . .F6	Santos E7
Fortaleza C8	São Luís B7
Goiânia D6	São Paulo E7
Maceió D9	Teresina C7
	Uberlândia E7

Country facts

	Area sq mi (sq km)	Population	Language	Religion	Currency
Brazil	3,286,470 (8,511,957)	171,853,126	Portuguese	Catholic	Real

A

B

C

D

E

F

G

Middle Andes

PERU, ECUADOR

A YOUNG BOY PLAYS ON A SIMPLE flute as he herds llamas. They pass between ancient stone walls and terraced fields built by the Inca people, who ruled most of the Andes Mountains before Spanish invaders conquered Peru in 1532. Sheer, forested peaks climb into the mist.

In Ecuador and Peru, the snowcapped peaks of the Andes soar to more than 20,000 feet (6,000 m) above sea level, a long chain of peaks, volcanoes, and glaciers. They tower over sweeping plateaus and cool lakes, which reflect blue skies. Potatoes are grown at these high altitudes and left for the sun and frost to freeze-dry them. They will be boiled later to make vegetable stew.

In the east, mountain streams drain into the brimming waterways of the hot and sticky Amazon rain forest. In the west, the foothills of the Andes drop to a narrow plain along the Pacific coast, a hot, dry region broken by fertile river valleys. Here are farms, fishing villages, and large, modern cities such as Lima, with its port of Callao. Ecuador also includes the distant Pacific islands of the Galápagos, where unique giant tortoises live.

Spanish is spoken throughout the region, but local languages such as Quechua or Aymara are also widespread. About 90 percent of the population is Roman Catholic, and religious festivals are marked with colorful processions and pilgrimages.

DISCOVER MORE

• Ecuador takes its name from the equator, on which it lies. However, its capital, Quito, is located so high above the hot lowlands that the climate there is mild all year round.

• The Peruvian railroad reaches 15,846 ft (4,830 m) in the Andes—the highest track anywhere in the world.

Long lines are scraped from the desert floor of the Nazca region in southern Peru. They are in the shapes of animals, birds, spirals, and other patterns. Many are best viewed from the air, and yet they were created more than 2,000 years ago. They probably marked routes for religious processions.

(Map labels) Punta Galera · Quito · ECUADOR · Chimborazo 20,561 ft (6,267 m) · Guayaquil · Cuenca · Gulf of Guayaquil · Napo · Marañón · Iquito · Piura · Punta Negra · ANDES · Chiclayo · Huallaga · Ucayali · Trujillo · Chimbote · Huascarán · MOUNTAINS · PER · PACIFIC OCEAN · Callao · Lima · Huancayo · Paracas Peninsula · Nazca · COLOMBIA

Highest mountains

Huascarán
22,205 ft
(6,768 m)

Mount McKinley
20,320 ft
(6,194 m)

Where in the world?

7 A.M.   noon   7 A.M.
Washington, DC   GMT   Lima

Washington, DC to Lima
3,508 mi (5,646 km)
6 hr 45 min

Lima lies on
12° 06'S latitude
76° 55'W longitude

Life facts

How long do people live?

U.S.A.   76 years

Peru   70 years

Ecuador   72 years

How many people in 100 own cars?

48

2

2

A young Ecuadorean holds up pods from a cacao tree. They contain the beans that are used to make chocolate. Cacao is a native plant of the American tropics.

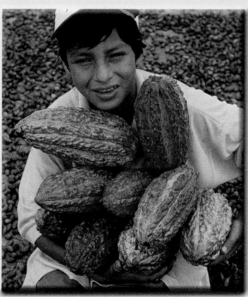

Search and find

Peru
Capital: Lima . . .E5
Arequipa F7
Callao E5
Chiclayo D4
Chimbote D4
Cuzco F6
Huancayo E5
Iquitos C6

Machu Picchu . . .F6
Nazca F6
Piura C4
Trujillo D4

Ecuador
Capital: Quito . .B4
Cuenca B4
Guayaquil B4

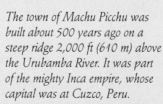

300 miles

500 km

The town of Machu Picchu was built about 500 years ago on a steep ridge 2,000 ft (610 m) above the Urubamba River. It was part of the mighty Inca empire, whose capital was at Cuzco, Peru.

Amazon

BRAZIL

Purus

achu cchu   Cuzco

El Misti
19,101 ft
(5,821 m)

Arequipa

BOLIVIA

L. Titicaca

CHILE

Peru

Ecuador

Country facts

	Area sq mi (sq km)	Population	Language	Religion	Currency
Peru	496,223 (1,285,218)	26,624,582	Spanish	Catholic	New Sol
Ecuador	105,037 (272,046)	12,562,496	Spanish	Catholic	US Dollar

Central South America

BOLIVIA, PARAGUAY

Bolivia

Paraguay

BOLIVIA AND PARAGUAY ARE two landlocked countries occupying the heart of the South American continent. Bolivia has two capitals, La Paz and Sucre, both high in the Andes mountain range, where dazzling snowfields tower above high plateaus and lakes. In these cities, modern high-rise buildings overlook old churches built by Spanish colonists. Country women in the streets wear long, full skirts; shawls and cloaks woven from llama wool; and round derby-style hats. Take a bus into Bolivia's Oriente, or eastern region, and find rough roads plunging down to the Amazon River basin, tropical forests, swamps, and farms producing bananas, coffee, and sugarcane.

The Gran Chaco, a scrub-covered plain that floods in the rainy season, extends into Paraguay. Here, roads are few and far between, and are best traveled on horseback. Most people live east of the Paraguay River, in the large city of Asunción or on the more fertile farmland of the east and south. Almost half of the labor force works on the land. Paraguay depends on its farmers for 90 percent of its exports. Major crops include wheat, cotton, and soybeans. A shrub called the Paraguay holly is grown to make a kind of tea called *yerba maté*, which is widely drunk in parts of South America.

Map labels: BRAZIL · Riberalta · Guaporé · PERU · Beni · Mamoré · San Miguel · L. Titicaca · Ancohume 20,958 ft ▲(6,388 m) · B O L I V · ⊕ La Paz · Cochabamba · Santa Cruz · Nevado ▲ Sajama 21,463 ft (6,542 m) · ●Oruro · Lake Poopó · ALTIPLANO · CHILE · ⊕Sucre · ●Potosí · ANDES MTS · ●Tarija · A R G

DISCOVER MORE

• Paraguayan lacework is so fine that it is known as ñandutí, which means "spider's web" in the Guarani language.

• The Itaipu Dam on the Paraná River is the world's biggest. The river's flow is used to power great turbines that generate electricity. It is jointly owned by Paraguay and Brazil.

The Brahman, or zebu, breed of cattle has a humped back, floppy ears, and upturned horns. It originated in southern Asia but now lives in warm, subtropical regions around the world. It is perfectly adapted for life in the warm areas of Bolivia and Paraguay.

Bolivia

Paraguay

Country facts

	Area sq mi (sq km)	Population	Language	Religion	Currency
Bolivia	424,162 (1,098,580)	7,982,850	Spanish/Quechua/Aymara	Catholic	Boliviano
Paraguay	157,046 (406,749)	5,434,095	Spanish/Guarani	Catholic	Guaraní

In Bolivia, the Andes Mountains form two long ranges called the Eastern and Western Cordilleras. Between the two lies the high plateau, or Altiplano. It is a treeless land with lakes and wide salt flats.

A

300 miles
500 km

GRAN
CHACO

PARAGUAY

Verde
Pilcomayo
Paraguay

Concepción

Ciudad Itaipu
del Este Dam

Asunción

Paraguay

Alto Paraná

Where in the world?

7 A.M.   noon   8 A.M.
Washington, DC GMT   La Paz

Washington, DC to La Paz
3,854 mi (6,203 km)
7 hr 25 min

La Paz lies on
16° 31'S latitude
68° 10'W longitude

Life facts

How long do people live?   **How many people in 100 own cars?**

U.S.A.
76 years   48

Bolivia
61 years   3

Paraguay
72 years   1

Women rest and talk after a day visiting La Paz. Native peoples such as the Quechua and Aymara make up two-thirds of the Bolivian population.

Search and find

Southern Andes

ARGENTINA, CHILE, URUGUAY

Chile
Uruguay
Argentina

THE JAGGED RIDGES and volcanoes of the Andes run southward from the tropics toward bleak, frozen coasts. The continent breaks up into ragged islands around Tierra del Fuego. Great gray-green seas power their way past Cape Horn.

West of the Andes lies Chile, a long, narrow country. Visitors remember it for its sunny vineyards and the crowds in Santiago, the capital. Few visit the deserts of the north, or the wilderness of the far south.

East of the Andes lie the farmland and cattle country of Argentina and Uruguay, on either side of the broad estuary of La Plata. Spanish invaders and settlers from Europe drove most of the people from these lands and founded the cities of Montevideo in Uruguay and Buenos Aires in Argentina, which is the home of a dramatic Latin dance called the tango.

The lasting image of Argentina is of cowboys called *gauchos* galloping across vast, lonely grasslands of the pampas. Times have changed, but gaucho folklore lives on whenever Argentineans barbecue beef on an open fire. Grapevines are grown in the fertile lands around Mendoza, but the remote, windswept grasslands of Patagonia are best suited for raising sheep.

DISCOVER MORE

• Chile's Atacama Desert is the driest place on earth, with no rainfall.

• The monkey puzzle tree, or Chile pine, can produce cones the size of a coconut. It grows in the southern Andes, often in bleak landscapes of volcanic ash and rocks.

The fishing port of Ushuaia is built at the southern limits of the Americas. This remote spot attracts visitors interested in seeing penguins and other wildlife.

500 miles

500 km

Arica
Iquique
ATACAMA DESERT
BOLIVIA
CHACO
PARAGUAY
Antofagasta
Salta
San Miguel de Tucumán
Formosa
Resistencia
Corrientes
Posadas
Bermejo
Ojos del Salado 22,575 ft (6,880 m)
Santiago del Estero
Catamarca
Salado
Paraná
GRAN
MESOPOTAMIA
Coquimbo
Mar Chiquita
Córdoba
Concordia
Salto
Punta Lengua de Vaca
San Juan
SIERRA DE CORDOBA
Santa Fé
Paysa
Cerro Aconcagua
Mendoza
Río Cuarto
Paraná
UR
Valparaíso
San Rafael
Buenos Aires
Santiago
Rancagua
PAMPAS
La Plata
PACIFIC OCEAN
Talca
A R G E N T I N A
Chillán
Salado
Concepción
Mar del Plata
Punta Lavapié
Bahia Blanca
CHILE
Neuquén
Colorado
Blanca Bay
Temuco
Valdivia
Negro
Punta de la Galera
Limay
San Matías Gulf
Osorno
PATAGONIA
Valdés Peninsula
Puerto Montt
Chiloé I.
Chubut
Cape Quilán
Chico
CHONOS ARCHIPELAGO
Comodoro Rivadavia
San Jorge Gulf
L. Buenos Aires
Deseado
Cape Tres Puntas
Gulf of Penas
Chico
FALKLAND ISLANDS (U.K.)
Santa Cruz
Wellington I.
Grande Bay
Stanley
West Falkland
East Falkland
REINA ADELAIDA ARCHIPELAGO
Punta Arenas
Strait of Magellan
Tierra del Fuego
Cape San Diego
Santa Inés I.
Ushuaia
Cape Horn

1 | 2 | 3 | 4 | 5

Highest mountains

Cerro Aconcagua
22,831 ft
(6,959 m)

Mount McKinley
20,320 ft
(6,194 m)

Where in the world?

7 A.M.   noon   9 A.M.
Washington, DC GMT   Buenos Aires

Washington, DC to Buenos Aires	Buenos Aires lies on
5,176 mi (8,330 km) 9 hr 55 min	34° 20'S latitude 58° 30'W longitude

Life facts

How long do people live?   **How many people in 100 own cars?**

U.S.A.   76 years   48

Argentina   75 years   13

Chile   75 years   6

Uruguay   76 years   14

The Atacama Desert is bone-dry and barren, but it is rich in nitrates, iodine, iron ore, and copper.

UAY
ontevideo
Plata

*TLANTIC
OCEAN*

Argentina

Chile

Uruguay

The folklore of the gauchos, Argentina's wild cowboys of the 1800s, lives on at a modern cattle roundup. Beef is still an important export.

Country facts

	Area sq mi (sq km)	Population	Language	Religion	Currency
Argentina	1,057,518 (2,738,972)	36,737,664	Spanish	Catholic	Peso
Chile	292,258 (756,948)	14,973,843	Spanish	Catholic	Peso
Uruguay	68,039 (176,221)	3,308,523	Spanish	Catholic	Peso

Search and find

Argentina
Capital:
  Buenos Aires .D6
Bahía Blanca . . .D5
Catamarca C4
Comodoro
  Rivadavia F5
Concordia C6
Córdoba C5
Corrientes B6
Formosa B6
La Plata D6
Mar del Plata . . .D6
Mendoza C4
Neuquén D4
Paraná C5
Posadas B6
Resistencia B6
Río Cuarto D5
Rosario C5
Salta B5
San Juan C4
San Miguel
  de Tucumán . .B5
San Rafael D4
Santa Fé C5

Santiago
  del Estero C5
Ushuaia G5

Chile
Capital: Santiago D4
Antofagasta B4
Arica A4
Chillán D4
Concepción D4
Coquimbo C4
Iquique A4
Osorno E4
Puerto Montt . . .E4
Punta Arenas . . .G4
Rancagua D4
Talca D4
Temuco E4
Valdivia E4
Valparaiso D4

Uruguay
Capital:
  Montevideo . . .D6
Paysandú C6
Salto C6

Atlantic Ocean
and Islands

THE ATLANTIC OCEAN DIVIDES EUROPE AND AFRICA
from the Americas. Its salty waters fill the hot and humid
lagoons of Africa's Guinea Coast and sparkle off the
Florida Keys. In mid-ocean its white-crested waves may
tower to terrifying heights.

The Atlantic is the world's second-largest ocean,
covering an area of about 31,744,015 square miles
(82,217,000 sq km). The North Atlantic spreads into the
freezing Arctic Ocean. It flows eastward to form the
North, Baltic, and Mediterranean seas, and westward to
form the Caribbean Sea. With an average depth of
11,729 feet (3,575 m), in the Puerto Rico Trench it plunges
to an awesome, pitch-black 30,223 feet (9,212 m). The
South Atlantic merges with the Pacific and Indian oceans.

Running north to south, the Mid-Atlantic Ridge is a
crack in the ocean floor. Molten rock bursts through,
creating underwater volcanoes. Islands, many of them
volcanic, rise from the ocean—Iceland, the Azores and
Madeira, the Canaries, St. Helena, Tristan da Cunha, and
Ascension.

In the extreme north and south, the ocean exchanges
cold polar waters with warm tropical waters through a
system of currents. The cool Benguela Current sweeps
down southern Africa, while the Americas are warmed by
the Brazil Current and the Gulf Stream. The North
Atlantic Drift warms the shores of northwestern Europe.

The trade winds (used by merchant ships in the days
of sail) blow in from the northeast and southeast toward
the equator, where there is a large windless area called the
doldrums. Westerly winds circle the far north and south.
In the South Atlantic they join the roaring forties,
powerful winds of the Southern Atlantic Ocean—the
waters of the South Pacific, South Atlantic, and Indian
Ocean, which surround Antarctica.

DISCOVER MORE

• The islanders of Tristan
da Cunha live in one of the
most remote places in the
world. Their home is
1,513 mi (2,435 km) from
the island of St. Helena and
1,702 mi (2,740 km) from
Africa.

Funchal is the chief city on the island of Madeira, which is
grouped with the African continent but governed as a part
of Portugal, in Europe. It rises from a fine, natural harbor.

Baffin Bay

Greenlan
(DENMAR

Cape Chidley

LABRADOR SEA

NORTH AMERICA

Newfoundland

Cape Race

Sable I.

Cape Sable

Cape Cod

Cape Fear

Bermuda
(U.K.)

Gulf of Mexico

CARIBBEAN SEA

SOUTH AMERICA

Cape Oran

PACIFIC OCEAN

Cape Corrientes

Cape Blanco

Falkland Is
(U.K.)

Cape Horn

SCOTIA SEA

A

B

C

D

E

F

G

NORWEGIAN SEA

ICELAND

Faroe Is
(DENMARK)

Shetland Is

Rockall
(U.K.)

*NORTH
SEA*

*NORTH
ATLANTIC
OCEAN*

**BRITISH
ISLES**

E U R O P E

ewell

Cape Finisterre

*MEDITERRANEAN
SEA*

Azores
(PORTUGAL)

Madeira
(PORTUGAL)

Canary Is
(SPAIN)

A F R I C A

**CAPE
VERDE**

St. Paul Rocks
(BRAZIL)

*Cape
Palmas*

Bioko

**SÃO TOMÉ
& PRÍNCIPE**

Fernando de Noronha I.
(BRAZIL)

Cape São Roque

Ascension I.
(St. Helena)

Trindade
(BRAZIL)

St. Helena
(U.K.)

*SOUTH
ATLANTIC
OCEAN*

Tristan da Cunha
(St. Helena)

*Cape
Agulhas*

Gough I.
(St. Helena)

uth Georgia
(U.K.)

Bouvet I.
(NORWAY)

South Sandwich Is
(U.K.)

1,000 miles

3,000 km

Where in the world?

7 A.M.
Washington, DC

noon
GMT

1 P.M.
Madeira

Washington, DC to Madeira
3,350 mi (5,391 km)
6 hr 25 min

Madeira lies on
32° 42'N latitude
16° 46'W longitude

The Bermudas are a group of about 300 low-lying, rocky islands in the
Atlantic Ocean. About 20 of the islands are inhabited, and the warm
climate attracts many tourists.

The port of Reykjavik, the capital of Iceland, is a center of fisheries,
business, and manufacturing. It has an average January temperature of
34°F (1°C) and a July average of 52°F (11°C).

Search and find

Europe

EUROPE IS A SMALL CONTINENT, BUT ONE OF GREAT variety. In wintry Finland, spruce forests and frozen lakes may be blanketed with thick snow, while parts of Spain are so hot that they are becoming desert. Northern France and the United Kingdom have a mild and moist climate, with green fields and woodlands.

The Netherlands are as flat as a pancake, while towering mountain ranges run through southern Europe, including the Pyrenees, the Alps, the Carpathians, and the Caucasus Mountains, where Elbrus rises to 18,510 feet (5,642 m) above sea level.

The European continent belongs to the same landmass as Asia, and together the two continents are often called Eurasia. They are, however, set apart by their different way of life and historical traditions. The dividing line between the two continents runs along the Russian Federation's Ural Mountains, and then follows the Caucasus range, between the Black and Caspian seas. The Strait of Gibraltar, between Morocco and Spain at the western end of the Mediterranean Sea, separates Europe from Africa.

The 47 European countries range in size from the Russian Federation which is by far the largest country, extending across Asia, to the Vatican City which is the smallest. A growing number of countries belong to a close political and economic alliance called the European Union, which provides common economic and other policies for all member countries.

DISCOVER MORE

• Europe has a longer coastline in proportion to its physical size than any other continent. This is because it has so many inlets, bays, and peninsulas.

• The Alps are the highest mountains in western Europe.

ICELAND

Faroe Is (DENMARK)

NORWEGIAN SEA

Shetland Is

SWEDEN

Gulf of Both

NORWAY

Hebrides

Orkney Is

Scotland

Northern Ireland

NORTH SEA

Skagerrak

BALTIC SEA

UNITED

IRELAND

KINGDOM

DENMARK

Wales

Kaliningra (RUSSIAN FED

England NETHERLANDS

POLAND

BELGIUM GERMANY

LUXEMBOURG

CZECH REPUBLIC

LIECHTENSTEIN

SLOVAK

Bay of Biscay

FRANCE

AUSTRIA

SWITZERLAND

HUNGAR

SLOVENIA

CROATIA

PORTUGAL

BOSNIA-HERZEGOVINA

UGOSLAVIA

ANDORRA

MONACO

SAN MARINO

S P A I N

Corsica (FRANCE)

ITALY

ALBANIA

Balearic Is

VATICAN CITY

Sardinia (ITALY)

Strait of Gibraltar **Gibraltar** (U.K.)

M E D I T E R R A N E A N

Sicily

The gondola is the traditional Venice boat. It is poled along the city's canals. Today, gondolas are mostly used by tourists who also use the motor boats and ferries around the waterways.

1 2 3 4 5

A

B

C

D

E

F

G

Kolguyev I.

Iceland is located just below the Arctic Circle. It is an island of bleak moors, scattered with snow in winter.

NLAND

TONIA

ATVIA

HUANIA

BELARUS

UKRAINE

MOLDOVA

ROMANIA

BULGARIA

ACEDONIA

REECE

Crete
E A

R U S S I A N
F E D E R A T I O N
★ Moscow

CASPIAN SEA

BLACK SEA

300 miles

500 km

The Parthenon in Greece was built between 447 and 432 B.C., and was dedicated to Athena, the patron goddess of the city of Athens.

Where in the world?

Washington, DC to Moscow
4,873 mi (7,842 km)
✈ 9 hr 20 min

| 7 A.M. | 3 P.M. |
| Washington, DC | Moscow |

Search and find

Albania E6	Lithuania C6
Andorra E4	Luxembourg D5
Austria D5	Macedonia E6
Balearic Islands .E4	Moldova D7
Belarus D7	Monaco E4
Belgium D4	Moscow C7
Bosnia-	Netherlands D5
Herzegovina . .E6	Norway B5
Bulgaria E7	Orkney Islands . .C4
Corsica E4	Poland D6
Crete F6	Portugal E3
Croatia E5	Romania E6
Czech Republic .D5	Russian
Denmark C5	Federation . . .C8
Estonia C6	San Marino E5
Faroe Islands . . .B4	Sardinia E5
Finland B6	Shetland
France D4	Islands B4
Germany D5	Sicily F5
Gibraltar F3	Slovakia D6
Greece F6	Slovenia E5
Hebrides C4	Spain E3
Hungary E6	Sweden B5
Iceland B4	Switzerland D5
Ireland C4	Ukraine D7
Italy E5	United Kingdom .C4
Kolguyev Island .A7	Vatican City E5
Latvia C6	Yugoslavia E6
Liechtenstein . . .D5	

Continent facts

	Area sq mi (sq km)	% of Earth's area	Population	Largest country by area sq mi (sq km)	Largest country by population
Europe	4,015,000 (10,400,000)	6.6	508,285,000	Ukraine* 233,089 (603,700)	Germany* 82,087,361

*largest country entirely in Europe

Scandinavia

SWEDEN, FINLAND, NORWAY, ICELAND, DENMARK

A
B
C
D
E
F
G

A trawlerman repairs nets on a small island off the coast of southern Iceland. The fishing industry is important, but like other nearby countries, Iceland faces decline in stocks of fish because of pollution and overfishing.

THE NORTH SEA AND THE Baltic Sea can be blue and sparkling on summer days, but they are often gray and stormy during the cold winters.

To the south of the Skagerrak strait is Denmark, which is made up of the Jutland Peninsula and some of the neighboring islands. Here the farmland is flat and dotted with wind turbines. Most Danes are city-dwellers. Seagulls squabble on the old docks of the capital, Copenhagen, a lively port whose Danish name means "merchants' harbor."

North of the Skagerrak, the mountainous Scandinavian peninsula stretches far beyond the Arctic Circle, the home of Saami reindeer herders. Norway, with its ragged coastline carved into fjords by the movements of ice, is in the western part of the peninsula. To the east is Sweden, a land of lakes and green forests, with heavy winter snows but milder summers. Most Norwegians and Swedes live in southern or coastal regions, often in large cities such as Oslo or Stockholm, where the climate is less severe. The Scandinavian peninsula is linked to the Russian Federation by Finland, whose snowy forests provide a rich resource of timber.

The people of Iceland, far away in the North Atlantic, are of Scandinavian descent. Their fascinating island is a land of bleak moors, fiery volcanoes, and hot springs.

Grimsey
Olafsfjördhur
Isafjördhur • Húsavik
Akureyri
Ólafsvik *Mývatn*
ICELAND Eskifjördhur
Hvítá *VATNAJÖKULL*
Borgarnes *Hvítá*
Reykjavik *Thorsá*
• Höfn
Keflavik
Hvannadalshnúkur
Heimaey • Vik *6,952 ft*
Surtsey *(2,119 m)*

1 inch to 130 miles

ATLANTIC OCEAN

Trom

VESTERÅLEN IS
LOFOTEN IS • Narvik
Mt Kebnekai 6,926 ft (2,111 m)
Bodø

Um

Trondheim Örnsköldsv

Kristiansund Östersund

Ålesund *Galdhøpiggen 8,100 ft* Sundsvall

NORWAY ▲*(2,469 m)* **SWEDEN**

Voss Lillehammer Söderhamn

Bergen Gjøvik Falun Gävl

Hageland **Oslo** Uppsa

Stavanger Drammen Karlstad Västerås

Skien *L. Vänern* Örebro

Fredrikstad Södertäl

Norrköping

Kristiansand Linköping

Skagerrak Göteborg *L. Vättern* Västerv

Borås Jönköping

Ålborg Växjö Borghol

Randers *Kattegat* Halmstad

Århus Helsingborg Karlsham

DENMARK Lund Karlskro

Esbjerg **Copenhagen**

Kolding Odense Malmö

GERMANY *BORNHOLM (DENMARK)*

NORTH SEA

DISCOVER MORE

• *Northern Scandinavia is often called the "Land of the Midnight Sun" because it stays light all night long in summer. During the bitter winters, it stays dark all day.*

• *Sweden has at least 90,000 lakes. They were created when great sheets of ice scarred and pitted the land during the Ice Age, more than 10,000 years ago.*

The Little Mermaid overlooks Copenhagen's harbor. This much-loved statue honors Hans Christian Andersen (1805–75), who wrote such famous children's tales as The Ugly Duckling, The Snow Queen, *and* The Little Mermaid.

1   2   3   4   5

ARCTIC OCEAN

North Cape

Hammerfest • Vadsø

L. Inari

Mt Haltiatunturi
4,344 ft (1,324 m)

LAPLAND

Kiruna

Gällivare Rovaniemi

Luleå • Kemi
Piteå
Skellefteå • Oulu

meå
Kokkola
Kuopio

Gulf of Bothnia

Vaasa   F I N L A N D

Jyväskylä
Tampere L. Saimaa
Pöri   Lahti
ÅLAND Hämeenlinna
IS
(FINLAND) Turku   Kotka
Espoo **Helsinki**

Mariehamn

ockholm

BALTIC SEA

GOTLAND
sby

Life facts

How long do people live?

U.S.A. 76 years

Sweden 79 years

Finland 77 years

Norway 78 years

Iceland 79 years

Denmark 76 years

How many people in 100 own cars?

48
41
37
37
46
32

Chain saws and powerful machinery make light work of logging in the conifer forests of Finland. The timber is used in building, furniture manufacture, and papermaking.

200 miles

200 km

Sweden   Finland   Norway   Iceland   Denmark

Where in the world?

7 A.M.   noon   1 P.M.
Washington, DC GMT Stockholm

Washington, DC to Stockholm
4,130 mi (6,646 km)
7 hr 55 min

Stockholm lies on
59° 23′ N latitude
18° 00′ E longitude

Search and find

Sweden
Capital: Stockholm .E6
Borås F5
Borgholm F6
Falun E6
Gällivare C6
Gävle E6
Göteborg F5
Halmstad F5
Helsingborg F5
Jönköping F5
Karlshamn F5
Karlskrona F6
Karlstad E5
Kiruna B6
Linköping F6
Luleå C6
Lund F5
Malmö F5
Norrköping E6
Örebro E5
Örnsköldsvik . . .D6
Östersund D5
Piteå C6
Skellefteå C6
Söderhamn E6
Södertälje E6
Sundsvall D6
Umeå D6
Uppsala E6
Västerås E6
Västervik F6
Växjö F5
Visby F6

Finland
Capital: Helsinki .E7
Espoo E7
Hämeenlinna . . .E7
Jyväskylä D7
Kemi C7
Kokkola D7
Kotka E7
Kuopio D7
Lahti E7
Mariehamn E6
Oulu C7
Pöri D7

Rovaniemi C7
Tampere D7
Turku E7
Vaasa D6

Norway
Capital: Oslo . . .E5
Ålesund D4
Bergen E4
Bodø C5
Drammen E5
Fredrikstad E5
Gjøvik E4
Hammerfest . . .B6
Haugesund E4
Kristiansand . . .E4
Kristiansund . . .D4
Lillehammer E5
Narvik B6
Skien E5
Stavanger E4
Tromsø B6
Trondheim D5
Vadsø B7
Voss E4

Iceland
Capital: Reykjavik .C4
Akureyri B4
Borgarnes C4
Eskifjördhur C5
Höfn C5
Húsavik B4
Isafjördhur B3
Keflavík C3
Olafsfjördhur . . .B4
Ólafsvik C3
Vik C4

Denmark
Capital:
 Copenhagen . .F5
Ålborg F5
Århus F5
Esbjerg F4
Kolding F4
Odense F5
Randers F5

Country facts

	Area sq mi (sq km)	Population	Language	Religion	Currency
Sweden	173,731 (449,963)	8,911,296	Swedish	E/Lutheran*	Krona
Finland	130,127 (337,029)	5,158,372	Finnish	E/Lutheran*	Euro
Norway	125,181 (324,219)	4,438,547	Norwegian	E/Lutheran*	Krone
Iceland	39,699 (102,819)	272,512	Icelandic	E/Lutheran*	Krona
Denmark	16,639 (43,095)	5,356,845	Danish	E/Lutheran*	Krone

* Evangelical/Lutheran

British Isles

UNITED KINGDOM, REPUBLIC OF IRELAND

Republic
of Ireland

United
Kingdom

BATTERED BY THE ATLANTIC
Ocean, the coastline of
northwest Europe breaks up
into the numerous channels
and islands of the British Isles.
The western shores have a
mild, often rainy, climate as a
result of the oceans and winds. The inhabitants of
these islands include English, Scots, Welsh, and
Irish, and large numbers of people of Asian and
Afro-Caribbean descent.

The capital of the United Kingdom is London,
England, a large city on the Thames River. Red
buses and black taxis roar past street markets,
fountains, theaters, old churches, royal palaces,
and green parks. Beyond London lie wheat
fields, rocky shores bordering coastlines, the
moors and lakes of northern England, and the
mountains of Wales and Scotland, England's
partner countries in Great Britain. The British
countryside is dotted with historic villages
and castles, but there are also large,
sprawling cities such as Birmingham,
Liverpool, Manchester, and Glasgow.

Across the Irish Sea, Northern
Ireland is ruled as part of the United
Kingdom, but the Republic of Ireland is
an independent country. Its capital is the
historic city of Dublin, through which
the Liffey River flows. The Irish
countryside is peaceful, with lush
farmland, peat bogs, and rocky
cliffs which tower above the
rolling Atlantic surf.

DISCOVER MORE

• About 10,000 years ago,
the British Isles were joined
with France. However, the
sea gradually flooded the
low-lying land to form the
English Channel. They were
not linked again until a rail
tunnel was opened in 1994.

100 miles

150 km

1   2   3   4   5

A

Where in the world?

7 A.M. noon noon
Washington, DC GMT London

Washington, DC to London	London lies on
3,674 mi (5,913 km)	51° 30'N latitude
7 hr 5 min	00° 07'W longitude

erwick

Edinburgh Castle stands on top of a large rocky hill overlooking the city.

NORTH SEA

ly I.

ewcastle upon Tyne
urham
Middlesbrough

Life facts

How long do people live?

U.S.A.
76 years

United Kingdom
77 years

Republic of Ireland
76 years

How many people in 100 own cars?

48

42

29

C

Flamborough Head

eds Hull

Spurn Head

heffield

NGLAND

Nottingham
Derby
eicester
Coventry Peterborough
Cambridge
orthampton Ipswich
xford Luton Colchester
London
Thames Canterbury
Reading
lisbury Dover
outhampton Folkestone
Portsmouth Brighton
of Wight

HANNEL

The prehistoric pillars of Stonehenge rise from the rolling fields and grassland of Salisbury Plain, in southern England. The site was in use from about 3100 to 1100 B.C.

United Kingdom   Republic of Ireland

Search and find

United Kingdom
Capital: London .F7
Aberdeen C6
Aberystwyth E5
Ayr D5
Belfast D4
Birmingham E6
Blackpool E5
Bournemouth . . .F6
Bradford E6
Brighton F7
Bristol F6
Cambridge F7
Canterbury F7
Cardiff F5
Carlisle D5
Carmarthen F5
Colchester F7
Coventry E6
Derby E6
Douglas D5
Dover F7
Dundee C5
Durham D6
Edinburgh C5
Exeter F5
Folkestone F7
Glasgow C5
Gloucester F6
Holyhead E5
Hull E6
Inverness C5
Ipswich F7
Kirkwall B5
Leeds E6
Leicester E6
Lerwick A6
Liverpool E5
Londonderry . . .D4

Luton F7
Manchester E6
Middlesbrough . .D6
Newcastle upon
    Tyne D6
Newport F5
Northampton . . .F6
Norwich E7
Nottingham E6
Oban C5
Oxford F6
Penzance G4
Perth C5
Peterborough . . .E6
Plymouth F6
Portsmouth F5
Reading F6
Salisbury F6
Sheffield E6
Southampton . . .F6
Stornoway B4
Stranraer D5
Swansea F4
Thurso B5
Wolverhampton .E6
Wrexham E5

Republic of Ireland
Capital: Dublin . .E4
Cork F4
Donegal D4
Dun Laoghaire . .E4
Dundalk E4
Galway E3
Killarney F3
Limerick E3
Sligo D4
Tipperary E4
Waterford F4

Country facts

	Area sq mi (sq km)	Population	Language	Religion	Currency
United Kingdom	94,525 (244,820)	59,113,439	English	Anglican	Pound
Republic of Ireland	27,135 (70,280)	3,632,944	English	Catholic	Euro

D

E

F

G

A

Low Countries
NETHERLANDS, BELGIUM, LUXEMBOURG

B

ONLY SEA WALLS AND RIVER barriers prevent the stormy North Sea from flooding into the Netherlands, for large areas of the country are below sea level. The best way to travel is by bicycle, because there are very few hills. Canals and rivers cross the flat farmland. Many fields are grazed by black-and-white Holstein cows, whose milk is used to make Dutch cheeses. In spring, other fields are brilliant with tulips. Many cities have elegant merchants' houses built in the 1600s. The Netherlands is still a center of business and trade, and Rotterdam is the world's busiest seaport. The capital is Amsterdam, but the center of government is at The Hague.

C

Belgium is another low-lying, mostly flat country with a rich history. It is a major industrial and commercial power, which is also famous for its handmade chocolates and lace. Southern Belgium rises to the hills of the Ardennes, which become the fields and woods of tiny Luxembourg.

D

The city of Luxembourg is an international center of finance. Brussels, the Belgian capital, and the city of Luxembourg are the headquarters of many of the institutions of the European Union (EU). Although Luxembourg is a small country, it has its own language, called Letzeburgish. Many people speak it there, in addition to French or German.

E

The Dutch landscape is still dotted with beautiful old windmills, which were once used to power pumps for draining waterlogged fields. Many are still in working order today.

Wearing traditional costume, a Belgian woman moves bobbins skillfully across a pillow to make delicate patterns of lace. Fine lace has been made in the city of Bruges since the Middle Ages.

Zeebrugge
Ostend Bruges
Roeselare
Kortrijk
Tourna

F

DISCOVER MORE

• *Over 40 percent of the Netherlands has been created by people. It is mostly polder—land that has been reclaimed from the sea and drained.*

• *The Belgian town of Spa has health-enhancing mineral springs, which were discovered more than 600 years ago. They became so famous that health resorts all over the world are now called spas.*

G

Amsterdam is built on marshy land, which lies just below sea level. More than 100 canals cross the city, helping to drain the land. The city's name means "dam of the Amstel"—referring to a dam that was built in the 13th century.

Netherlands

Belgium

Luxembourg

Country facts					
	Area sq mi (sq km)	Population	Language	Religion	Currency
Netherlands	16,033 (41,525)	15,807,641	Dutch	Catholic	Euro
Belgium	11,780 (30,510)	10,182,034	Flemish/French	Catholic	Euro
Luxembourg	999 (2,587)	429,080	French	Catholic	Euro

WEST FRISIAN ISLANDS

Ameland

Terscheling

Vlieland

Waddenzee

Texel

Barrier Dam

Leeuwarden

Groningen

Assen

Emmen

NORTH SEA

Alkmaar

L. IJssel

Northeast Polder

Zwolle

Almelo

Haarlem

Amsterdam

Hilversum

Apeldoorn

Enschede

Marken L.

Flevoland Polder

NETHERLANDS

Leiden

Gouda

Utrecht

Amersfoort

Arnhem

The Hague

Delft

Rotterdam

Lek

Waal

Nijmegen

GERMANY

Dordrecht

Maas

's Hertogenbosch

Breda

Tilburg

Venlo

Vlissingen

Eindhoven

Antwerp

Genk

Sittard

Ghent

Mechelen

Hasselt

Maastricht

Aalst

Leuven

Vaalserberg 1,053 ft (321 m)

Brussels

Liège

Verviers

Waterloo

Spa

Botrange 2,277 ft (694 m)

BELGIUM

Meuse

Sambre

Schelde

Mons

Namur

ARDENNES

Charleroi

Dinant

Buurgplaatz 1,835 ft (559 m)

FRANCE

GERMANY

Bastogne

LUXEMBOURG

Luxembourg

Esch-sur-Alzette

50 miles

50 km

Where in the world?

7 A.M. Washington, DC | noon GMT | 1 P.M. Amsterdam

Washington, DC to Amsterdam	Amsterdam lies on
3,855 mi (6,203 km)	52° 21'N latitude
7 hr 25 min	04° 52'E longitude

Life facts

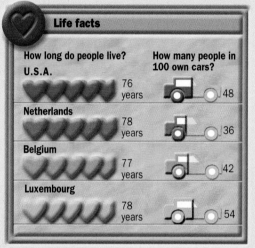

How long do people live?

How many people in 100 own cars?

U.S.A.	76 years	48
Netherlands	78 years	36
Belgium	77 years	42
Luxembourg	78 years	54

Search and find

Netherlands

Capitals:

Amsterdam . . C7
The Hague . . .C7
Alkmaar B7
Almelo C9
Amersfoort C8
Apeldoorn C8
Arnhem C8
Assen B9
Breda D7
Delft C7
Dordrecht C7
Eindhoven D8
Emmen B9
Enschede C9
Gouda C7
Groningen A9
Haarlem C7
Hilversum C8
Leeuwarden A8
Leiden C7
Maastricht E8
Nijmegen C8
Rotterdam C7
Sittard E8
's Hertogenbosch .D8
Tilburg D8
Utrecht C7
Venlo D8
Vlissingen D6

Zwolle B8

Belgium

Capital: Brussels E7

Aalst E6
Antwerp D7
Bastogne F8
Bruges D6
Charleroi E7
Dinant F7
Genk E8
Ghent E6
Hasselt E8
Kortrijk E6
Leuven E7
Liège E8
Mechelen E7
Mons E6
Namur E7
Ostend D5
Roeselare E6
Spa E8
Tournai E6
Verviers E8
Waterloo E7
Zeebrugge D6

Luxembourg

Capital:

Luxembourg . .F9
Esch-sur-Alzette .G8

France and Its Neighbors

FRANCE, ANDORRA, MONACO

Southeastern France includes the western end of the Alps, the highest mountain range in western Europe.

THE CITY OF PARIS, CAPITAL OF France, is built on the islands and banks of the Seine River, which winds across France's northern plain. On land, traffic pours though the city, along broad, tree-lined avenues to the grand memorial, the Triumphal Arc.

Here in Paris you can see the soaring iron arches of the Eiffel Tower. You will find the world-famous art museum of the Louvre, and the arts complex of the Beaubourg Center. There is also the ancient cathedral of Nôtre Dame, and the old artists' quarter of Montmartre, with its fashionable crowds and small restaurants serving *haute cuisine*— fine cooking.

France lies at the heart of western Europe. Its cool north coast is on the English Channel. Its west coast is formed by the stormy Bay of Biscay, but its sunny south coast borders the Mediterranean Sea. Mountains make up its eastern border—from the Vosges and Jura to the icy peaks and glaciers of the Alps. The Rhône River forms a valley running north to south almost through the center of France.

Although French is spoken everywhere, several other languages may be heard too. They include Breton, Catalán, Basque, and Arabic.

Two tiny independent states border France. Monaco, on the Mediterranean coast, is famous for its casinos and automobile racing. The mountain state of Andorra, high in the Pyrenees, attracts thousands of skiers and walkers.

DISCOVER MORE

• *Corsica is a French island in the Mediterranean Sea. It was the birthplace of Napoleon Bonaparte, the French general and emperor.*

• *The world's toughest bicycle race is the Tour de France. It includes mountains and plains and has exceeded 3,540 mi (5,700 km).*

France

Andorra

Monaco

Country facts

	Area sq mi (sq km)	Population	Language	Religion	Currency
France	211,208 (547,029)	58,978,172	French	Catholic	Euro
Andorra	181 (469)	65,939	Catalán	Catholic	Euro
Monaco	0.75 (1.95)	32,149	French	Catholic	Euro

*Map labels:*
Dunkerque, Calais, Roubaix, Boulogne, Lille, Douai, Valenciennes, ENGLISH CHANNEL, Dieppe, Amiens, St.-Quenti, CHANNEL IS (U.K.), Bay of the Seine, Le Havre, Cherbourg, Rouen, Reims, Caen, St.-Denis, Gulf of St.-Malo, NORMANDY, Versailles, **Paris**, Marn, Ouessant I., Brest, St.-Malo, Chartres, Seine, BRITTANY, Rennes, Le Mans, Fontainebleau, Troy, Quimper, Lorient, Orléans, Auxerr, Angers, Tours, Loir, St.-Nazaire, BURGUN, Belle-Île, Nantes, Cher, Loire, Bourges, Yeu I., Poitiers, **FRANCE**, Ré I., La Rochelle, Montluçon, Oléron I., Cognac, Limoges, Clermont-Ferrand, ATLANTIC OCEAN, Angoulême, Puy de Sancy 6,188 ft (1,887 m), Gironde, Périgueux, MASSIF, Bay of Biscay, Bordeaux, Bergerac, Lot, CENTRAL, Dordogne, LANDES, Garonne, Montauban, Adour, Tarn, Montpellie, Bayonne, Toulouse, Castres, Béziers, Pau, Carcassonne, Sèt, Tarbes, Ariège, Aude, Lourdes, Perpignan, PYRENEES, SPAIN, **ANDORRA Andorra la Vella**, ME

100 miles
150 km

Life facts

How long do people live?

How many people in 100 own cars?

U.S.A. — 76 years — 48

France — 78 years — 43

Andorra — 76 years — 56

Monaco — 79 years — 53

Where in the world?

7 A.M. — noon — 1 P.M.
Washington, DC — GMT — Paris

Washington, DC to Paris
3,839 mi (6,203 km)
7 hr 25 min

Paris lies on
48° 52'N latitude
02° 20'E longitude

Highest mountains

Mount McKinley
20,320 ft
(6,194 m)

Mont Blanc
15,771 ft
(4,807 m)

BELGIUM
LUXEMBOURG
Meuse
Verdun
Châlons-sur-Marne
Metz
Nancy
Strasbourg
LORRAINE
VOSGES MTS
Rhine
GERMANY
Dijon
Saône
Mulhouse
Besançon
SWITZERLAND
JURA MTS
Rhône
Mâcon
Bourg-en-Bresse
Chamonix
Lyon
Chambéry
St.-Étienne
Mont Blanc
Grenoble
Valence
ITALY
Montélimar
Avignon
Durance
Nîmes
Aix-en-Provence
MONACO
Monaco
Nice
Antibes
Cannes
Arles
Marseille
St.-Tropez
Gulf of Lion
Toulon
MEDITERRANEAN SEA

Cape Corse
Bastia
Gulf of Sagone
CORSICA
Ajaccio
Strait of Bonifacio

Monte Carlo basks in the warm Mediterranean sunshine. This wealthy, built-up residential area takes up most of the tiny principality of Monaco.

Search and find

France
Capital: Paris . . . C5
Aix-en-Provence . F7
Amiens B5
Angers D4
Angoulême E4
Antibes F7
Arles F6
Auxerre D6
Avignon E6
Bayonne F4
Bergerac E5
Besançon D7
Béziers F6
Bordeaux E4
Boulogne B5
Bourg-en-Bresse D7
Bourges D5
Brest C3
Caen C4
Calais B5
Cannes F7
Carcassonne . . . F5
Castres F5
Châlons-sur-Marne. C6
Chambéry E7
Chamonix D7
Chartres C5
Cherbourg C4
Clermont-Ferrand E6
Cognac E4
Dieppe B5
Dijon D6
Douai B5
Dunkerque B5
Fontainebleau . . C5
Grenoble E7
La Rochelle D4
Le Havre C5
Le Mans C5
Lille B5
Limoges D5
Lorient C3
Lourdes F4
Lyon E6
Mâcon D6
Marseille F7
Metz C7

Montauban E5
Montélimar E6
Montluçon. D5
Montpellier F6
Mulhouse C7
Nancy C7
Nantes D4
Nice F7
Nîmes F6
Orléans C5
Pau F4
Périgueux E5
Perpignan F5
Poitiers D5
Quimper C3
Reims C6
Rennes C4
Roubaix B6
Rouen C5
Sète F6
St.-Denis C5
St.-Étienne E6
St.-Malo C4
St.-Nazaire D4
St.-Quentin B6
St.-Tropez F7
Strasbourg C7
Tarbes F4
Toulon F7
Toulouse F5
Tours D5
Troyes C6
Valence E6
Valenciennes . . . B6
Verdun C6
Versailles C5

Andorra. F5
Capital: Andorra
la Vella F5

Monaco F7
Capital:
Monaco F7

Corsica
Ajaccio G7
Bastia F7

Iberian Peninsula

SPAIN, PORTUGAL

The Torre de Belém guards the entrance to Lisbon's harbor. When it was built in 1520, Portugal was building up a South American empire. That is why today more than 165 million Brazilians speak the Portuguese language.

SOUTHWESTERN EUROPE IS A great area of land called the Iberian Peninsula, which sweeps around from the Bay of Biscay into the Atlantic Ocean. The sheer rock face of Gibraltar, just 8 miles (13 km) from the African coast, guards the western approach to the Mediterranean Sea. Spain's northern coast is green and moist, but the southern region of Andalusia is extremely hot in summer. It is a land of red soil and brown rock, with cactuses, olive groves, orange trees, and whitewashed villages. Central Spain is a dry, dusty plateau known as the Meseta. This is framed by the peaks of the Cantabrian, Pyrenees, and Sierra Nevada mountains.

Spain is a land of distinct cultural regions, with the Basque, Catalán, and Galician peoples all retaining their own languages and customs. The country is famous for its fiery, foot-stamping flamenco dances, for its bullfighting, and for colorful Christian processions in which statues of saints are carried through village streets.

In Portugal, the white buildings and red-tiled roofs of many towns face the Atlantic Ocean. One-third of the population lives in cities, such as Lisbon, Coimbra, and Porto. However, most people are country dwellers. Portugal is a land of hills, cork-oak forests, and vineyards, descending to coastal inlets and river estuaries. The rivers provide irrigation and hydroelectric power.

DISCOVER MORE

• During the annual San Fermín festival in Pamplona, Spain, six bulls are released into the streets each morning. They chase the crowds of people, who try to show off their daring and escape the bulls' sharp horns.

The massive Rock of Gibraltar towers over the narrow entrance to the Mediterranean Sea. It is linked to the Spanish mainland by a neck of low-lying sand.

Life facts

How long do people live?

U.S.A.
76 years

Spain
78 years

Portugal
76 years

How many people in 100 own cars?

48

37

27

In swirling, traditional dress, young girls learn how to dance to the flamenco music of the Andalusia region. The occasion is the Feria, a spectacular festival held each April in the city of Seville.

Where in the world?

7 A.M. — Washington, DC
noon — GMT
1 P.M. — Madrid

Washington, DC to Madrid
3,791 mi (6,101 km)
7 hr 15 min

Madrid lies on
40° 26'N latitude
03° 42'E longitude

San Sebastián
FRANCE
PYRENEES
Pamplona
ANDORRA
Pico de Aneto
11,168 ft
(3,405 m)
Girona
Manresa
Lleida
Mataró
Tarrasa
Costa Brava
Saragossa
Reus
Barcelona
Ebro
Tarragona
Costa Dorada
Tortosa
Cape Tortosa
Morella
Costa del Azahar
Teruel
Castellón de la Plana
Menorca
Sagunto
Mallorca
Cuenca
Palma
Valencia
Gulf of Valencia
Ibiza
BALEARIC IS
Júcar
Albacete
Ibiza
Alcoy
Formentera
Segura
Alicante
Costa Blanca
Murcia
Elche
Cartagena
MEDITERRANEAN SEA
Lorca
Cape Palos
Almería
Cape Gata
Arga
Gállego
Cinca
Jalón
Tajo
Turia
Cuenca

200 miles
300 km

Spain

Portugal

Olive trees dot the rolling red earth near Córdoba in southern Spain. This part of Spain has hot, dry summers and mild winters.

Country facts

	Area sq mi (sq km)	Population	Language	Religion	Currency
Spain	195,364 (505,993)	39,167,744	Spanish	Catholic	Euro
Portugal	35,672 (92,390)	9,918,040	Portuguese	Catholic	Euro

Search and find

Spain
Capital: Madrid . .D5
Albacete E6
Alcalá de Henares . .D6
Alcoy E7
Algeciras F5
Alicante E7
Almería F6
Antequera F5
Aranjuez D5
Arcos F4
Ávila D5
Badajoz E4
Barcelona C8
Bilbao B6
Burgos C5
Cáceres D4
Cádiz F4
Cartagena E7
Castellón de la
   Plana D7
Ceuta F5
Ciudad Real . . .E5
Córdoba E5
Cuenca D6
El Ferrol B4
Elche E7
Gijón B5
Glrona C8
Granada F5
Guadalajara D6
Huelva F4
Ibiza E8
Jaén E5
Jerez de la Frontera .F4
La Coruña B3
León C5
Lleida C7
Linares E5
Logroño C6
Lorca E6
Lugo B4
Málaga F5
Manresa C8
Marbella F5
Mataró C8
Melilla G6

Mérida E4
Morella D7
Morón de la
   Frontera F5
Motril F5
Murcia E7
Orense C4
Oviedo B4
Palencia C5
Palma D8
Pamplona C6
Puente Genil F5
Puertollano E5
Reus C7
Ronda F5
Sagunto D7
Salamanca D5
San Sebastián . .B6
Santander B5
Santiago de
   Compostela . . .C3
Saragossa C7
Segovia D5
Seville F4
Soria C6
Tarragona C7
Tarrasa C8
Teruel D7
Toledo D5
Tortosa D7
Valdepeñas E6
Valencia D7
Valladolid C5
Vigo C3
Vitória C6
Zamora C5

Portugal
Capital: Lisbon . .E3
Aviero D3
Braga C3
Coimbra D3
Évora E4
Faro F4
Lagos F3
Porto C3
Setúbal E3

Germany

Germany

Small towns and villages sit beneath peaks dusted with snow. They are popular for exploring the lakes and forests of the Alps.

CRANES TOWER OVER THE LEAFY avenues of the German capital, Berlin. New glass buildings rise on the skyline, as the city is rebuilt after long years in which Germany was divided into separate countries, East Germany and West Germany. Berlin lies on a great plain, which stretches from eastern Germany to the Russian Federation. It has cold, snowy winters, while the warm summers are ideal for swimming in the woodland lakes.

Germany has sandy coasts on the North and Baltic seas. In the west, the Rhine River winds through steep-sided valleys, where sunny slopes are covered in vineyards. Central Germany is mountainous, but the country's highest peaks are in the Bavarian Alps in the south. Germany has many large cities and factories producing chemicals, electrical goods, and cars.

Although the German language is spoken everywhere, there are many different dialects and accents because it is such a large country. There are also immigrants from Turkey and Eastern Europe. The German people have a very strong sense of region, with each part of the country having its own way of preparing food and drink, its own newspapers, and its own way of celebrating traditional festivals. Carnival, the week before the Christian period of Lent, is marked by wild parties and fancy dress.

DISCOVER MORE

- Germany produces 1,500 different types of sausage.

- The spire of Ulm cathedral soars to 528 ft (161 m). It is the tallest in the world.

- The Black Forest, in southwest Germany, is named after the dark rows of fir trees that cover higher ground. Beech and oak trees cover the lower-lying ground.

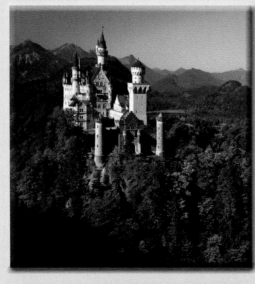

The tall granite turrets of Neuschwanstein date back to 1869, when it was built for King Ludwig II of Bavaria, which is now a state in southeastern Germany.

Map labels:

Sylt I.
Schleswig
Kie
Ba
Ki
Helgoland I.
Cuxhaven
Lübec
EAST FRISIAN IS
Bremerhaven
Wilhelmshaven
Hamburg
Bremen
Lünebur
Oldenburg
Weser
NETHERLANDS
Ems
Osnabrück
Hannover
Hameln
Münster
TEUTOBURGER FOREST
Bielefeld
Brunswic
Hamm
Paderborn
Leine
Ha
Duisburg
Dortmund
Krefeld
Essen
Kassel
Göttinge
Düsseldorf
Wuppertal
Leverkusen
Solingen
G E R M A N
Cologne (Köln)
Eisenac
Aachen
Bonn
Siegen
Fulda
Werra
BELGIUM
Koblenz
Wetzlar
Rhine
Fulda
LUXEMBOURG
Moselle
Wiesbaden
Frankfurt am Main
HUNSRÜCK
Mainz
Offenbach
Ma
Trier
Worms
Darmstadt
Würzbur
Saar
Ludwigshafen
Mannheim
Kaiserslautern
Heidelberg
Saarbrücken
Karlsruhe
Heilbronn
Baden-Baden
Pforzheim
FRANCE
Stuttgart
Rhine
Tübingen
BLACK FOREST
Reutlingen
SWABIAN JURA
Ulm
Freiburg
L. Constance
SWITZERLAND
BAVARI

Life facts

How long do people live?

U.S.A.
76 years

Germany
77 years

How many people in 100 own cars?

U.S.A. 48

Germany 50

Where in the world?

7 A.M.
Washington, DC

noon
GMT

1 P.M.
Berlin

Washington, DC to Berlin
4,177 mi (6,723 km)
8 hr

Berlin lies on
52° 31'N latitude
13° 25'E longitude

Fehmarn
Mecklenburg Bay
Rügen
• Rostock
Schwerin •
Neubrandenburg •
Müritz L.
Elbe
POLAND
Brandenburg •
Berlin ☆
Fürstenwalde •
Wolfsburg •
Potsdam •
Frankfurt •
Oder
• Magdeburg
Dessau •
Cottbus •
Elbe
Halle •
Leipzig •
Meissen •
Görlitz •
Weimar •
Chemnitz •
Dresden •
Erfurt • Jena •
Gera •
• Zwickau
Plauen •
CZECH REPUBLIC
Bayreuth •
Bamberg •
Nuremberg •
ürth •
BOHEMIAN FOREST
Regensburg •
Ingolstadt •
Danube
Passau •
ugsburg •
Inn
• Munich
ALPS
Berchtesgaden •
AUSTRIA
ugspitze 9,721 ft (2,964 m)

The pretty medieval town of Rothenburg ob der Tauber was once famous for its textile industry. It lies to the south of Würzburg, in southern Germany. It is visited by tourists from all over the world.

Germany

100 miles

150 km

This tollhouse, on an island, was built in 1326 for ships passing up and down the Rhine. This river remains a busy commercial waterway today.

Search and find

Germany
Capital: Berlin . . C7
Aachen D4
Augsburg F6
Baden-Baden . . .E5
Bamberg E6
Bayreuth E6
Berchtesgaden . .F7
Bielefeld C5
Bonn D4
Brandenburg . . .C7
Bremen B5
Bremerhaven . .B5
Brunswick C6
Chemnitz D7
Cologne (Köln) . .D4
Cottbus C8
Cuxhaven B5
Darmstadt E5
Dessau C7
Dortmund D4
Dresden D7
Duisburg D4
Düsseldorf D4
Eisenach D6
Erfurt D6
Essen D4
Frankfurt C8
Frankfurt
  am Main D5
Freiburg F4
Fulda D5
Fürstenwalde . . .C7
Fürth E6
Gera D7
Görlitz D8
Göttingen D5
Halle D7
Hamburg B6
Hameln C5
Hamm C4
Hannover C5
Heidelberg E5
Heilbronn E5
Ingolstadt E6
Jena D6
Kaiserslautern . .E4

Karlsruhe E5
Kassel D5
Kiel B6
Koblenz D4
Krefeld D4
Leipzig D7
Leverkusen D4
Lübeck B6
Ludwigshafen . .E5
Lüneburg B6
Magdeburg C6
Mainz E5
Mannheim E5
Meissen D7
Munich F6
Münster C4
Neubrandenburg B7
Nuremberg E6
Offenbach E5
Oldenburg B5
Osnabrück C5
Paderborn C5
Passau F7
Pforzheim E5
Plauen D7
Potsdam C7
Regensburg E7
Reutlingen F5
Rostock B7
Saarbrücken . . .E4
Schleswig A5
Schwerin B6
Siegen D5
Solingen D4
Stuttgart E5
Trier E4
Tübingen F5
Ulm F5
Weimar D6
Wetzlar D5
Wiesbaden E5
Wilhelmshaven .B5
Wolfsburg C6
Worms E5
Wuppertal D4
Würzburg E5
Zwickau D7

Country facts

	Area sq mi (sq km)	Population	Language	Religion	Currency
Germany	137,803 (356,910)	82,087,361	German	Protestant/Catholic	Euro

The Alps

AUSTRIA, SWITZERLAND, LIECHTENSTEIN

IN SUMMER THE ALPS ARE A world of sunny meadows filled with wildflowers, dark forests, lakeshores, and villages of broad-roofed, wooden chalets. The air is filled with the clanking of cowbells and the rush of waterfalls. Glistening peaks form the skyline. In winter all this is transformed: Snow fills the valleys, attracting skiers and snowboarders.

The Alpine region of Europe has famous cities, too. In Switzerland there is Geneva, headquarters of the International Committee of the International Red Cross and Crescent Movement (ICRC), the World Health Organization (WHO), and the World Trade Organization (WTO); and Zürich, a world center of banking. In Austria, Salzburg's music festival celebrates the composer Wolfgang Amadeus Mozart. Vienna, Austria's capital, is a grand city on the Danube River. It is renowned for its theaters, cafés, museums, parks and gardens.

Switzerland is famous for its cheeses, its precision instruments, and its clocks, while Austria produces timber, paper, steel, and glass. Liechtenstein, a tiny nation set between these two countries, relies on tourism. It uses Swiss currency, and its lenient tax laws attract many companies to register there.

The Alps are a meeting place between northern and southern Europe, and the region is shared by several peoples with different cultures and languages.

Salzburg was the birthplace of the great composer Wolfgang Amadeus Mozart (1756–91). It is a fine old Austrian city on the banks of the Salzach River, dominated by the towers of Hohensalzburg Castle.

DISCOVER MORE

• The Austrian composer Johann Strauss the Younger (1825–99) wrote over 400 waltzes, romantic dances which were pop hits of his day. The most famous was called "The Blue Danube," after the Danube River that flows through Vienna.

The Matterhorn rises in the Alps on Switzerland's border with Italy. Its distinctive peak, 14,688 ft (4,478 m) above sea level, has claimed many lives.

Highest mountains

Mount McKinley
20,320 ft
(6,194 m)

Monte Rosa
15,203 ft
(4,634 m)

Life facts

How long do people live?

U.S.A.
76 years

Austria
77 years

Switzerland
80 years

Liechtenstein
78 years

How many people in 100 own cars?

U.S.A. 48

Austria 45

Switzerland 45

Liechtenstein n.a.

Where in the world?

7 A.M. Washington, DC | noon GMT | 1 P.M. Bern

Washington, DC to Bern
4,109 mi (6,613 km)
7 hr 55 min

Bern lies on
46° 55'N latitude
07° 25'E longitude

Once the winter snows have melted, tall grasses and wildflowers grow in sunny meadows high in the Swiss Alps.

CZECH REPUBLIC

Zwettl Stadt

Krems

Klosterneuburg

Linz

Danube

Wels

Sankt Pölten

★Vienna

Braunau

Amstetten

Baden

Bruck

Steyr

Wiener Neustadt

Neusiedler L.

Salzburg   Gmunden

SLOVAKIA

Bad Ischl

AUSTRIA

Hallein

Leoben

Kapfenberg

Kufstein

Inn

Enns

NIEDERE TAUERN

Knittelfeld

Kitzbühel

chwaz

Salzach

Judenburg

Mur

Graz

Gleisdorf

HUNGARY

▲ HOHE TAUERN

Köflach

Grossglockner
12,457 ft
(3,797 m)

Spittal

Wolfsberg

Klagenfurt

Villach

Drau

SLOVENIA

100 miles

150 km

 Austria

 Switzerland

 Liechtenstein

Search and find

Austria		Switzerland	
Capital: Vienna	.C9	*Capital*: Bern	. . .D3
Amstetten	. . . . .C8	Aarau	. . . . . . .D4
Bad Ischl	. . . . . .D7	Andermatt	. . . . .E4
Baden	. . . . .D9	Baden	. . . . .D4
Braunau	. . . . . .C7	Basel	. . . . . . .D4
Bregenz	. . . . . .D5	Bellinzona	. . . . .E4
Brenner	. . . . . .D6	Biel	. . . . .D3
Bruck	. . . . .C9	Brig	. . . . .E4
Feldkirch	. . . . . .D5	Chur	. . . . .E5
Gleisdorf	. . . . . .D9	Davos	. . . . . . .E5
Gmunden	. . . . . .D7	Fribourg	. . . . . .E3
Graz	. . . . .D8	Geneva	. . . . . . .E3
Hallein	. . . . . . .D7	Interlaken	. . . . .E4
Innsbruck	. . . . .D6	Lausanne	. . . . .E3
Judenburg	. . . . .D8	Locarno	. . . . . .E4
Kapfenberg	. . . .D8	Lucerne	. . . . . .D4
Kitzbühel	. . . . . .D7	Lugano	. . . . . . .E4
Klagenfurt	. . . . .E8	Montreux	. . . . .E3
Klosteneuberg	. .C9	Neuchâtel	. . . . .D3
Knittelfeld	. . . . .D8	Olten	. . . . .D4
Köflach	. . . . . . .D8	Schaffhausen	. .D4
Krems	. . . . .C8	Sion	. . . . .E3
Kufstein	. . . . . .D7	Solothurn	. . . . .D3
Leoben	. . . . . . .D8	St. Gall	. . . . . .D5
Linz	. . . . .C8	St. Moritz	. . . . .E5
Saizburg	. . . . . .D7	Thun	. . . . .E4
Sankt Pölten	. . .C8	Winterthur	. . . .D4
Schwaz	. . . . . . .D6	Yverdon	. . . . . .E3
Spittal	. . . . . . .E7	Zermatt	. . . . . .E4
St. Anton	. . . . .D5	Zug	. . . . .D4
Steyr	. . . . .C8	Zürich	. . . . . . .D4
Villach	. . . . . . .E7		
Wels	. . . . .C8	**Liechtenstein**	
Wiener Neustadt .D9		*Capital*: Vaduz	. .D5
Wolfsberg	. . . . .D8		
Zwettl Stadt	. . . .C8		

Country facts

	Area sq mi (sq km)	Population	Language	Religion	Currency
Austria	32,374 (83,849)	8,139,299	German	Catholic	Euro
Switzerland	15,942 (41,290)	7,275,467	German/French/Italian	Catholic/Protestant	Franc
Liechtenstein	62 (161)	32,057	German	Catholic	Swiss Franc

Italy and Its Neighbors

ITALY, MALTA, SAN MARINO, VATICAN CITY

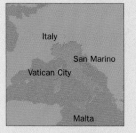

TRUCKS AND CARS ENTER Italy through the road tunnels of the Alps, emerging into a region of high peaks and shining lakes. They descend to the floodplain of the Po River, a flat patchwork pattern of open fields. Northern cities include wealthy, industrial Milan and beautiful Venice, built on the lagoons and islands of the Adriatic coast.

The Apennine Mountains run down the center of the Italian peninsula. The regional hilltop towns date from the Middle Ages. Grapevines are cultivated on the lower slopes. The Italian capital, Rome, is built beside the Tiber River. Its ruins are a reminder that Roman rule once stretched from Egypt to the British Isles. To the south is Naples and the fertile surrounding region. The south is poorer than the north, dry and dusty with hot summers.

Vatican City is a district of Rome which is recognized internationally as an independent state. It is the headquarters and center of the Roman Catholic Church. The tiny republic of San Marino is completely surrounded by Italy, lying on the slopes of the Apennine Mountains of northeastern Italy.

Beyond the volcanic island of Sicily are the islands of Malta, an independent state whose main industries are tourism and clothing manufacturing.

Valletta is the capital and chief seaport of Malta. The city's stone ramparts date back to wars between Christians and Turkish Muslims in the 1500s.

DISCOVER MORE

- *Italy produces more wine than any other country in the world.*

- *San Marino is one of the smallest states in the world. It claims to be the oldest state in Europe.*

Country facts

	Area sq mi (sq km)	Population	Language	Religion	Currency
Italy	116,305 (301,230)	56,735,130	Italian	Catholic	Euro
Malta	124 (321)	381,603	Maltese/English	Catholic	Lira
San Marino	23 (60)	25,061	Italian	Catholic	Euro
Vatican City	0.17 (0.44)	860	Italian/Latin	Catholic	Euro

A
B
C
D
E
F
G

Where in the world?

7 A.M. noon 1 P.M.
Washington, DC GMT Rome

Washington, DC to Rome
4,501 mi (7,244 km)
8 hr 40 min

Rome lies on
41° 52'N latitude
12° 37'E longitude

The Colosseum has stood in Rome since A.D. 80. In ancient times this was an amphitheater, where crowds came to watch gladiators fight to the death or wild animals being slaughtered.

ADRIATIC SEA

ramo
•Pescara

100 miles

150 km

Italy

Malta

San Marino

Vatican City

Campobasso •Foggia Gulf of
Manfredonia
Benevento Ofanto
•Benevento
aples
▲Vesuvius 4,026 ft
(1,227 m)
•Salerno
Gulf of •Bari
Salerno •Brindisi
Taranto•
Lecce•
Gulf of
Taranto

Cosenza•

•Crotone

Stromboli I.
Salina I. Catanzaro Gulf of
Lipari I. Squillace
LIPARI Vulcano I.
IS
•Messina •Reggio di
Etna 10,958 ft Calabria
(3,340 m)▲
•Catania Gulf of
Caltanissetta• Catania
Sicily •Siracusa
ulf of •Ragusa
ela

MALTA CHANNEL

✪Valletta
MALTA

Search and find

Italy
Capital: Rome . .D5
Adria B5
Agrigento F6
Alessandria . . .B4
Ancona C6
Aosta A3
Arezzo C5
Bari D7
Benevento D6
Bergamo A4
Bologna B5
Bolzano A5
Brescia B5
Brindisi D8
Cagliari E4
Caltanissetta . .F6
Campobasso . . .D7
Carpi B5
Carrara B4
Catania F7
Catanzaro E7
Chioggia B5
Civitavecchia . . .C5
Como B4
Cosenza E7
Cremona B4
Crotone E8
Empoli C5
Ferrara B5
Florence C5
Foggia D7
Forli B5
Genoa B4
Grosseto C5
La Spezia B4
Latina D6
Lecce D8
Lecco A4
Livorno C5
Lodi B4
Mantua B5
Massa B5
Messina F7
Milan B4
Monza A4
Naples D6

Novara B4
Nuoro D4
Padua B5
Palermo F6
Parma B5
Pavia B4
Perugia C5
Pesaro B5
Pescara C6
Piacenza B4
Piombino C5
Pisa C5
Pistoia B5
Prato C5
Ragusa F7
Ravenna B5
Reggio di
  Calabria F7
Reggio nell'
  Emilia B5
Rimini B5
Salerno D7
Sassari D4
Savona B4
Siena C5
Siracusa F7
Taranto D8
Teramo C6
Terni C5
Trapani F5
Trento A5
Treviso A5
Trieste A6
Turin B4
Udine A6
Venice B5
Verona B5
Viareggio C5
Vicenza B5

Malta
Capital: Valletta .G6

San Marino
Capital: San Marino B5

Vatican City . . .D5

Life facts

How long do people live?	How many people in 100 own cars?
U.S.A. 76 years	48
Italy 79 years	54
Malta 78 years	32
San Marino 81 years	98
Vatican City	not available

Northern Central Europe

POLAND, CZECH REPUBLIC, SLOVAKIA

Bridge after bridge crosses the Vltava River in Prague, capital of the Czech Republic.

SOUTH OF THE BALTIC COAST, a wide, level plain stretches across central and eastern Europe, broken only by broad rivers such as the Oder and Vistula, by lakes, and by evergreen forests, whose branches bend under the weight of winter snows. Farmers work in the flat fields, digging up sugar beets or potatoes. In the center of this region is the city of Warsaw, capital of Poland.

South of the city of Kraków, which has many beautiful buildings dating back to the 1300s, lie wooded hills, where in summer, farming families rake out hay in the fields beside large, wood-shingled houses. Farther south, high mountains rise along Poland's southern border. For a wedding in these highland regions, traditional costume is worn. Dancing to fiddle music, the men wear vests over their clothes, and round felt hats, while the women wear embroidered bodices and swirling skirts.

The Czech Republic is bordered by the Sudeten Mountains in the north and the Bohemian Forest in the west. There is good farmland here, around the Elbe and Vltava rivers, and industrial areas produce steel and glass. The capital is historic Prague. Slovakia, between the Tatra Mountains and the Danube River, is a center of farming and mining.

Poles, Czechs, and Slovaks all belong to the Slavic group of peoples, and the region is also home to many Roma, commonly known as Gypsies.

DISCOVER MORE

• Every day, a trumpeter blows a lament from the tower of the Mariacki Church in Kraków, Poland. This ancient custom dates back more than 700 years, when a watchman on the tower was hit by the arrow of a Tartar invader.

A Polish horse-drawn wagon comes in from the fields piled high with hay. Twenty-two percent of the Polish labor force works on the land.

Highest mountains

Mount McKinley
20,320 ft
(6,194 m)

Gerlachovsky Peak
8,711 ft
(2,655 m)

Where in the world?

7 A.M. noon 1 P.M.
Washington, DC GMT Warsaw

Washington, DC to Warsaw
4,461 mi (7,179 km)
8 hr 35 min

Warsaw lies on
52° 15'N latitude
21° 00'E longitude

100 miles

100 km

A castle towers over Bratislava, the Slovakian capital. Originally built in the Middle Ages, it was rebuilt several times, up until the eighteenth century.

Life facts

How long do people live?

U.S.A.
76 years

Poland
73 years

Czech Republic
74 years

Slovakia
73 years

How many people in 100 own cars?

48

19

43

18

 Poland   Czech Republic   Slovakia

KALININGRAD (RUSSIAN FEDERATION)

LITHUANIA

BELARUS

Narew

Bug

Białystok

Bug

Warsaw

Pilica

Vistula

Lublin

Vistula

San

UKRAINE

raków

Gerlachovsky Peak

Prešov

Košice

Search and find

Poland
Capital: Warsaw .D6
Bialystok C7
Bydgoszcz C5
Bytom E5
Częstochowa ...E5
Gdańsk B5
Gliwice E5
Katowice E5
Kraków E6
Łódź D6
Lublin E7
Poznań D5
Sosnowiec E5
Szczecin C4
Wroclaw E5
Zabrze E5

Czech Republic
Capital: Prague .E4
Brno F4
České Budějovice F4

Hradec Králové .E4
Jihlava F4
Karlovy Vary E3
Liberec E4
Olomouc F5
Ostrava E5
Pardubice E4
Plzeň E3
Ústí nad Labem .E3
Zlin F5

Slovakia
Capital: Bratislava F5
Banská Bystrica .F5
Komárno G5
Košice F7
Levice F5
Martin F5
Nitra F5
Prešov F6
Trnava F5
Žilina F5

This city square, in Warsaw, Poland, is often filled with street performers and horse-drawn carriages.

Country facts

	Area sq mi (sq km)	Population	Language	Religion	Currency
Poland	120,727 (312,683)	38,608,929	Polish	Catholic	Zloty
Czech Republic	30,387 (78,702)	10,280,513	Czech	Catholic	Koruna
Slovakia	18,859 (48,845)	5,396,193	Slovak	Catholic	Koruna

A B C D E F G

The Lower Danube

ROMANIA, BULGARIA, HUNGARY

Longest rivers

Nile	4,145 mi (6,670 km)
Mississippi	3,741 mi (6,020 km)
Danube	1,777 mi (2,860 km)

THE BROAD, SWIFT DANUBE River runs like a silver thread through Central Europe. It crosses Hungary, loops through Yugoslavia, and runs along the borders of Romania and Bulgaria. Finally the thread unravels, the river dividing into a delta as it joins the Black Sea.

The Hungarian capital, Budapest, is a grand city on the banks of the Danube. To its west are highlands, forests, and Lake Balaton. To the east are the plains where the soil is fertile and the climate is mild enough to support vineyards and orchards, as well as wheat, corn, potatoes, and sugar beets.

Romania's two forested mountain ranges, the Carpathians and the Transylvanian Alps, form a great horseshoe. They ring a high plateau but descend in the east and south to the plains near the capital, Bucharest. South of Romania is Bulgaria, a part of the Balkan peninsula. Here, the northern and central plains are divided by the Balkan Mountains, and the high Rhodope range in the southwest. The capital, Sofia, lies in the west. Rose petals, used to make perfumes, are one of the region's best-known crops.

Living in this part of Europe are Hungarian Magyars, Turks, Bulgarian Slavs, Romanians, and Roma (Gypsies). The Romanian language is partly derived from Latin, which was spoken in this region 1,800 years ago when the Roman Empire extended to the Black Sea.

The eroded, rocky spires of the Belogradchik crags rise to heights of 330 ft (100 m). They can be seen near the River Danube in northwestern Bulgaria.

DISCOVER MORE

• *Hungary has many health resorts, or spas, where people can bathe in mineral water from hot springs. Some hot springs, such as those near Miskolc in the north of the country, are found inside caves.*

The Hungarian parliament meets in the capital, Budapest, beside the Danube River. The parliament building is also home to a public library and various art treasures.

A farmer plows his fields in Transylvania. This region of Romania is made up of forested mountains and fertile valleys. Crops include grain and grapes.

Where in the world?

7 A.M.   noon   2 P.M.
Washington, DC   GMT   Bucharest

Washington, DC to Bucharest
4,973 mi (8,004 km)
✈ 9 hr 35 min

Bucharest lies on
44° 23'N latitude
26° 10'E longitude

Life facts

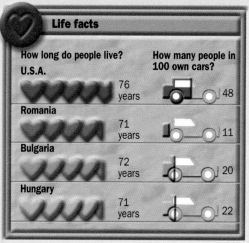

How long do people live?

U.S.A.		76 years
Romania		71 years
Bulgaria		72 years
Hungary		71 years

How many people in 100 own cars?

U.S.A.	48
Romania	11
Bulgaria	20
Hungary	22

UKRAINE

Satu Mare

Someş

Cluj-Napoca

CARPATHIAN MTS.

Târgu Mureş

Bacău

Iaşi

Prut

MOLDOVA

Mureş

ROMANIA

Siret

Sibiu

Braşov

Galaţi

TRANSYLVANIAN ALPS

Brăila

Tulcea

Olt

Ploiesti

Jiu

Pitesti

Craiova

✪Bucharest

Constanţa

Danube

BLACK SEA

Danube

Ruse

Dobrich

Iskŭr

Pleven

Varna

BALKAN MOUNTAINS

BULGARIA

Sliven

✪Sofia

Burgas

Musala Peak
9,596 ft (2,924 m)

Stara Zagora

Plovdiv

Strum

Maritsa

RHODOPE MTS

TURKEY

NIA

GREECE

200 miles

300 km

Romania

Bulgaria

Hungary

Search and find

Romania
Capital:
  Bucharest D8
Arad C6
Bacău C8
Brăila D8
Braşov D8
Cluj-Napoca . . . C7
Constanţa D9
Craiova D7
Galati D8
Iaşi C8
Oradea C6
Piteşti D7
Ploiesti D8
Satu Mare B6
Sibiu D7
Timişoara D6
Târgu Mureş . . . C7
Tulcea D9

Bulgaria
Capital: Sofia . . . E7
Burgas E8
Dobrich E8
Pleven E7
Plovdiv F7
Ruse E8
Sliven E8
Stara Zagora . . . F7
Varna E9

Hungary
Capital: Budapest C5
Debrecen C6
Győr B4
Kecskemét C5
Miskolc B5
Nyíregyhaza . . . B6
Pécs C4
Szeged C5
Székesfehérvár . C4
Szombathely . . . C4

Country facts

	Area sq mi (sq km)	Population	Language	Religion	Currency
Romania	91,699 (237,423)	22,334,312	Romanian	Romanian Orthodox	Leu
Bulgaria	42,822 (110,909)	8,194,772	Bulgarian	Non-religious	Lev
Hungary	35,919 (93,030)	10,186,372	Hungarian	Catholic	Forint

A   B   C   D   E   F   G

South Central Europe

CROATIA, BOSNIA-HERZEGOVINA, SLOVENIA

White-water rivers and rushing streams are common sights in the mountains of Bosnia. Many pass through old, pretty villages.

SOUTH CENTRAL EUROPE IS A region of forested mountains, limestone crags, and caves full of stalactites and stalagmites, pillars of limestone formed by dripping water. The mountains plunge abruptly into the warm, blue Adriatic Sea. Offshore there is a maze of islands.

The region is rich in minerals, including iron and coal. There are vineyards and fields of sunflowers. The sunny Dalmatian Coast and islands attract tourists from northern Europe, and major road and rail routes between Greece and Western Europe pass through here.

Slovenia borders the high mountain passes of the Austrian and Italian Alps, while Croatia forms a U-shape, with the Pannonian Plains in the north and the Dinaric Alps running through the coastal region of Dalmatia. To the east, Bosnia is mountainous and Herzegovina has hills and plains. These two form a single country.

The inhabitants of the Lower Danube belong to many different ethnic groups and religions. In Croatia, the people are mainly Roman Catholic Croats. In Slovenia, Roman Catholic Slovenes make up almost 90 percent of the population. In Bosnia, the majority of people are Bosnian Muslims; however, Serbian Orthodox Serbs also make up a significant proportion of the population.

The Balkan region, the poorest part of Europe's Mediterranean coast, has a long history of conquest—by Romans, Byzantines, Turks, Austrians, and Germans. It was an assassination in Sarajevo (capital of Bosnia-Herzegovina) that triggered World War I in 1914.

100 miles

150 km

DISCOVER MORE

• Slovenia is known for its beautiful beaches, lakes and ski resorts. However, it is also an important industrial center. It lies on the main road and rail routes between Western Europe and the Balkans.

Zagreb is a manufacturing city on the Sava River. Since 1991 it has been capital of independent Croatia.

A cable car climbs to dizzying heights. Slovenia flanks the eastern limits of Western Europe's Alpine ranges.

Where in the world?

7 A.M.   noon   1 P.M.
Washington, DC   GMT   Zagreb

Washington, DC to Zagreb
4,505 mi (7,251 km)
8 hr 40 min

Zagreb lies on
45° 48'N latitude
15° 58'E longitude

Life facts

How long do people live?		How many people in 100 own cars?
U.S.A.	76 years	48
Croatia	74 years	15
Bosnia-Herzegovina	63 years	n.a.
Slovenia	75 years	33

HUNGARY

Varaždin

CROATIA

Bjelovar

Sisak

Drava

Osijek

Sava

Slavonski Brod

Prijedor

Vrbas

Bosna

Brčko

Banja Luka

Bijeljina

YUGOSLAVIA

BOSNIA-HERZEGOVINA

Tuzla

Zenica

Srebrenica

ALPS

Livno

Sarajevo

Drina

Split

Foča

Brac

Mostar

Ivar

Korcula

Neum

Lastovo

Mljet

Dubrovnik

Croatia

Bosnia-Herzegovina

Slovenia

Search and find

Croatia
Capital: Zagreb .C6
Bjelovar C6
Dubrovnik F8
Gospić D5
Karlovac C5
Osijek C8
Pula D4
Rijeka C5
Sibenik E6
Sisak C6
Slavonski Brod . .D7
Split E6
Varaždin B6
Zadar E5

Bosnia-Herzegovina
Capital: Sarajevo E8
Banja Luka D7

Bihac D6
Bijeljina D8
Brčko D8
Foča E8
Livno E7
Mostar F7
Neum F7
Prijedor D6
Srebrenica E9
Tuzla D8
Zenica E7

Slovenia
Capital: Ljubljana .C5
Celje B5
Koper C4
Kranj B4
Maribor B6
Novo Mesto C5

Country facts

	Area sq mi (sq km)	Population	Language	Religion	Currency
Croatia	21,829 (56,537)	4,676,865	Croatian	Catholic	Kuna
Bosnia-Herzegovina	19,781 (51,233)	3,370,000	Serb and Croat	Sunni Islam/Serbian Orthodox/Catholic	Marka
Slovenia	7,821 (20,256)	1,970,570	Slovenian	Catholic	Tolar

A B C D E F G

Central Balkans

YUGOSLAVIA, ALBANIA, MACEDONIA

THESE SMALL CENTRAL NATIONS lie between the western Balkans, Bulgaria, and Greece. The northernmost of these nations is Yugoslavia, and it is made up of the territories of Serbia and Montenegro. In fact, there is pending legislation in the federal parliament to change the nation's name to Serbia and Montenegro. People of different ethnic origins and religious beliefs live scattered throughout the different areas of the country. Muslims form 19 percent of the total population.

Albania has long been a very poor country. Recently, exploiting resources such as iron, natural gas, and oil is helping to increase the country's wealth.

The constant changes that have affected the Balkan region for centuries have taken place against a backdrop of snowy winter mountains and sunbaked summer fields and orchards. Plums are used to make a brandy called *slivovitz*. Tractors and horses still haul farm carts.

Villages with tiled roofs cluster around old stone bridges. There are minarets of mosques and domed churches, too, for this region is home to both Muslims and Christians. Major cities such as Belgrade, Skopje, and Tiranë have suffered from earthquakes, for this region lies on the border of two sections of the earth's crust: the Turkish-Aegean plate and the Eurasian plate.

DISCOVER MORE

• *Albania has twice the altitude of the average European country, with about 70% of the country being mountainous.*

• *Beautiful Lake Ohrid, 938 ft (286 m) deep, lies on the highland border between Albania and Macedonia. It is famous for its clear waters. It is possible to see down to a depth of 65 ft (20 m).*

A patchwork of fields rises to folds of barren rock. Much of Albania is mountainous, and agriculture is difficult in many regions.

HUNGARY

CROATIA

ROMANIA

Subotica

Tisa

Vojvodina

Zrenjanin

Novi Sad

Danube

Pancevo

Belgrade

Šabac

Sava

Smederevo

Smederevska Palanka

Drina

Valjevo

S e r b i a

Užice

Čačak   Kragujevac

BOSNIA-HERZEGOVINA

YUGOSLAVIA

Kruševac

Mor

Novi Pazar

Kosovska Mitrovica

Montenegro

Nikšic   Ivangrad

Peć

Kosovo   Prištin

CROATIA

Podgorica

Dakovica

Cetinje

Prizren

L. Scutari   *Drin*

Bar

Shkodër

ADRIATIC SEA

Drin Gulf

Mt Korab 9,025 ft (2,751 m) ▲

▲ Rudoka 9,016 ft (2,748 m)

Sko

Durrës   ☉ **Tiranë**

M A C

Prile

ALBANIA

L. Ohrid   Bitol

Elbasan

L. Prespa

Korçë

G R

•Vlorë

Many of the villages in Macedonia are situated in the Vardar basin, a region given over to agriculture and dairy farming.

Where in the world?

7 A.M.   noon   1 P.M.
Washington, DC   GMT   Belgrade

Washington, DC to Belgrade
4,730 mi (7,613 km)
9 hr

Belgrade lies on
44° 48'N latitude
20° 32'E longitude

The minaret of a mosque forms part of the Belgrade skyline along with skyscrapers and industrial buildings.

Life facts

How long do people live?

U.S.A.	76 years	
Yugoslavia	75 years	
Albania	69 years	
Macedonia	73 years	

How many people in 100 own cars?

	48
	9
	n.a.
	13

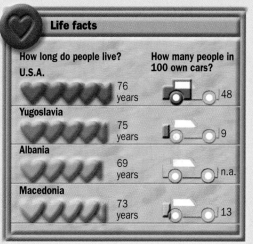

Search and find

Yugoslavia
Capital: Belgrade B5
Bar E4
Čačak C5
Cetinje E4
Dakovica E5
Ivangrad D5
Kosovska
   Mitrovica . . .D5
Kragujevac C5
Kruševac C6
Leskovac D6
Negotin C6
Nikšic D4
Nis D6
Novi Pazar D5
Novi Sad B5
Pancevo B5
Peč D5
Podgorica D4
Priština D6
Prizren E5
Sabac B5

Smederevo B5
Smederevska
   Palanka C5
Subotica A5
Užice C5
Valjevo C5
Vranje D6
Zajecar C6
Zrenjanin B5

Albania
Capital: Tiranë . .E5
Durrës F4
Elbasan F5
Korçë F5
Shkodër E4
Vlorë F4

Macedonia
Capital: Skopje . .E6
Bitola F6
Kumanovo E6
Prilep F6

Negotin●
ajecar ●
Nis
Leskovac
●Vranje
manovo
ONIA

Sunflowers open up in the Serbian summer sunshine. They are cultivated in many parts of the Balkans. The flowers are densely packed with edible seeds, which can be processed into margarine or cooking oil.

BULGARIA

C E

100 miles
150 km

Country facts

	Area sq mi (sq km)	Population	Language	Religion	Currency
Yugoslavia	39,517 (102,349)	11,206,847	Serb	Serbian Orthodox	ND*/DM**
Albania	11,100 (28,749)	3,364,571	Albanian	Muslim	Lek
Macedonia	9,781 (25,333)	2,022,604	Macedonian	Mac Orthodox***	Denar

*New Dinar **Deutsche Mark ***Macedonian Orthodox

Yugoslavia   Albania   Macedonia

Greece

The Erechtheion is one of several ancient temples built on the Acropolis, the great rock of Athens. It dates back to about 420 B.C. The roof is supported by columns, shaped like women, called caryatids.

Greece

THIS SMALL COUNTRY OCCUPIES the southern part of the Balkan peninsula. Its major industries include tourism, shipping, foodstuffs, and oil refining.

Greece is a land of rugged mountains rising from dusty plains and olive groves, very hot in summer and mostly mild in winter. The mainland is almost divided in two by the Gulf of Corinth, with an earthquake-prone peninsula in the south. Chains of rocky islands are scattered across dark blue seas. Whitewashed villages and tourist cafés surround fishing harbors.

Ferries travel between the islands and Piraeus, south of Athens. The Greek capital is a sprawling city, noisy with honking cars. In its squares one may see old men arguing about politics, bearded Greek Orthodox priests in tall black hats, children buying comics from a newsstand, and vendors of traditional foods such as pretzel rings. Looking out over the city is the great rock of the Acropolis, topped by ancient buildings, including the Parthenon, completed around 438 B.C. At that time, Greece was a center of civilization, home to great sculptors, architects, writers, and thinkers.

MACEDONIA
Palikastron
Sérra
Edessa
Kilkís
Florina
Náousa
Yiannitsa
Kastoria
Veroia
Thessaloní
Ptolemaïs
ALBANIA
Kozáni
Kateríni
Gulf of Salonika
Aliakmon
PINDUS
Mt Olympus
9,570 ft
(2,917 m)
Stómion
Kérkira
Ioánnina
Metéora
Corfu
Tríkala
Piniós
Larissa
Párga
Kardhitsa
Vólos
Arta
Akhelöós
G R E E C E
Skíat
Préveza
MTS
Lamía
Lím
Levkás
Agrínion
Mt Parnassus
▲ 8,061 ft
(2,456 m)
Cephalonia
Ithaca
L. Trichonis
Thérmon
Mesalóngion
Thebes
Sámi
Gulf of Corinth
Mega
Pátrai
Aíyion
Peloponnese
Corinth
Amaliás
Lambia
Salami
Zákinthos
Olympia
Corinth Canal
Árgos
Pyrgos
Trípolis
Nauplia
Alpheus
Megalópolis
TAÏYETOS MTS
Kalamata
Sparti
Neápo
Kíthira

Windmills rise above the whitewashed houses of Mykonos, a tiny island just off the coast of mainland Greece. In the last 30 years this small Greek island has become a major international tourist destination.

Greece

Country facts					
	Area sq mi (sq km)	Population	Language	Religion	Currency
Greece	50,942 (131,940)	10,707,135	Greek	Greek Orthodox	Euro

1   2   3   4   5

A

Some Greek Orthodox monasteries have been built on pillars of rock since the Middle Ages at Metéora in central Greece.

B U L G A R I A

Drama   Xánthi   Ørestiás

Komotiní   T U R K E Y

Kaválla

Alexandroúpolis

Thásos

Samothrace

▲ *Mt Athos*
6,670 ft
(2,033 m)

Lemnos

100 miles

150 km

ópelos

Skíros

Mytilene

Lesbos

A E G E A N
S E A

boea
Kími

halkís
arathon

Káristos   *Andros*

thens
raeus

Kéa   *Tínos*

Khíos
Chios

Sámos
Vathí

T
U
R
K
E
Y

Ikaría

Kíthnos   Syros   Mykonos   *Pátmos*

Sérifos   Páros   Náxos   Leros
Kálimnos

Sífnos   *Náxos*   *Amorgos*   Kos

Íos

Melos   *Astipálaia*

Thíra   *Tílos*

Rhódos

Lindos

Rhodes

Kárpathos

S E A   O F   C R E T E

Khaniá

Réthimnon   Iráklion   Áyios Nikólaos

C r e t e

7 A.M.   noon   2 P.M.
Washington, DC   GMT   Athens

Washington, DC to Athens
5,138 mi (8,269 km)
✈ 9 hr 50 min

Athens lies on
38° 01´N latitude
23° 44´E longitude

B

❤ **Life facts**

How long do people live?   How many people in 100 own cars?

U.S.A.
76 years   48

Greece
78 years   22

C

🔍 **Search and find**

Greece		
Capital: Athens	.E6	Megalópolis E5
Agriníon	.......D4	Megara E6
Aíyion	........D5	Mesalóngion ...D4
Alexandroúpolis	.B8	Mytilene D8
Amaliás	.......E4	Náousa C5
Árgos	.........E5	Nauplia E5
Arta	.........D4	Náxos F7
Áyios Nikólios	..G7	Neápolis F5
Corinth	.......E5	Olympia E5
Drama	........B7	Orestiás B8
Edessa	.......B5	Palikastron ...B5
Florina	.......B5	Párga D4
Ioánnina	......C4	Pátrai E5
Iráklion	.......G7	Piraeus E6
Kalamata	......E5	Préveza D4
Kardhitsa	.....D5	Ptolemaïs C5
Káristos	.......E7	Pyrgos E4
Kastoría	......C4	Réthimnon G7
Kateríni	......C5	Rhódos F9
Kaválla	.......B7	Salamis E6
Kérkira	.......C3	Sámi D4
Khalkís	.......D6	Sérrai B6
Khaniá	.......G6	Sparti E5
Khíos	........E8	Stómion C5
Kilkís	.......B5	Thebes D6
Kími	.........D6	Thérmon D5
Komotiní	.....B7	Thessaloníki ...C6
Kozáni	.......C5	Tríkala C5
Lambia	.......E5	Trípolis E5
Lamía	........D5	Vathí E8
Larissa	.......C5	Veroia C5
Límni	........D6	Vólos D6
Lindos	........F9	Xánthi B7
Marathon	......E6	Yiannitsa B5

D

E

F

G

Baltic States

LITHUANIA, LATVIA, ESTONIA

CHILLY WINDS BLOW ACROSS the Baltic Sea and the gulfs of Finland and Riga. The eastern Baltic coast is fringed by chains of islands and pale sand dunes. Inland from the coast are three small independent nations, Estonia, Latvia, and Lithuania, which border the Russian Federation in the east. A small enclave, or pocket, of territory around the seaport of Kaliningrad is Russian territory.

The peoples of the region love choral music, folk dance, and festivals, and many of these celebrate regional languages and costumes. The three countries are largely Christian, represented by the Roman Catholic, Protestant, and Orthodox churches. Russians, Belarusians, and Ukrainians also live in the Baltic states, alongside Estonians, Latvians (also known as Letts), and Lithuanians.

Estonia is a low-lying land of farms, peat bogs, and forests, part of the great plain that extends eastward across Russia. Lake Peipus lies on Estonia's eastern border. Latvia, too, lies on the plain, and here, farmers raise pigs and dairy cattle. Many Latvians work in factories, but there are few local resources, and fuel has to be imported from Russia. The lakes, moors, and pine forests of Lithuania lie to the south, extending toward the capital, Vilnius, and the borders of Poland and Belarus. Winters are extremely cold and snowy, while summers are mostly mild and moist.

The Daugava River flows through the Latvian capital, 8 mi (13 km) above its mouth on the Gulf of Riga. In the Middle Ages, Riga was part of a Baltic trading network called the Hansa, and the city still contains many fine buildings from that period.

Kärdla
Hiiumaa

Saaremaa
Kuressaare

Ruhnu

BALTIC SEA • Ventspils

Venta

Auce

Liepāja

100 miles

150 km

• Klaipeda

Kaliningrad
(RUSSIAN FEDERATION
• Kaliningrad

P O L A N

DISCOVER MORE

• *The Baltic coasts have long been famous for their fine amber. The fossilized resin from plants comes in beautiful browns and yellows and is used to make jewelry. Some amber contains insects from prehistoric times trapped in the sticky sap.*

• *Despite its small size, Lithuania has no fewer than 3,000 small lakes.*

A cluster of domed roofs in Tallinn, the Estonian capital, shows Russian influence. Many Estonian Christians belong to the Eastern Orthodox Church, but the great majority are Lutheran Protestants.

1 2 3 4 5

Gulf of Finland

●Narva

Kohtla-Järve ●

★**Tallinn**

Haapsalu

E S T O N I A

L. Peipus

● Tartu

Viljandi ●

L. Vórts

● Pärnu

● Vóru

Kihnu I.

Gauja

Valmiera ●

Gulf of Riga

● Cesis

L A T V I A

● Ergli

⊛**Riga**

Jūrmala ●

Daugava

● Jelgava

Daugavpils ●

● Šiauliai

● Panevėžys

L I T H U A N I A

Nemunas

● Kaunas

★ **Vilnius**

● Alytus

R U S S I A N   F E D E R A T I O N

B E L A R U S

Where in the world?

7 A.M.
Washington, DC   noon GMT   2 P.M. Vilnius

Washington, DC to Vilnius
4,530 mi (7,842 km)
9 hr 20 min

Vilnius lies on
55° 45′N latitude
37° 37′E longitude

Life facts

How long do people live?

U.S.A. 76 years

Lithuania 69 years

Latvia 67 years

Estonia 69 years

How many people in 100 own cars?

48

18

11

24

Search and find

Lithuania
Capital: Vilnius . .F8
Alytus F7
Kaunas F7
Klaipéda E5
Panevėžys E7
Šiauliai E6

Latvia
Capital: Riga . . .D7
Cesis C7
Daugavpils E8
Ergli D7
Jelgava D6
Jūrmala D6
Liepāja D5
Valmiera C7
Ventspils D5

Estonia
Capital: Tallinn . .A7
Haapsalu B6
Kärdla B5
Kohtla-Järve A8
Kuressaare C5
Narva A8
Pärnu B7
Tartu B8
Viljandi B7
Vóru C8

Kaliningrad (Russian Federation)
Kaliningrad F5

Lithuania

Latvia

Estonia

Country facts

	Area sq mi (sq km)	Population	Language	Religion	Currency
Lithuania	25,174 (65,201)	3,584,966	Lithuanian	Catholic	Litas
Latvia	24,749 (64,100)	2,353,874	Latvian/Russian	Lutheran/NR*	Lat
Estonia	17,462 (45,227)	1,408,523	Estonian	Lutheran/NR*/EO**	Kroon

*Non-religious   **Estonian Orthodox

Eastern Europe
UKRAINE, BELARUS, MOLDOVA

A

BELARUS IS PART OF THE GREAT plain that stretches eastward from Germany into the Russian Federation. The flat lands rise to low hills in the center of the country, drained by the Dnieper and Pripyat' rivers. There are marshes, too, and dark forests. Winter snows weigh down the trees' boughs, but summers are warm and sunny. Men and women work in the fields, growing potatoes and beets, but most Belarussians are town dwellers. Many work in industrial cities, such as Minsk.

Ukraine, too, is an industrial country. The capital, Kiev, lies on bluffs above the Dnieper River. Southern Ukraine is a land of rolling steppes where wheat is grown in the rich, black earth. In the south, Ukraine borders the warm waters of the Black Sea. The ports of Odessa and Yalta, on the Crimean Peninsula, are popular resorts for tourists, many of whom are from eastern Europe.

Moldova is a small country, situated between Ukraine and Romania. Its forests and hills descend to the western edge of the steppes. Most Moldovans belong to the same ethnic group as their neighbors, the Romanians, and they speak the same language.

DISCOVER MORE

• Optimisticekaja ("optimists' cave") in Ukraine is the second-longest cave system in the world, with 125 mi (201 km) mapped so far.

• Ukraine is the largest nation to lie entirely within the European continent.

A Belarussian woman lights a candle in an Eastern Orthodox church. Sixty percent of the Belarussian population follows the Orthodox form of Christianity. Other Christians include Roman Catholics and Protestants.

Ferries moor on the banks of the Dnieper River, in Kiev, capital of Ukraine. This is a large industrial city which produces textiles, machinery, chemicals, and processed foods.

Where in the world?

7 A.M.   noon   2 P.M.
Washington, DC   GMT   Minsk

Washington, DC to Minsk
4,636 mi (7,461 km)
8 hr 55 min

Minsk lies on
53° 54'N latitude
27° 34'E longitude

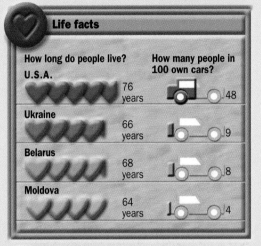

Life facts

How long do people live?	How many people in 100 own cars?
U.S.A. 76 years	48
Ukraine 66 years	9
Belarus 68 years	8
Moldova 64 years	4

Search and find

Ukraine
Capital: Kiev . . .D5
Dnipropetrovs'k .D7
Donetsk E8
Kharkiv D7
Kherson F6
Kryvyy Rih E7
Lviv D3
Mariupol E8
Odessa F6
Poltava D7
Sevastopol F7
Vinnytsya D5

Yalta F7
Zaporizhzhya . . .E7

Belarus
Capital: Minsk . .B4
Homyel' C5
Hrodna B3
Mahilyow B5
Vitsyebsk B5

Moldova
Capital: Chişinău E5
Tiraspol F5

•Kharkiv

•Poltava

Dnieper

Dnipropetrovs'k

Donetsk

Zaporizhzhya

Kryvyy Rih

Mariupol•

Kherson

SEA OF AZOV

CRIMEA

Sevastopol• •Yalta

200 miles

300 km

Ukraine   Belarus   Moldova

Country facts

	Area sq mi (sq km)	Population	Language	Religion	Currency
Ukraine	233,089 (603,701)	49,811,174	Ukrainian	NR*/Russian Orthodox	Hryvnya
Belarus	80,154 (207,599)	10,235,000	Belarussian/Russian	NR*/ Orthodox	Ruble
Moldova	13,012 (33,701)	4,460,838	Moldovan	NR*/Romanian Orthodox	Leu

*Non-religious

Western Russia

The ornate, onion-shaped domes of St. Basil's cathedral rise from Red Square, at the heart of Moscow.

RED SQUARE LIES AT THE HEART of Moscow, capital of the Russian Federation. The square is dominated by the red walls of the Kremlin, a medieval fortress that towers over the Moscow River and distant skylines of apartment blocks and factory chimneys. The Kremlin's walls surround government buildings and splendid Russian Orthodox churches with golden domes. Outside the walls are the colorful onion-shaped domes of St. Basil's Cathedral. Away from the river and square, the Kremlin is flanked by wooded slopes, where children go to toboggan in the snow.

Moscow's winters are extremely cold. Outdoors, people in the Moscow crowds are well wrapped and wear fur hats for protection against the icy wind. One way to escape the wind is to travel on the city's elegant, old-fashioned subway, or metro. Visitors come to the city from the Caucasus region, far to the south, from the Arctic north, and from distant Siberia.

The Russian Federation is the largest country in the world. Its western part lies in Europe, but its eastern part stretches across northern Asia. European Russia is a vast plain, with seemingly endless forests of spruce and birch. The region is crossed by great rivers such as the Don and the Volga. Most people live in big cities. Russia's second-largest city is St. Petersburg, which was founded in the 1700s. It has grand palaces, the world's biggest art gallery, a famous opera and ballet theater, factories, and shipbuilding yards.

DISCOVER MORE

• Moscow's subway system is the world's busiest. It carries about 3.2 billion passengers each year.

• Russia's chief Arctic port, Arkhangel'sk, freezes over in winter. From November to May, icebreakers must be used to keep the shipping lanes open.

Swirling clouds and rugged peaks form a dizzying spectacle at more than 18,000 ft (5,500 m). Mount Elbrus rises from Russia's border with Georgia, in the Caucasus Mountains.

Gulf of Finland
FIN
ESTONIA
LATVIA
BELARUS
UKRAINE
L. Ladoga
St. Petersburg
L. One
RUSSIAN
Smolensk
Tver'
Rybins
Yaroslav
Bryansk
Moscow
Tula
Ryazan
Volga
Nizhniy
Novgoro
Lipetsk
Simbir
Don
Penza
Voronezh
Saratov
Volga
SEA OF AZOV
Rostov-na-Donu
Volgograd
BLACK SEA
Krasnodar
Stavropol
Mt Elbrus
Astrakhan
CAUCASUS MTS
Grozny
CASPIAN SEA
GEORGIA
AZERBAIJAN

Franz Josef Land

A R C T I C   O C E A N

B A R E N T S
SEA

Novaya Zemlya

K A R A
SEA

Kolguyev I.

Murmansk

*Kola
Peninsula*

WHITE SEA

• Arkhangel'sk

N D

F E D E R A T I O N

*evernaya
Dvina*

Pechora

U R A L   M O U N T A I N S

Kirov

Perm

Izhevsk

Kazan

Kama

Tolyattigrad
Samara

• Ufa

Magnitogorsk

Orenburg

Ural

• Orsk

A K H S T A N

400 miles

650 km

Russian
Federation

*Nizhniy Novgorod, although a
modern manufacturing center,
has many ancient churches.*

Where in the world?

7 A.M. | noon | 3 P.M.
Washington, DC | GMT | Moscow

Washington, DC to Moscow
4,873 mi (7,842 km)
9 hr 20 min

Moscow lies on
55° 45'N latitude
37° 37'E longitude

Life facts

How long do people live?
U.S.A.
76 years
Russian Federation
65 years

How many people in
100 own cars?
48
9

Highest mountains

Mount McKinley
20,320 ft
(6,194 m)

Mount Elbrus
18,510 ft
(5,642 m)

Search and find

Western Russia
Capital: Moscow D5
Arkhangel'sk . . .C7
Astrakhan F5
Bryansk D4
Grozny F5
Izhevsk D7
Kazan E6
Kirov D6
Krasnodar F4
Lipetsk D5
Magnitogorsk . . .E7
Murmansk B7
Nizhniy
  Novgorod D6
Orenburg F6
Orsk F7
Penza E5

Perm E7
Rostov-na-Donu .E4
Ryazan D5
Rybinsk D5
Samara E6
Saratov E5
Simbirsk E6
Smolensk D5
St. Petersburg . .C5
Stavropol F4
Tolyattigrad E6
Tula D5
Tver' D5
Ufa E7
Volgograd E5
Voronezh E5
Yaroslavl' D5

Country facts

	Area sq mi (sq km)	Population	Language	Religion	Currency
Russian Federation	6,592,800 (17,075,352)	146,393,569	Russian	Russian Orthodox	Ruble

A

Asia

FROM THE TOP OF THE HIGHEST POINT IN THE WORLD,
Mount Everest, on the borders of China and Nepal,
range after range of snow-white peaks fade into the
blue distance. Far below lies Asia, the largest
continent on Earth. It takes up one-third of the
planet's land area, stretching from the Mediterranean
Sea to the Pacific Ocean, from the pack ice of the
Arctic to the tropical beaches of the Timor Sea. It is
part of the vast Eurasian landmass, bordering the
continent of Europe along the Ural and Caucasus
mountains and separated from Africa only by the
Suez Canal. Asia includes desolate wildernesses,
from the frozen wastes of Siberia to the fierce heat
of Saudi Arabia's Empty Quarter, but it also has
fertile lands, such as the lush green rice paddies of
the Mekong River and the rich farmland of
China's Huang River valley.

With its beautiful coat and muscular body, the
Siberian tiger is an impressive sight. There are
now less than 500 living in the wild.

These lands gave birth to ancient civilizations
and most of the world's major religions, including
Hinduism, Buddhism, Judaism, Christianity, and
Islam. Craft workers still produce fine Iranian
carpets, Japanese pottery, and Chinese and Indian
silk, using traditional skills, while people in modern
factories manufacture cars and computers.

About one-third of all Asians live in towns.
Millions pour into crowded cities such as Bombay,
Calcutta, Shanghai, and Tokyo. The continent has a
population of 3.6 billion, and that is expected to
double within 50 years.

DISCOVER MORE

• *Ninety percent of the
world's rice is grown in Asia.*

• *More than one-fifth of all
the people in the world live
in China.*

• *Northern Asia has the
largest area of conifer forest
in the world, in the Russian
region of Siberia.*

• *Asia is home to the highest
and lowest points on Earth:
Mount Everest and the
Dead Sea.*

Vast areas of southwest Asia form a hot, barren wilderness of sand.
The southeastern region of Saudi Arabia is called Rub'al-Khali, the
Empty Quarter.

1   2   3   4   5

OCEAN

SEA OF OKHOTSK

SIAN
ATION

MONGOLIA

SEA OF JAPAN

CHINA

NORTH KOREA

JAPAN

✪ TOKYO

SOUTH KOREA

EAST CHINA SEA

TAIWAN

PACIFIC OCEAN

BHUTAN

BANGLADESH

engal

MYANMAR (BURMA)   LAOS

THAILAND

VIETNAM

CAMBODIA

PHILIPPINES

SOUTH CHINA SEA

CELEBES SEA

BRUNEI

MALAYSIA

SINGAPORE

INDONESIA

BANDA SEA

JAVA SEA

EAST TIMOR

TIMOR SEA

W E N S

600 miles

1,000 km

Where in the world?

Washington, DC to Tokyo
6,790 mi (10,927 km)
✈ 13 hr

7 A.M.   9 P.M.
Washington, DC Tokyo

Search and find

Afghanistan D5	Mongolia C7
Armenia C4	Myanmar E7
Azerbaijan C4	Nepal E6
Bahrain D4	North Korea . . .D8
Bangladesh E6	Oman E4
Bhutan E6	Pakistan D5
Brunei F8	Philippines E8
Cambodia E7	Qatar D4
China D7	Russian
Cyprus C3	Federation . . .B6
East Timor F8	Saudi Arabia . .D4
Georgia C4	Singapore F7
India E5	South Korea . . .D8
Indonesia F8	Sri Lanka F5
Iran D4	Syria C4
Iraq D4	Taiwan E8
Israel D3	Tajikistan D5
Japan C8	Thailand E7
Jordan D3	Tokyo D8
Kazakhstan C5	Turkey C3
Kuwait D4	Turkmenistan . . .D5
Kyrgyzstan D5	U.A.E. E4
Laos E7	Uzbekistan D5
Lebanon C4	Vietnam E7
Malaysia F7	Yemen E4
Maldives F4	

Throughout Asia, religion plays a key part in people's lives. In Thailand, more than 95 percent of the population is Buddhist. Beautiful temples dedicated to Buddhism can be seen throughout the country.

Continent facts

	Area sq mi (sq km)	% of Earth's area	Population	Largest country by area sq mi (sq km)	Largest country by population
Asia	17,400,000 (45,066,000)	30.1	3,527,969,000	Russian Fed. 6,592,800 (17,075,352)	China 1,250,066,000

A
B
C
D
E
F
G

Eastern Russia

The gray wolf thrives in the wilderness of Siberia, where it has survived thousands of years of being hunted. It lives in tundra and forest regions, gathering in packs of up to 30 during the harsh winters.

Eastern Russia

IN THE WEST OF RUSSIA, AT Moscow's Yaroslavsky Station, passengers board an eastbound train on the world's longest railroad, the Trans-Siberian. Once past the Ural Mountains, the train enters the region of Siberia, in the Asian part of the Russian Federation. It halts at sprawling industrial cities such as Omsk and rushes past small villages of wooden houses, their carved roof gables hung with icicles in winter. Borscht—beet soup—is served in the dining car.

Vast forests continue eastward, and many westbound locomotives may be seen hauling loads of timber. At Lake Baykal the track divides, southward to Mongolia or eastward to the Pacific coast and the seaport of Vladivostok, more than six days from Moscow, traveling at 35 mph (60 km/h).

Western Siberia forms a great plain, drained by the Ob River. Beyond the Yenisey River is the Central Siberian Plateau, bordered to the east and south by high mountains. Asian Russia has vast mineral wealth, but its great distance from the industrial cities in the west makes transportation expensive. The most fertile region is southwest of Siberia.

Siberian winters are among the most severe on Earth. Milk is delivered in solid blocks, and trucks use frozen rivers as highways. Siberia is sparsely populated, but it is home to many ethnic groups— Kets, Khants, Mani, Yakuts, Evenks, Koryaks, and Chukchi, as well as Russians. Some Arctic groups live by hunting, fishing, and reindeer herding.

Severnaya Zemlya

LAPTE

Nordvik

Dikson

Central Siberian Platea

Salekhard

Yenisey

RUSSIAN F

Ob

Siberian Lowland

Lower Tunguska

Surgut

Nizhniy Tagil

Ob

Yenisey

Tobol'

Tyumen'

Tobol'sk

Angara

Yekaterinburg

Chelyabinsk

Kurgan

Tomsk

Bratsk

Omsk

Kemerovo

Krasnoyarsk

KAZAKHSTAN

Novosibirsk

Novokuznetsk

Irkutsk

Barnaul

Yenisey

SAYAN MTS

MONGO

DISCOVER MORE

• Siberian temperatures have been known to drop to below –140°F (–60°C).

• Lake Baykal is the world's oldest surviving lake, dating back over 25 million years. Many of its plant and animal species, such as the rare Baykal seal, are found nowhere else on earth.

Yakutsk is located by the Lena River, in remote Siberia. It experiences bitterly cold winters, but is home to about 200,000 people.

1 2 3 4 5

ARCTIC OCEAN

Wrangel I.

EAST
SIBERIAN
SEA

Anadyr

BERING
SEA

w Siberian
Is

SEA

elta of
e Lena

Kolyma

KOLYMA MTS

Indigirka

Kolyma
Lowland

Komandorskiye I.

CHERSKIY RANGE

VERKHOYANSKIY MTS

Kamchatka
Peninsula

Magadan

Lena

Okhotsk

Petropavlovsk-
Kamchatskiy

DZHUGDZHUR MTS

Yakutsk

SEA OF
OKHOTSK

Olekminsk
ensk

D E R A T I O N

Aldan
Plateau

Lena

STANOVOY MTS

Sakhalin I.

Tatar Strait

YABLONOVYY MTS

Amur

Yuzhno-Sakhalinsk

.Baykal

SIKHOTE-ALIN MTS

C H I N A

Khabarovsk

SEA OF
JAPAN

Ulan-Ude

A

Vladivostok

A cone of gray rock called andestite, striped with
snow, rises from clouds on Russia's Kamchatka
Peninsula. Like many other parts of the Pacific Rim,
Kamchatka is a region of intense volcanic activity.

Where in the world?

7 A.M.
Washington, DC

noon
GMT

10 P.M.
Vladivostok

Washington, DC to Vladivostok	Vladivostok lies on
6,507 mi (10,471 km)	43° 06'N latitude
12 hr 30 min	131° 47'E longitude

Life facts

How long do people live?

U.S.A.
76 years

Russian Federation
65 years

**How many people in
100 own cars?**

48

9

Search and find

Eastern Russia

Anadyr A8	Novosibirsk E4
Barnaul E4	Okhotsk C8
Bratsk D6	Olekminsk D7
Chelyabinsk D3	Omsk E4
Dikson C5	Petropavlovsk-
Irkutsk E6	Kamchatskiy . .C9
Kemerovo E5	Salekhard C4
Khabarovsk D8	Surgut D4
Krasnoyarsk E5	Tobol'sk D4
Kurgan D4	Tomsk D5
Lensk D6	Tyumen' D3
Magadan C8	Ulan-Ude E6
Nizhniy Tagil D3	Vladivostok E8
Nordvik B6	Yakutsk C7
Novokuznetsk . .E5	Yekaterinburg . .D3
	Yuzhno-SakhalinskD9

A
B
C
D
E
F
G

500 miles

500 km

Russian
Federation

Country facts

	Area sq mi (sq km)	Population	Language	Religion	Currency
Russian Federation	6,592,800 (17,075,352)	146,393,569	Russian	Russian Orthodox	Ruble

A

The Caucasus

AZERBAIJAN, GEORGIA, ARMENIA

B

DAZZLING WHITE SNOWFIELDS can be seen above forests in the Caucasus range, which rises to some of Europe's highest peaks. Melting snows feed mountain streams and fast-flowing rivers, and these drain westward into the Black Sea. Eastward they drain into the Caspian Sea—a lake holding the largest volume of fresh water in the world.

C

The region is known as Trans-Caucasia, and the Caucasus Mountains form a meeting point between Europe and Asia, with the continental border passing through northern Georgia.

Armenia, known as the Land of Stones, contains very dry areas. However, river valleys and the warmer mountain foothills offer fertile land. Lowland crops include grapes, peaches, and figs. At higher altitudes, wheat, tobacco, and potatoes grow.

D

Trans-Caucasian factories produce chemicals, machinery, textiles, and leather goods. Azerbaijan has seen its oil industry thrive and decline over the years, but it seems likely that the Caspian Sea still has large reserves of oil to be exploited. Oil production is based around Baku, the best situated but most polluted harbor on the Caspian Sea.

E

More than 500 different ethnic groups live on the slopes of the Caucasus Mountains. Most people in Azerbaijan are Muslims, while Armenia and Georgia hold ancient Orthodox Christian traditions.

Georgian national costume may still be worn for special festivals. Men wear high leather boots, tunics, and round caps or hats of sheepskin.

DISCOVER MORE

• *The Caucasus range has more than 2,000 glaciers.*

F

• *Horseback riders gallop at breakneck speed in a Georgian game called* tskhenburi, *which is rather like polo. Teams of players hit a ball with a long racket.*

• *Oil reserves in Baku, the capital of Azerbaijan, once supplied half the world's oil.*

G

High-rise apartments tower over farmland on the outskirts of Yerevan, Armenia. The city is close to the Turkish border, a region prone to earthquakes.

Map labels:
Gagra · Sukhumi · Ochamchira · Zugdidi · Kutaisi · Poti · Batumi · Rioni · Kura · Mt Elbrus 18,510 ft (5,642 m) · RUSSIA · CAUCAS · BLACK SEA · GEORGIA · Tbilis · TURKEY · Vanadzor · Gyumri · Dilizh · ARME · Ejmiadzin · Yereva · Arak

1   2   3   4   5

With banners held high, priests of the Armenian Church lead a procession through the ancient town of Ejmiadzin to celebrate Easter. Armenia was the first country in history to make Christianity its state religion.

Where in the world?

7 A.M. — Washington, DC
noon — GMT
3 P.M. — Baku

Washington, DC to Baku
5,816 mi (9,360 km)
11 hr 10 min

Baku lies on
44° 22'N latitude
49° 53'E longitude

Life facts

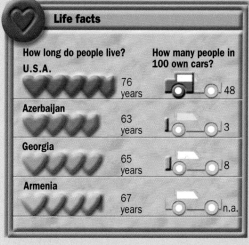

How long do people live?

U.S.A.	76 years
Azerbaijan	63 years
Georgia	65 years
Armenia	67 years

How many people in 100 own cars?

U.S.A.	48
Azerbaijan	3
Georgia	8
Armenia	n.a.

The Caucasus Mountains are home to the highest point in Europe, Mount Elbrus. Many geographers consider the Caucasus range to be the dividing line between Europe and Asia.

FEDERATION

Alazani
Rustavi
Şäki
Kuba
Gyandzha
Mingäçevir
A Z E R B A I J A N
Sumgait
Baku ✪
CASPIAN SEA
Nagorno-Karabakh
Stepanakert
Kura
Qazimämmäd
Araks
Salyan
RBAIJAN
Naxçivan
I R A N
Lenkoran'

300 miles
400 km

Azerbaijan   Georgia   Armenia

Search and find

Country facts

	Area sq mi (sq km)	Population	Language	Religion	Currency
Azerbaijan	33,4367 (86,599)	7,908,224	Azeri	Shia Muslim	Manat
Georgia	26,911 (69,911)	5,066,499	Georgian	Georgian Orthodox	Lavi
Armenia	11,506 (29,801)	3,409,234	Armenian	Armenian Apostolic	Dram

Central Asia

KAZAKHSTAN, TURKMENISTAN, UZBEKISTAN, KYRGYZSTAN, TAJIKISTAN

A little boy tries the reins of a horse in Kyrgyzstan. Most Kyrgyz people live by farming and herding in rural areas.

CENTRAL ASIA STRETCHES from the salty waters of the Caspian Sea to high mountain ranges such as the Pamirs, on the border with western China. Although the region lies at the heart of the Eurasian landmass, it is thinly populated. Its rocky plateaus and empty deserts are freezing in winter, but shimmer in the extreme heat of summer. These are crossed by two-humped Bactrian camels, as they pad and snort along ancient trading routes. There are wide, open, windswept grasslands called steppes, shallow lakes, and bleak mountain passes.

The newly independent nations of Central Asia take their names from the Muslim peoples of the region—the Kazakhs, Turkmen, Uzbeks, Tajiks, and Kyrgyz. Some of these people still lead a nomadic life, pitching tents wherever their goats and sheep can graze. Turkmen women make wool into beautiful, intricately patterned carpets. Some people are farmers, harvesting cotton, grain, melons, or wheat from irrigated land. Others work in a growing industry that is rapidly opening up the region— oil and natural gas.

DISCOVER MORE

• *The Aral Sea, on the Kazakh-Uzbek border, is vanishing fast. Today, it covers barely one-third of its original area. This is mainly because huge amounts of water have been drained away to irrigate crops.*

A young woman sets to work at a carpet factory in Ashkhabad, the capital of Turkmenistan. Central Asia and the Middle East have been a center of carpet making for thousands of years.

Kazakhstan

Turkmenistan

RUSSI

•Aqtöbe

•Baykonur

ARAL
SEA

K A Z A

TURANIAN
PLATEAU

Syr Dar'ya

Dashhowuz •

UZBEKISTAN

Shymke

TURKMENISTAN

✪**Ashkhabad**

Bukhara

Amu Dar'ya

✪**Tashke**

Samarkand

Dushanbe
✪
TAJIK

I
R
A
N

AFGHANISTAN

C A S P I A N   S E A

1   2   3   4   5

The tomb of Timur the Lame, or Tamerlane, may still be seen in the ancient trading city of Samarkand, in Uzbekistan. Timur led armies of Turks and Mongols to conquer land from Europe to India. He died in 1405.

Where in the world?

7 A.M. Washington, DC | noon GMT | 7 P.M Astana

Washington, DC to Astana
5,942 mi (9,563 km)
11 hr 25 min

Astana lies on
51° 11'N latitude
71° 26'E longitude

Life facts

How long do people live?

U.S.A. 76 years

Kazakhstan 64 years

Turkmenistan 61 years

Uzbekistan 64 years

Kyrgyzstan 64 years

Tajikistan 65 years

How many people in 100 own cars?

U.S.A. 48
Kazakhstan 6
Turkmenistan n.a.
Uzbekistan 4
Kyrgyzstan 4
Tajikistan 3

N
F E D E R A T I O N

Irtysh

★ **Astana**

• Qaraghandy

I S T A N

ETPAQDALA DESERT

L. Balkhash

C H I N A

• Almaty

☆ **Bishkek**
KYRGYZSTAN

ngan

TIAN SHAN

TAN

AMIRS

300 miles
500 km

Search and find

Kazakhstan
Capital: Astana .C7
Almaty E7
Aqtöbe C4
Baykonur D5
Qaraghandy D7
Shymkent E6

Turkmenistan
Capital:
  Ashkhabad . . .F4
Dashhowuz E4

Uzbekistan
Capital: Tashkent F6
Bukhara F5
Namangan F6
Samarkand F5

Kyrgyzstan
Capital: Bishkek .E7

Tajikistan
Capital:
  Dushanbe F5

Uzbekistan

Kyrgyzstan

Tajikistan

Country facts

	Area sq mi (sq km)	Population	Language	Religion	Currency
Kazakhstan	1,052,100 (2,724,939)	16,824,825	Kazakh/Russian	Sunni Muslim/NR*	Tenge
Turkmenistan	188,455 (488,098)	4,366,383	Turkmen	Muslim	Manat
Uzbekistan	172,741 (447,399)	24,102,473	Uzbek	Sunni Muslim	Som
Kyrgyzstan	76,641 (198,500)	4,546,055	Kyrgyz	Sunni Muslim	Som
Tajikistan	55,251 (143,100)	6,102,854	Tajik	Sunni Muslim	Ruble

*Non-religious

A B C D E F G

Northwest Asia

TURKEY, CYPRUS

Turkey

Cyprus

A LONG, GRACEFUL SUSPENSION bridge crosses the narrow, windy stretch of sea called the Bosporus. It separates the small European part of Turkey from the broad Anatolian plateau, known since ancient times as Asia Minor. Clustered on the steep, western shores of the Bosporus is the walled city of Istanbul. The beautiful domes of the Blue Mosque and Hagia Sophia mark its skyline. The covered bazaar is a maze of alleys where shops sell gleaming copper pots and carpets. Black tea and coffee are drunk wherever business is done; the coffee is served thick and very strong. Topkapi, the old palace of the Turkish rulers, or sultans, looks out over blue seas.

Anatolia's sunny coasts, with their fishing villages and ancient ruins, attract many tourists. Inland, dusty plains stretch eastward to Iran. Hot in summer but freezing in winter, they are broken by saltwater lakes and mountains. Ankara is Turkey's capital and second-largest populated city.

The beautiful Mediterranean island of Cyprus rises from a plateau to the Troodos Mountains in the southwest. The country is divided between its Greek and Turkish populations.

The landscape of Cappadocia, in the Turkish region of Anatolia, was created more than 8 million years ago by volcanic eruptions. Lava and ash were eroded by the weather into rocky pinnacles. Homes were later built into the rock face.

BULGARIA

GREECE

BLACK SEA

Edirne

Bosporus

Zonguldak

Bartin

Karabük

Tekirdağ

Istanbul

Izmit

Gerede

Kizil

Çoru

Sea of Marmara

Adapazari

Ankara

Bursa

Sakarya

Eskişehir

Porsuk

Kirikkale

Balikesir

Kütahya

ANATOLIAN PLATEAU

Tuz L.

Manisa

Uşak

Cappadoc

Izmir

Aydin

Nazilli

Konya

Denizli

Isparta

Bodrum

Antalya

TAURUS MOUNTAIN

Adar

Tarsus

Mersin

MEDITERRANEAN SEA

Nicosia

CYPRUS

TROODOS MTS

Larnaca

Limassol

This village in the center of the island of Cyprus lies on the eastern edge of the Troodos mountain range.

DISCOVER MORE

• *Millions of birds belonging to about 200 species use Cyprus as a stopping point on their annual migrations. They are attracted by the wetlands of Cyprus's lakes.*

• *Turkey is known for its ancient hamams, or public baths, containing steam rooms, washrooms, and massage rooms for men and women.*

1 2 3 4 5

A
B
C
D
E
F
G

Highest mountains

Mount McKinley
20,320 ft
(6,194 m)

Mount Ararat
17,011 ft
(5,186 m)

Ice-capped Mount Ararat is the highest point in Turkey, near the frontiers with Armenia and Iran. Ararat is an extinct volcano.

Where in the world?

7 A.M.   noon   2 P.M.
Washington, DC GMT Ankara

Washington, DC to Ankara
5,431 mi (8,740 km)
✈ 10 hr 25 min

Ankara lies on
40° 02'N latitude
32° 54'E longitude

Life facts

How long do people live?
U.S.A.
76 years

How many people in 100 own cars?
48

Turkey
73 years
5

Cyprus
77 years
30

Search and find

Turkey
Capital: Ankara .D5
Adana E6
Adapazari C4
Adiyaman E7
Antakya E6
Antalya E4
Aydin E4
Balikesir D4
Bartin C5
Batman E8
Bodrum E3
Bursa D4
Çorum D6
Denizli E4
Diyarbakir E8
Edirne C3
Elâzığ D7
Erzincan D7
Erzurum D8
Eskişehir D4
Gaziantep E7
Isparta E4
Istanbul C4
Izmir D3
Izmit C4

Karabük C5
Kars D9
Kayseri D6
Kirikkale D5
Konya E5
Kütahya D4
Malatya D7
Manisa D3
Mersin E6
Nazilli E4
Ordu C7
Osmaniye E6
Samsun C6
Sivas D6
Tarsus E6
Tekirdağ C3
Trabzon C7
Urfa E7
Uşak D4
Van D9
Zonguldak C5

Cyprus
Capital: Nicosia .F5
Larnaca F5
Limassol F5

A group of Turkish women ride in a tractor-trailer on their way to work in the fields. Forty-five percent of the Turkish labor force is employed in agriculture.

Turkey

Cyprus

Country facts

	Area sq mi (sq km)	Population	Language	Religion	Currency
Turkey	301,382 (780,579)	65,599,206	Turkish	Sunni Muslim	Lira
Cyprus	3,571 (9,249)	754,064	Greek/Turkish	Greek Orthodox/Sunni Muslim	Pound

100 miles
150 km

A

B

C

D

E

F

G

Western Asia

SYRIA, LEBANON

Lebanon's long, green Bekáa Valley lies at an altitude of 3,247 ft (990 m). About 12 mi (20 km) across, it is bordered in the west by the Lebanon Mountains. Often streaked with snow, the mountains rise to 10,115 ft (3,083 m) above sea level.

LEBANON'S COAST ROAD RUNS alongside the warm, blue Mediterranean Sea, through the ancient ports of Tyre and Sidon, and northward to the white apartment blocks and bright lights of the capital, Beirut. The city is being rebuilt after long years of war, and some districts remain badly damaged or ruined. Beirut hopes to regain its reputation for style and entertainment, attracting new tourists and investment. Roads cross the Lebanon Mountains and the fertile Bekáa Valley to the Anti-Lebanon Mountains on the Syrian border.

Syria and Lebanon include many Christians and Druze (a religious movement that broke away from Islam), but most people of the region are Muslim Arabs. Calls to prayer are broadcast five times daily from the loudspeakers of mosques in Damascus, the Syrian capital. They echo and boom around modern high-rise buildings, bustling covered markets, and narrow alleys. Syria extends westward to the orchards of the Mediterranean coast and eastward to the wheat and cotton fields of the fertile valley of the Euphrates River. Much of the country is hot, sandy desert, crossed by camel herders.

This man is a Druze. About one-half million of these people live in Lebanon, Syria, and Israel.

DISCOVER MORE

• Damascus is the oldest capital city in the world. People have lived there for at least 4,500 years.

• Lebanese cedar was used by craftspeople in ancient Egypt and Israel. Today very few cedars have survived, so millions of the trees are being grown to replace the forests. The cedar of Lebanon appears on the national flag.

Al Bāb

Aleppo

Asad Reservoi

Latakia

Apamea

Hamāh

Krak des Chevaliers

Tartus

Homs

Palmyra

MEDITERRANEAN SEA

Kebir

Tripoli

Qurnatas as Sawdā 10,115 ft (3,083 m)

LEBANON

Beirut

Sidon

Tyre

Damascus

Al Kiswah

Al Qunaytirah

Golan Heights

Shahbā

Dar'ā

As Suwayda

Busrā ash-Shām

ISRAEL

JORDAN

Syrian

A

In the heart of the city of Damascus, Syria, shops open directly onto the street. They are often festooned with all kinds of produce and household goods to tempt customers. Many of the women wear the long, dark robes and veils of the Islamic religion.

Where in the world?

7 A.M.	noon	2 P.M.
Washington, DC	GMT	Damascus

Washington, DC to Damascus
5,875 mi (9,454 km)
11 hr 20 min

Damascus lies on
33° 31'N latitude
36° 18'E longitude

B

Life facts

How long do people live?

U.S.A.
76 years

Syria
68 years

Lebanon
71 years

How many people in 100 own cars?

48

0.8

31

C

T U R K E Y

Al Qāmishli

Al Hasakah

Ar Raqqah

Euphrates

Khābūr

Dayr az Zawr

R I A

Abū Kamāl

Q

A

R

I

Desert

Cedars of Lebanon spread their ancient branches against the evening sky in Lebanon. The trees are evergreen conifers with a fragrant wood.

D

E

F

200 miles

300 km

Syria   Lebanon

Search and find

G

Country facts

	Area sq mi (sq km)	Population	Language	Religion	Currency
Syria	71,498 (185,180)	17,213,871	Arabic	Sunni Muslim	Pound
Lebanon	4,015 (10,399)	3,562,699	Arabic	Muslim	Pound

Southwest Asia

JORDAN, ISRAEL

These Jews are worshipping at the Western Wall in Jerusalem. The stone blocks supported the Second Temple built by King Herod more than 2,000 years ago. It was destroyed by Roman troops in A.D. 70.

Israel Jordan

JERUSALEM IS A HOLY CITY TO three faiths. Jews worship at the 2,000-year-old Western Wall, while Christian pilgrims sing hymns as they follow the route along which Jesus Christ is believed to have walked to his crucifixion. The golden Dome of the Rock is a magnificent mosque where it is believed the prophet Muhammad rode to heaven on a winged horse.

Israel is a land of orange, olive, and cypress trees, beside the warm shores of the eastern Mediterranean Sea. Much of the soil is very dry and has to be irrigated to produce crops. The south of the country is occupied by the sand dunes and rocks of the Negev Desert. Eight out of ten Israelis are Jews, many of them settlers who have come from other parts of the world. Most of the rest are Palestinian Arabs.

To the east is Jordan, a Muslim Arab kingdom. This country, too, has many ancient monuments, such as the beautiful city of Petra, carved from rock about 2,400 years ago. The land is mostly desert, where camels pad over rippling sand and four-wheel-drive vehicles kick up dust. Only the valley of the Jordan River is fertile enough to produce fruit and vegetables.

DISCOVER MORE

• *The Dead Sea is actually a lake. Its shores form the deepest exposed depression on Earth, lying some 1,300 ft (400 m) below sea level. The floor of the lake itself plunges to 2,390 ft (728 m) below sea level. The Dead Sea is eight times as salty as other seawater.*

• *Israel has no shortage of sunshine. The country is a world leader in solar energy research, and many houses now use the power of the sun to heat their water.*

A young pupil walks to Koranic school to learn the holy scriptures of Islam. He is from Gaza, a self-governing territory, which is home to about one million Palestinian Arabs.

MEDITERRANEAN SEA

LEBANON

Nahariyya
Acre • Sakhnin
Haifa • Tiberias
Nazareth
'Afula
Hadera • Janin
Netanya • Tul Karm
Herzliyya
Tel Aviv • Nābulus
Rishon le-Ziyyon • Rām Allāh
Rehovot
Ashdod • Jericho
Ashqelon • Jerusalem
Gaza • Gaza
Strip • Bethlehem
Khan Yunis • Hebron

Golan Heights
Sea of Galilee
Irbid
Ajlun
Al-Mafra
Jordan
Zarqa
West Bank
Salt • Az-Zarq
✪ **Ammān**
Ma'dabā
Dhībān
Mujib
Al-Mazra'ah
DEAD SEA
Al-Karak
JO

Beersheba

I S R A E L
Dimona

Negev Desert

At-Tafilah
JEBA
Wadi al Hasa
Ard a

E G Y P T

Wadi al Arabah

Petra
Ma'ān

Yotvata

Elat
'Aqaba
Gulf of 'Aqaba

S A U D I   A R A B I A

Israel's Sea of Galilee is also known as Lake Tiberias. The lake lies about 690 ft (210 m) below sea level and is filled and drained by the Jordan River.

Where in the world?

7 A.M.   noon   2 P.M
Washington, DC   GMT   Ammān

Washington, DC to Ammān
5,935 mi (9,552 km)
11 hr 25 min

Ammān lies on
31° 57'N latitude
35° 57'E longitude

Life facts

How long do people live?
U.S.A.
76 years

How many people in 100 own cars?
48

Jordan
73 years
4

Israel
78 years
21

SYRIAN DESERT

IRAQ

SYRIA

SAUDI ARABIA

DAN

ADHIRIYAT

w w a n

50 miles

50 km

Jordan   Israel

Petra is a desert city. In ancient times, it controlled the trade route between the Mediterranean region and the Indian Ocean.

Search and find

Jordan
Capital: Ammān .D5
Ajlun C5
Al-Karak E5
Al-Mafraq C6
Al-Mazra'ah D5
At-Tafílah E5
'Aqaba G4
Az-Zarqā C5
Dhíbān D5
Irbid C5
Ma'ān F5
Ma'dabā D5
Salt C5

Israel
Capital:
  Jerusalem . . .D4
Acre B4
'Afula C5
Ashdod D4
Ashqelon D4
Beersheba D4

Bethlehem D4
Dimona E4
Elat G4
Gaza D4
Hadera C4
Haifa B4
Hebron D4
Herzliyya C4
Janin C5
Jericho D5
Khan Yunis D3
Nābulus C4
Nahariyya B4
Nazareth C5
Netanya C4
Rām Allāh D4
Rehovot D4
Rishon le-Ziyyon .D4
Sakhnin B4
Tel Aviv C4
Tiberias C5
Tul Karm C4
Yotvata F4

Country facts

	Area sq mi (sq km)	Population	Language	Religion	Currency
Jordan	34,445 (89,213)	4,561,147	Arabic	Sunni Muslim	Dinar
Israel	7,876 (20,400)	5,749,760	Hebrew	Jewish	New Shekel

Northern Arabia

SAUDI ARABIA, KUWAIT

WITH A HEADDRESS AND flowing robes, a Saudi Arabian talks to his brother about hunting with birds of prey. A hooded falcon fidgets on his gloved hand. Inside his car parked on a desert highway, his wife is hidden within black robes. She wears a face veil, revealing only her eyes. Many women in Islamic countries cover their faces, believing that it frees them from the unwelcome attention of men. Other women think that remaining uncovered gives them freedom to carry out everyday work and feel comfortable.

Oil wells rise from the horizon, for Saudi Arabia has become rich through petroleum. This "black gold" has funded the building of modern cities, royal palaces, hospitals, and airports. However, vast areas of Saudi Arabia remain lonely, empty desert, crossed only by nomadic camel herders, many of whom remain poor.

The city of Mecca, in western Saudi Arabia, is the birthplace of the prophet Muhammad, and is visited by tens of thousands of white-robed Muslims from all over the world, during the annual pilgrimage, known as the *hajj*.

Kuwait, Saudi Arabia's neighbor on the Persian Gulf coast, is also a desert country that relies on oil for its wealth. Its people, too, are Muslim Arabs.

DISCOVER MORE

• *One part of Saudi Arabia is so barren and remote that it is known simply as the "Rub 'al-Khali," the "Empty Quarter." Here there are no plants, just gravel and endlessly shifting dunes.*

• *King Khalid airport, Riyadh, is the biggest international airport in the world, covering an area of 87 sq mi (225 sq km).*

These Saudi Arabian nomads have spread rugs on the ground outside their tent. The elderly man sips strong coffee. He wears a headdress called a ghutra. The woman wears a black robe and silver jewelry.

IRAQ

JORDAN

Al Jawf • • Sakākah

Nafud Desert

Gulf of Aqaba

Buraydah•

Shaqra

H E J A Z

NEJD

•Medina

R E D

S A U D I

•Jidda
•Mecca
•Taif

S E A

A S I R

Tihama

Jīzān•

The desert landscape of Kuwait is dominated by the oil industry. Petroleum and other related products account for more than 90 percent of this small country's exports. Since 1946, oil production has transformed Kuwait from a country of little means into one of the world's most prosperous nations.

Where in the world?

7 A.M. Washington, DC
noon GMT
3 P.M. Riyadh

Washington, DC to Riyadh
6,760 mi (10,879 km)
13 hr

Riyadh lies on
24° 31'N latitude
46° 47'E longitude

Life facts

How long do people live?

U.S.A. — 76 years
Saudi Arabia — 70 years
Kuwait — 77 years

How many people in 100 own cars?

48
8
28

It is the dream of every Muslim to make the pilgrimage to Mecca at least once in a lifetime. Beside the Great Mosque of this Saudi Arabian city is a small, square building called the Kaaba. Set into its eastern corner is the Black Stone, to which Muslims all over the world turn when they pray.

KUWAIT
✪ Kuwait

Persian Gulf

Ad Dabnā'

Al Qatīf
Ad-Dammām
BAHRAIN
QATAR
Al-Hufūf

✪ Riyadh

● Harad

A R A B I A

UNITED ARAB
EMIRATES

As-Sulayyil

O M A N

R u b ' a l - K h a l i

Y E M E N

200 miles

300 km

Saudi Arabia   Kuwait

Country facts

	Area sq mi (sq km)	Population	Language	Religion	Currency
Saudi Arabia	864,000 (2,240,350)	21,504,613	Arabic	Sunni Muslim	Riyal
Kuwait	6,880 (17,819)	1,991,115	Arabic	Sunni Muslim	Dinar

Search and find

Saudi Arabia
Capital: Riyadh .D6
Ad-Dammām . . .C7
Al-Hufūf D7
Al Jawf B4
Al Qatīf C7
As-Sulayyil E6
Buraydah C5
Harad D7
Jidda E4

JPẕan F5
Mecca E4
Medina D4
Sakākah B4
Shaqra D6
Taif E4

Kuwait
Capital: Kuwait . .B7

A
B
C
D
E
F
G

Southern Arabia
YEMEN, OMAN

CAMEL CARAVANS HEADING south from the deserts of Saudi Arabia enter the baking, rocky plateaus and mountain ranges of Yemen. Descending from the highlands, the slopes become greener, for they catch moist winds from the Indian Ocean. Coffee and cotton can be grown at this level. The coastal plains beside the Red Sea and the Gulf of Aden shimmer in a heat haze. Yemen's capital is Sanaa, where minarets, the slender towers of mosques, soar above rectangular, four-story buildings built of mud brick trimmed with white, looking like slabs of iced gingerbread.

Oman, too, is a land of mountains and gravelly deserts, beneath a blazing sun. Its territory includes several offshore islands and an enclave, or separate patch of territory, on the Musandam Peninsula, which extends into the Strait of Hormuz. Camels and goats graze on the scrub of the interior. Most nomadic herders belong to the Jebali of the southern region. The only cultivated area of any size is in the far north, where dates are grown. Fishermen sail large wooden boats out of coastal ports. Oil tankers make up most of the sea traffic between the Gulf of Oman and the port of Aden.

Maṭraḥ was an ancient trading center that outgrew the Omani capital until the two towns merged into a single urban area.

DISCOVER MORE

• *Southern Arabia and the Horn of Africa were the original home of the coffee plant. It was later introduced to India, Southeast Asia, East Africa, and Central and South America.*

• *Desert valleys called* wadis *have no rainfall for years and, baked by the sun, they become as hard as concrete. When it does rain, the water cannot soak into the ground, and can form a violent flash flood.*

This old Yemeni palace in Sanaa perches on top of an eroded pillar of rock. Over the ages, desert landscapes have been worn down into strange and fantastic shapes by windborne sand.

1   2   3   4   5

Strait of Hormuz

Musandam Peninsula

Persian Gulf

UNITED ARAB EMIRATES

Gulf of Oman

Şuḥār

Maţraḥ ○✪ **Muscat**

Jabal ash Sham
9,957 ft
(3,035 m) ▲

Nizwā

Şūr

O M A N

Khaluf

Maşīrah

A R A B I A

Ras al Madrakah

ARABIAN
SEA

Salālah

Kuria Muria Is

Ras Fartak

Socotra

Abd al-Kuri

INDIAN
OCEAN

200 miles

300 km

Where in the world?

7 A.M.
Washington, DC GMT | noon | 3 P.M. Sanaa

Washington, DC to Sanaa
7,102 mi (11,430 km)
13 hr 40 min

Sanaa lies on
15° 27′N latitude
44° 12′E longitude

Life facts

How long do people live?

U.S.A.	76 years
Yemen	60 years
Oman	71 years

How many people in 100 own cars?

U.S.A.	48
Yemen	1
Oman	9

When they go out, most Yemeni Muslim women wear long, dark robes and a veil that covers their faces, with only their eyes showing. However, country women do not normally cover their faces when they are working on the land.

Yemen

Oman

Search and find

Yemen
Capital: Sanaa E4
Aden F4
Al-Hudaydah E4
Al Mukallā E6
Shaqrā' F5
Ta'izz F4
TarPm E5

Oman
Capital: Muscat .B8
Khaluf C8
Maţraḥ B9
Nizwā C8
Salālah D7
Şuḥār B8
Şūr C9

Country facts

	Area sq mi (sq km)	Population	Language	Religion	Currency
Yemen	207,286 (536,871)	16,942,230	Arabic	Muslim	Rial
Oman	118,150 (306,009)	2,446,645	Arabic	Ibadhi Muslim	Rial Omani

Gulf States

UNITED ARAB EMIRATES, QATAR, BAHRAIN

FLY INTO THE GLEAMING, air-conditioned international airports of Abu Dhabi or Dubayy, and the landscape below the plane makes up flat patterns of yellow-brown and emerald-blue. Desert lands stretch westward into the sandy, stony wilderness of Saudi Arabia. The blue is the water of the Persian Gulf, which separates the Arabian Peninsula from Iran. The salt flats, islands, and peninsulas of the Persian Gulf's southern shore are occupied by three small countries—Qatar, Bahrain, and a federation of six tiny states and one large state, Abu Dhabi, called the United Arab Emirates (U.A.E.). An emirate is a region ruled by an emir, or prince. The people are mostly Muslim Arabs.

The Persian Gulf coast is mostly barren, but oil has brought wealth to the region, with giant supertankers carrying the precious fuel eastward through the Strait of Hormuz. Oil has paid for the building of modern cities and for the development of other industries such as fish processing. It has also paid for a factory that removes salt from seawater, an expensive but useful way of producing vital drinking water and irrigating the desert region.

Qatar occupies a peninsula, while Bahrain is an island country, made up of more than thirty different small islands.

This Bahraini girl wears elaborate jewelery and traditional robes. The people of the island of Bahrain are mostly Arabs. They belong to both the Sunni and Shia branches of the Islamic religion.

DISCOVER MORE

• The world's largest natural gas reserve, North Field, lies off the shores of Qatar.

• Camel racing is a popular sport in the United Arab Emirates. Dromedaries (single-humped camels) ridden by jockeys are raced over courses at speeds of more than 12 mph (20 km/h).

• The Gulf region contains more than half of the world's supply of oil and gas.

Traditional wooden ships anchor in Dubayy creek, an inlet of the Persian Gulf that winds through the modern high-rise offices and hotels of Dubayy, the chief port and business center of the U.A.E.

Manama
BAHRAIN

QATAR
Ad-Dawhah

Persian

SAUDI ARABIA

This traditional mosque, a Muslim house of worship, is in Dubayy. People flock here daily to pray. Dubayy is one of the small emirates bordering the Persian Gulf. Ninety-six percent of the population in the U.A.E. is Muslim.

UNITED ARAB EMIRATES

United Arab Emirates   Qatar   Bahrain

100 miles

100 km

Country facts

	Area sq mi (sq km)	Population	Language	Religion	Currency
U.A.E.	32,000 (82,880)	2,344,402	Arabic	Sunni Muslim	Dirham
Qatar	4,416 (11,437)	723,542	Arabic	Sunni Muslim	Riyal
Bahrain	268 (694)	629,090	Arabic	Shia Muslim	Dinar

Where in the world?

7 A.M.   noon   4 P.M.
Washington, DC   GMT   Abu Dhabi

Washington, DC to Abu Dhabi
7,046 mi (11,340 km)
13 hr 35 min

Abu Dhabi lies on
24° 28'N latitude
54° 25'E longitude

Life facts

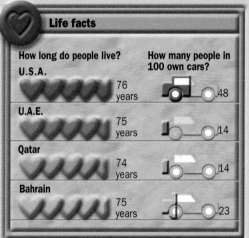

How long do people live?

U.S.A.	76 years	
U.A.E.	75 years	
Qatar	74 years	
Bahrain	75 years	

How many people in 100 own cars?

U.S.A. 48
U.A.E. 14
Qatar 14
Bahrain 23

Cannons guard the gate of an old fortress in Abu Dhabi. The pirate ships that once sailed along the Gulf Coast have today been replaced by oil tankers.

Search and find

The Middle East

IRAN, IRAQ

Men gather for Friday prayers in Tehrān, capital of Iran. Ninety-five percent of Iranians belong to a branch of Islam called Shia, while four percent belong to the Sunni branch.

IN THE HOLY CITY OF Mashhad, in eastern Iran, a group of turbaned travelers wait for a kettle to boil on glowing embers. It is a cold morning, and soon they are gulping down hot, sweet, black tea. A baker brings out round loaves of flat bread. With the sun risen, a bus takes the travelers westward across flat desert, toward snowy mountains and the hot, bustling streets of the capital, Tehrān. During the day the bus stops several times to allow people to climb out to pray. As in other strict Islamic countries, women are expected to wear a veil and men to wear beards, according to religious tradition.

Iraq is another Islamic country. Its capital, Baghdad, is one of the ancient trading centers of the Arab world. Once famous for its camel caravans and bazaars, it is now built of concrete and is noisy with traffic. The Tigris and Euphrates rivers flow through green lands, fringed with date palms and traditional villages of flat-roofed, mud-brick dwellings. Beyond the river valleys lie deserts. In the mountains of the north, stretching across the border into Turkey and Iran, lies the traditional homeland of a people called the Kurds. Iraq and Iran are oil-producing countries.

DISCOVER MORE

• *A rare kind of sturgeon from the Caspian Sea, called the beluga, weighs up to 2,200 lb (1,000 kg). The black eggs of this fish are used to make a delicacy called caviar.*

• *The Marsh Arabs live in the wetlands of southern Iraq. Their large houses are made of reeds and are built on artificial islands of reeds.*

At the center of Eşfahān, Iran's third-largest populated city, stands the impressive Royal Mosque. It is covered with beautiful enameled tiles, and dates back to the 1600s.

1   2   3   4   5

Highest mountains

Mount McKinley
20,320 ft
(6,194 m)

Mount Damāvand
18,386 ft
(5,605 m)

A carpet gradually lengthens on the loom, as an Iranian woman skillfully weaves in the elaborate pattern. Her craft dates back at least 2,500 years, but she is paid less than the equivalent of $1 a day.

Where in the world?

7 A.M.   noon   3.30 P.M.
Washington, DC   GMT   Tehrān

Washington, DC to Tehrān	Tehrān lies on
6,337 mi (10,198 km)	35° 40'N latitude
12 hr 10 min	51° 26'E longitude

Life facts

How long do people live?
U.S.A.
76 years

Iran
68 years

Iraq
67 years

How many people in 100 own cars?
48
2
3

Longest rivers

Nile   4,145 mi (6,670 km)

Mississippi   3,741 mi (6,020 km)

Euphrates 1,700 mi (2,740 km)

200 miles

300 km

T U R K M E N I S T A N

Bābol
M T S
Mt Damāvand

Mashhad

Dasht-e-Kavīr

I R A N

Yazd

A F G H A N I S T A N

Dasht-e-Lut

Kermān

Zāhedān

Shīrāz

P A K I S T A N

Bandar 'Abbās

Bandar-e Lengeh

Strait of Hormuz

Jāsk

N
W   E
S

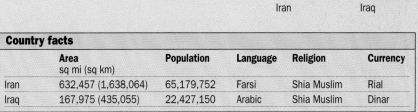

Iran   Iraq

Search and find

Iran	
Capital: Tehrān . .D6	Qom D6
Abādan E5	Rasht C5
Ahvāz E5	Shīrāz E6
Bābol C6	Tabrīz C5
Bākhtarān D5	Yazd D7
Bandar 'Abbās . .F7	Zāhedān E8
Bandar-e Lengeh F7	**Iraq**
Būshehr E6	*Capital*: Baghdad D4
Eşfahān D6	An Nasiriya E5
Hamadān D5	Arbīl C4
Jāsk F7	Basra E5
Kāshān D6	Karbalā' D4
Kermān E7	Kirkūk D4
Mashhad C8	Mosul C4

Country facts

	Area sq mi (sq km)	Population	Language	Religion	Currency
Iran	632,457 (1,638,064)	65,179,752	Farsi	Shia Muslim	Rial
Iraq	167,975 (435,055)	22,427,150	Arabic	Shia Muslim	Dinar

A
B
C
D
E
F
G

Kabul to the Indus

PAKISTAN, AFGHANISTAN

THE KHYBER PASS IS AN ancient route through rock-strewn hills, on the border between Afghanistan and Pakistan. Old-fashioned trucks, decorated in bright colors, line up at the frontier. The drivers—tall, bearded men with baggy trousers and round felt hats—chat with one another.

Northbound trucks are soon lurching around hairpin bends above dizzying gorges. The Afghan capital, Kabul, is surrounded by mountains, which are cold and snowy in winter. Roads lead north to the Hindu Kush range and loop westward to the cities of Qandahār and Herāt. This is a land of mud-brick forts, bazaars, and mosques. In the southwestern area of Afghanistan, the Helmand River flows toward the Iranian border. Crops such as barley, corn, and wheat are grown in this region.

Neighboring Pakistan, too, is a land of snow-covered peaks and deserts. One highway climbs through the bleak Karakoram Range to China. Rivers flow south across a plain to join the mighty Indus River. Wheat, rice, and cotton are grown on the plain. Railroads link large industrial cities such as Karachi and Lahore. City streets are hot and crowded. Men cycle by, wearing white tunics over loose trousers. A group of girls comes out of school, each one wearing brightly colored trousers, with a shawl over her thick braid of hair.

DISCOVER MORE

• Until 2001 massive statues of Gautama Buddha, founder of the Buddhist faith, towered over a valley 80 mi (130 km) northwest of Kabul. They were first mentioned by a Chinese monk who traveled to see them 1,370 years ago.

A flute seller demonstrates his wares on the busy streets of Karachi, in Pakistan. Wind instruments, including a wide range of bamboo flutes known as bansuri, are a very important part of the traditional music of Pakistan and northern India.

Longest rivers

River	Length
Nile	4,145 mi (6,670 km)
Mississippi	3,741 mi (6,020 km)
Indus	1,800 mi (2,897 km)

Where in the world?

7 A.M.   noon   5 P.M.
Washington, DC GMT   Islamabad

Washington, DC to Islamabad	Islamabad lies on
7,088 mi (11,406 km)	33° 37'N latitude
13 hr 40 min	73° 06'E longitude

Life facts

How long do people live?

U.S.A.	76 years
Pakistan	59 years
Afghanistan	48 years

How many people in 100 own cars?

	48
	1
	0.1

Highest mountains

K2
28,250 ft
(8,611 m)

Mount McKinley
20,320 ft
(6,194 m)

200 miles

300 km

Housing and mosques have been built along a valley floor and slopes not far from Kabul, the capital of Afghanistan. Fewer than one in five Afghans are town dwellers.

Pakistan

Afghanistan

Search and find

Country facts

	Area sq mi (sq km)	Population	Language	Religion	Currency
Pakistan	307,374 (796,099)	138,123,359	Urdu	Sunni Muslim	Rupee
Afghanistan	251,825 (652,227)	25,824,882	Pashto	Sunni Muslim	Afghani

Map labels: TAJIKISTAN, CHINA, KARAKORAM RANGE, K2, DISPUTED AREA, Kabul, Mardan, Khyber Pass, Peshawar, Islamabad, Rawalpindi, SULAIMAN RANGE, Indus, Gujranwala, Sargodha, Lahore, Jhang Maghiana, Faisalabad, Sahiwel, Sutlej, Multan, Bahawalpur, INDIA, Mirpur Khas

Southern Asia

INDIA, NEPAL, SRI LANKA, BHUTAN

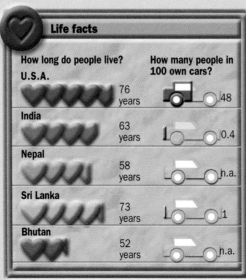

This woman comes from northwestern India where women wear silver jewelry and colorful dresses embroidered with mirror sequins.

A BUDDHIST SHRINE RISES from the outskirts of Kathmandu, the capital of Nepal. Its golden tower is decorated with four pairs of eyes, staring north, south, east, and west. They face north to the Himalayas, the world's highest mountain range, pink in the dawn. They face eastward to the terraced fields of the small mountain kingdom of Bhutan. They face west and south to the sacred Ganges River as it winds its way across the vast plains of northern India.

India is a large and beautiful country of many different peoples and faiths. It has a long tradition of fine crafts, sculpture, dance, music, and poetry. The land is parched by a burning sun and drenched by monsoon rains. This is a land of dusty villages and overcrowded cities, of heavy industry and aged railroads. On every street there is noise from shouting street vendors, and motor-tricycle taxis buzz like hornets. There are the brilliant colors of the women's saris and the smells of exotic spices and fruits sold in outdoor markets.

Southern India's coastal mountains, surrounding the Deccan plateau, converge to a point. Across the Palk Strait are the tropical forests and peaks of Sri Lanka.

DISCOVER MORE

• There are more than 400 different languages spoken throughout India.

• India is the world's largest democracy. More than 300 million people vote in the general elections.

• Elephants, decorated with electric lightbulbs, glow in the dark during the Esala Perahera festival held each year in Kandy, Sri Lanka. This festival is held to honor the Sacred Tooth of the Buddha, a relic preserved in a temple on the island.

Life facts

How long do people live?	How many people in 100 own cars?
U.S.A. 76 years	48
India 63 years	0.4
Nepal 58 years	n.a.
Sri Lanka 73 years	1
Bhutan 52 years	n.a.

A

Highest mountains

Mount Everest
29,028 ft
(8,848 m)

Mount McKinley
20,320 ft
(6,194 m)

Where in the world?

7 A.M.   noon   5:30 P.M.
Washington, DC GMT   Delhi

Washington, DC to Delhi
7,480 mi (12,038 km)
14 hr 25 min

Delhi lies on
28° 54'N latitude
77° 13'E longitude

B

300 miles

500 km

Longest rivers

Nile ～～～ 4,145 mi (6,670 km)

Mississippi ～～～ 3,741 mi (6,020 km)

Ganges ～ 1,560 mi (2,510 km)

C

CHINA

Annapurna ▲

Mt Everest

Thimphu ★ **B H U T A N**

Kathmandu

Biratnagar

Phuntsholing

Guwahati

H I M A L A Y A S

CHINA

NAGA HILLS

MYANMAR (BURMA)

Imphal

icknow

llahabad

Varanasi   Patna   *Ganges*

on

BANGLADESH

Jamshedpur

Haora

A

Calcutta

Mouths of the Ganges

aipur   *Mahanadi*

Cuttack

S

Vishakhapatnam

Bay of Bengal

India

Nepal

Sri Lanka

Bhutan

D

Search and find

India
Capital: Delhi ..B5
Agra C5
Ahmadabad C4
Ajmer C5
Allahabad C6
Bangalore F5
Bhavnagar D4
Bhopal C5
Calcutta D7
Calicut F4
Chennai
 (Madras) F5
Cochin F4
Coimbatore ...F5
Cuttack D7
Guwahati C8
Haora D7
Hubli-Dharwar ..E4
Hyderabad E5
Imphal C8
Indore C5
Jabalpur D6
Jaipur C5
Jamnagar C4
Jamshedpur ...D7
Jodhpur C5
Kalyan D4
Kanpur C6
Kolhapur E4
Kurnool E5
Lalitpur C5
Lucknow C6
Ludhiana B5

Madurai F5
Mumbai
 (Bombay) D4
Mysore F5
Nagpur D5
Nellore E5
Patna C7
Poona D4
Raipur D6
Solapur D5
Srinagar A5
Surat D4
Tiruchchirappalli .F5
Udaipur C5
Vadodara D4
Varanasi C6
Vijayawada E6
Vishakhapatnam E6

Nepal
Capital:
 Kathmandu ...C7
Biratnagar C7

Sri Lanka
Capital: Colombo G5
Galle G5
Jaffna F5
Kandy G5
Trincomalee G5

Bhutan
Capital: Thimphu C8
Phuntsholing ...C8

E

Country facts

	Area sq mi (sq km)	Population	Language	Religion	Currency
India	1,222,243 (3,165,609)	1,000,848,550	Hindi	Hindu	Rupee
Nepal	56,827 (147,182)	24,302,653	Nepali	Hindu	Rupee
Sri Lanka	25,332 (65,610)	19,144,875	Sinhala	Buddhist	Rupee
Bhutan	18,417 (47,000)	1,951,965	Dzongkha	Lamaistic Buddhist	Ngultrum

F

ANDAMAN IS (INDIA)

NICOBAR IS (INDIA)

G

The Taj Mahal was built in India at Agra by Emperor Shāh Jāhan for his wife in the 1600s. It took over 20,000 workers 23 years to build.

Bay of Bengal

MYANMAR, BANGLADESH

GREAT RIVERS CARRYING meltwater from the Himalayas spills across low-lying plains before entering the Bay of Bengal. In Bangladesh, the Ganges and Brahmaputra rivers merge and form a maze of waterways and small islands. Tropical storms called cyclones rage across the Bay of Bengal, and large areas of land are often flooded.

Bangladesh is a hot, humid country, with lush, fertile land. It is very crowded, and its people struggle to make a living by growing jute, tea, and rice. Most are Bengali, who follow the Islamic faith.

Myanmar, formerly known as Burma, lies to the east of Bangladesh. The Irrawaddy River flows north to south through the country and forms a broad delta where it meets the sea. Here, many of the wooden houses are built on stilts above the water. Rice, sugarcane, and rubber trees grow in this warm, wet region, and teak forests cover the cooler northern hills. Myanmar exports oil, natural gas, and gemstones. The golden-roofed Shwe Dagon pagoda in Yangon is one of the holiest temples of the Buddhist faith. Most of the population are Burmese, but minority peoples include the Chin, Kachin, Shan, and Karen.

A monk reads in front of ancient statues at a Buddhist monastery in Mandalay. The ornate carvings are made from teak, a precious tropical hardwood grown in the forests of Myanmar.

200 miles

300 km

DISCOVER MORE

• *The Brahmaputra and Ganges rivers form the world's largest delta region, occupying about 29,000 sq mi (75,000 sq km).*

• *More than half of Bangladesh can be under water at times of severe flooding. Three-quarters of the country is less than 9 ft (3 m) above sea level.*

• *Every five days on a lake in central Myanmar, farmers, craftworkers, and other people gather in boats. They trade items such as rice cakes, farm tools, silk, fish, fruits, and vegetables.*

In Bangladesh and other coastal regions of the Bay of Bengal, it is often hard to know where the land ends and the water begins. Tropical storms and monsoon rains often create disastrous floods.

Country facts					
	Area sq mi (sq km)	Population	Language	Religion	Currency
Myanmar	261,969 (678,500)	48,081,302	Burmese	Buddhist	Kyat
Bangladesh	55,598 (143,999)	127,117,967	Bengali	Sunni Muslim	Taka

MYANMAR (BURMA)

INDIA

KUMON RANGE

CHINA

DESH

Chittagong

nges

ARAKAN RANGE

Irrawaddy

PEGU RANGE

Mandalay

Sittwe

TANEN MTS

VIETNAM

THAILAND

Prome

Henzada

Pegu

Bassein

Yangon (Rangoon)

Moulmein

Mouths of the Irrawaddy

Gulf of Martaban

BILAUKTAUNG RANGE

Tavoy

ANDAMAN SEA

Mergui

MERGUI ARCHIPELAGO

Myanmar   Bangladesh

Where in the world?

7 A.M.
Washington, DC GMT

noon

6.30 P.M.
Yangon

Washington, DC to Yangon
8,576 mi (13,801 km)
16 hr 30 min

Yangon lies on
16° 46'N latitude
96° 09'E longitude

Life facts

How long do people live?

U.S.A.   76 years

Myanmar   55 years

Bangladesh   57 years

How many people in 100 own cars?

U.S.A.   48

Myanmar   0.1

Bangladesh   0.1

Wooden cargo vessels head from the shore, their square sails swelling in the wind. Myanmar's Irrawaddy River is an important trading route, used to transport teak logs, petroleum, rice, and crops.

Search and find

Myanmar
Capital: Yangon .E8
Bassein E7
Henzada D7
Mandalay C8
Mergui F9
Moulmein E8
Pegu E8
Prome D7

Sittwe D7
Tavoy F8

Bangladesh
Capital: Dhaka . .B6
Chittagong C6
Khulna C6
Rajshahi B6
Rangpur B6

A
B
C
D
E
F
G

Southeast Asia

THAILAND, VIETNAM, LAOS, CAMBODIA

SOUTH OF CHINA AND EAST OF
Myanmar, the Asian continent
bulges out, forming a long
peninsula in the west. This hot and
sometimes humid area is occupied
by Thailand and the countries
sometimes grouped together as
"Indochina"—Laos, Cambodia, and Vietnam.

This part of Asia is home to many different
peoples, including Thais, Karen, Shan, Hmong, Lao,
Khmer, Chinese, and Vietnamese. In the lush river
valleys and plains, men and women work in flooded
rice paddies. Many wear broad straw hats to keep off
the hot sun or the monsoon rains. In the mountains
and hills, villagers grow sweet potatoes and hunt in
the forests.

There are big cities, too, such as Bangkok,
Phnom Penh, Ho Chi Minh City, and Hanoi. Here
there are noisy motorcycles and minibuses, street
markets, and canal-side boats selling tropical fruits.
Among the crowds are orange-robed, shaven-
headed Buddhist monks.

Many tourists now come to the region. Some of
them are here to visit the ancient ruins of
Cambodia's Khmer civilization, others come to see
the turquoise seas and limestone rocks that form
part of the Thai coast.

DISCOVER MORE

• The Black River, which
flows through northern
Vietnam, has carved out a
narrow, sheer-sided gorge
about 2,600 ft (800 m)
deep. The light of day barely
reaches the gloomy floor of
the Laichau Canyon.

• Limestone caves in
southwest Thailand are
home to the world's smallest
mammal, Kitt's hog-nosed
bat. It is also called the
bumblebee bat because of its
tiny size: about 1 in (3 cm)
long, with a wingspan
of about 5 1/2 in (14 cm).

*Two Cambodians, wearing the saffron-colored robes of
Buddhist monks, sit in the ancient temple of Angkor
Wat. Situated to the northwest of the Cambodian
capital, Phnom Penh, the temple is one of many dating
back to the thousand-year-old Khmer civilization.*

Longest rivers

River	Length
Nile	4,145 mi (6,670 km)
Mississippi	3,741 mi (6,020 km)
Mekong	2,600 mi (4,180 km)

In the Far East, small wooden boats may be used for fishing or carrying goods to market. They are called sampans—these boats are in Vietnam.

Where in the world?

7 A.M.   noon   7 P.M.
Washington, DC   GMT   Bangkok

Washington, DC to Bangkok
8,799 mi (14,160 km)
16 hr 55 min

Bangkok lies on
13° 50'N latitude
100° 29'E longitude

Life facts

How long do people live?

Country	Years
U.S.A.	76 years
Thailand	69 years
Vietnam	68 years
Laos	54 years
Cambodia	48 years

How many people in 100 own cars?

Country	Cars
U.S.A.	48
Thailand	3
Vietnam	0.1
Laos	0.1
Cambodia	0.1

Search and find

Thailand
Capital: Bangkok D5
Chiang Mai B4
Hat Yai G5
Khon Kaen C6
Nakhon
  Ratchasima . .D5
Nakhon Si
  Thammarat . . .F5
Phuket F4
Songkhla G5
Ubon Ratchathani D7

Ho Chi Minh City E7
Hue C7
Nam Dinh B7
Nha Trang E8
Qui Nhon D8
Thai Nguyen A7
Vinh B7

Laos
Capital: Vientiane C6
Luang Prabang . .B6
Savannakhet . . .C6

Vietnam
Capital: Hanoi . .B7
Can Tho E7
Da Nang C8
Haiphong B7

Cambodia
Capital:
  Phnom Penh . .E6
Battambang D6
Kampong Cham .E7

Thailand

Vietnam

Laos

Cambodia

Country facts

	Area sq mi (sq km)	Population	Language	Religion	Currency
Thailand	198,455 (513,998)	61,210,000	Thai	Buddhist	Baht
Vietnam	127,243 (329,559)	77,311,210	Vietnamese	Buddhist	Dong
Laos	91,428 (236,799)	5,407,453	Lao	Buddhist	Kip
Cambodia	69,900 (181,041)	10,750,000	Khmer	Theravada Buddhist	Riel

200 miles

300 km

Eastern Seas

INDONESIA, MALAYSIA, EAST TIMOR, BRUNEI, SINGAPORE

SOUTHEAST ASIA IS mostly made up of islands, the majority forming part of Indonesia or Malaysia. A small motorbike is a good way to get around on the Indonesian island of Bali. Roads pass through green, terraced rice fields fringed with palm trees, forests with waterfalls and monkeys, and villages of thatched wooden houses. Craft workers carve wood or produce beautiful textiles, woven with dyed yarns or dyed with a wax method called batik. Young girls take lessons in graceful, swaying dance movements. Ducks swim in the moats of palaces and ornate temples that celebrate the Hindu beliefs of the Balinese people. Most other Indonesians are Muslims.

East Timor broke away from Indonesia in 2000. The small, oil-rich state of Brunei is located on the north coast of Borneo. While Southeast Asia contains vast areas of remote forest, it also includes centers of international business, with soaring skyscrapers, such as Kuala Lumpur (capital of Malaysia) and the port of Singapore, a city that is an independent state in its own right.

300 miles

400 km

DISCOVER MORE

• When the twin Petronas Towers building in Kuala Lumpur, Malaysia, was opened in 1996, it became the world's tallest building, at 1,483 ft (452 m).

• The Komodo dragon, a monitor lizard growing to 8 ft (2.5 m) in length, is the largest reptile in the world. It lives on several Indonesian islands, including the island of Komodo.

• The Indonesian archipelago is the biggest on Earth. It is made up of more than 17,000 islands.

Life facts

How long do people live?	How many people in 100 own cars?
U.S.A.	76 years	48
Indonesia	63 years	1
Malaysia	71 years	14
Brunei	72 years	46
Singapore	79 years	11
East Timor	not available	

Highest mountains

Mount McKinley
20,320 ft
(6,194 m)

Puncak Jaya
16,503 ft
(5,031 m)

1   2   3   4   5

A

B

C

D

E

F

G

Where in the world?

7 A.M. noon 7 P.M.
Washington, DC GMT Jakarta

Washington, DC to Jakarta
10,163 mi (16,355 km)
19 hr 30 min

Jakarta lies on
06° 10'S latitude
106° 48'E longitude

Kota
Kinabalu ▲ Mt Kinabalu 13,431 ft (4,095 m)
gawan Sandakan

Sabah

*C E L E B E S
SEA*

Makassar Strait

Manado

MOLUCCA SEA

Halmahera

Sorong

Jayapura

Balikpapan

Palu

Sulawesi

CERAM SEA

Ceram

Irian Jaya

PAPUA NEW GUINEA

Barito

I N D O N E S I A

Ambon

Buru

Puncak Jaya

Digul

Banjarmasin

Ujungpandang

Baubau

B A N D A   S E A

Aru Is

F L O R E S   S E A

Wetar

Tanimbar Is

Bali *Lombok* *Komodo F l o r e s*

Dili

Mataram *Sumbawa*

Ende

EAST
TIMOR

*A R A F U R A
SEA*

Sumba

Timor

Kupang

The skyscrapers of Singapore's business district rise from a small island,
which is linked to the Malay Peninsula by a causeway over the Johore
Strait. The population of Singapore is a mixture of peoples of Chinese,
Malay, and Indian descent.

Search and find

Indonesia	Ujungpandang ..C7
Capital: Jakarta .D5	
Ambon C8	**Malaysia**
Balikpapan C6	*Capital*:
Bandung D5	Kuala Lumpur .B4
Banjarmasin ...C6	Ipoh B4
Baubau C8	Johor Baharu ..B4
Ende D7	Kelang B4
Jambi C4	Kota Kinabalu ..A6
Jayapura C11	Kuala
Kupang D8	Terengganu ...B4
Malang D6	Sandakan A6
Manado B8	
Mataram D6	**East Timor**
Medan B3	*Capital*: Dili D8
Padang C4	
Palembang C4	**Brunei**
Palu C7	*Capital*: Bandar
Pontianak C5	Seri Begawan .B6
Semarang D5	
Sorong C9	**Singapore** B4
Surabaya D6	

Indonesia Malaysia

East Timor Brunei Singapore

Country facts

	Area sq mi (sq km)	Population	Language	Religion	Currency
Indonesia	735,309 (1,904,450)	202,110,000	Javanese	Sunni Muslim	Rupiah
Malaysia	127,316 (329,748)	20,932,901	Malay	Sunni Muslim	Ringgit
East Timor	5,743 (14,874)	845,000	Tetum	Catholic	Escudo
Brunei	2,228 (5,771)	315,292	Malay	Sunni Muslim	Dollar
Singapore	250 (648)	3,490,356	Chinese	Buddhist	Dollar

Philippines

Philippines

Rice has been grown on flooded terraces, cut from hillsides on the largest island, Luzon, for more than 2,000 years. It remains the chief crop and a major part of the inhabitants' diet.

SOUTHEAST ASIA'S BORDER with the wide Pacific Ocean is formed by a scattering of more than 7,000 tropical islands made of coral and volcanic rocks. These make up a nation called the Philippines. The Filipino people, as they are called, include more than 100 different ethnic groups, many of them from Malaysia. Most of them share Christian beliefs, and many are Roman Catholics.

The Philippine climate is warm and humid, but pleasantly fresh in the mountains. Coconut palms bend during violent storms, and monsoon rains drench the islands between June and October each year. Some of the islands have volcanoes that erupt from time to time, filling the air with choking fumes and showering ash over the countryside. The islands often experience earthquakes, too.

The Philippine landscape is very beautiful. Water buffalo plow the terraced rice paddies, which snake around lush green hillsides. Some Filipinos live in the country, but most live in the hustle and bustle of the towns and cities. Manila, the capital, is on the island of Luzon. The city has many manufacturing industries, which include textiles, garments, electrical goods, cane ("rattan") furniture, and food processing.

On a hot day in Manila, street vendors sell jasmine flowers to churchgoers attending a Holy Week service. Eighty-three percent of Filipinos are Roman Catholic, while the rest are Protestant or Muslim.

SOUTH CHINA SEA

Palawan Passage
Palawan • Puerto Princesa

Balabac
Balabac Strait

DISCOVER MORE

• *Pineapples are a major crop in the Philippines and are not harvested only for their fruit. Their fiber is used to weave a fabric that is made into the embroidered shirts worn by many men at the religious festivals for which the islands are famous.*

• *Mount Mayon, in the south of Luzon, is one of the world's most beautiful and most dangerous volcanoes. Its perfect cone shape was spoiled by a massive eruption in 1993.*

Public transportation in Manila is often provided by customized "jeepneys." Half-jeep, half-bus, they sparkle with polished chrome, mirrors, and every imaginable kind of accessory.

Philippines

Country facts					
	Area sq mi (sq km)	Population	Language	Religion	Currency
Philippines	115,830 (300,000)	79,345,812	Pilipino	Catholic	Peso

1   2   3   4   5

Calayan
Dalupiri
Fuga
Babuyan
BABUYAN IS
Camiguin
Escarpada Point
Laoag
Aparri
Vigan
Ilagan
CORDILLERA CENTRAL
SIERRA MADRE
Luzon
Dagupan
Mt Pinatubo
5,770 ft
(1,759 m)
Cabanatuan
Polillo
PHILIPPINE SEA
Olongapo
Quezon City
Manila Bay
Manila
Daet
San Pablo
Catanduanes
Batangas
Naga
Lubang
Calapan
Marinduque
Ragay Gulf
Mt Mayon
Legazpi
Mindoro
Sibuyan
Sea
Burias
Mindoro Strait
Tablas Strait
Tablas
Sibuyan
Masbate
Calbayog
Samar
CALAMIAN
GROUP
Visayan
Sea
PHILIPPINES
Tacloban
Cuyo
Panay
Cadiz
Ormoc
Iloilo
Leyte
Dinagat
Dumaran
Bacolod
Cebu
Cebu
Siargao
Panay Gulf
Negros
Bohol
Dumaguete
Bohol Sea
Camiguin
Butuan
Siquijor
Gingoog
Dipolog
Cagayan de Oro
SULU SEA
Agusan
Pagadian
Mindanao
Illana
Bay
Cotabato
Davao
Mati
Zamboanga
Moro
Gulf
Mt Apo
Davao Gulf
Basilan
General Santos
Pangutaran
Group
Jolo
Samales
Group
SULU ARCHIPELAGO
Sarangani Is
Tapul
Group
CELEBES
SEA

Highest mountains

Mount McKinley
20,320 ft
(6,194 m)

Mount Apo
9,692 ft
(2,954 m)

100 miles

100 km

Where in the world?

7 A.M.
Washington, DC
noon
GMT
8 P.M.
Manila

Washington, DC to Manila
8,570 mi (13,792 km)
16 hr 30 min

Manila lies on
14° 35'N latitude
121° 00'E longitude

Life facts

How long do people live?

U.S.A.
76 years

Philippines
66 years

How many people in
100 own cars?

48

1

This woman is gathering pumice stone from the
volcano Mount Pinatubo. Pumice is a porous rock
made from frothy lava. It serves as an abrasive, or
rubbing material, and may be used to clean the skin.

Search and find

A
B
C
D
E
F
G

A | B | C | D | E | F | G

Mongolia

Mongolia

A TRAIN FROM RUSSIA ON ITS journey southward to the Chinese border pulls in at the sprawling apartment blocks and factories that make up Ulaanbaatar, the Mongolian capital. Old men stand by the gray-and-white station entrance, wearing traditional Mongol dress—high boots with upturned toes, woolen tunics with sashes. From the capital, a four-wheel-drive vehicle or a galloping horse takes a rider out into the emptiest landscape imaginable.

This is a vast expanse of bare, rolling hills and grasslands, bordering the wasteland of the Gobi Desert. The summer sun produces average temperatures of 70°F (21°C), while winter temperatures average –16°F (–27°C). Two-humped Bactrian camels, with their shaggy coats, are well suited to this harsh climate. So is the *ger*, the circular tent of Mongol sheep herders. It is made of thick felted wool and sometimes canvas, placed over a wooden frame. Inside, mutton stew may simmer slowly on the stove. Today the family may be watching television, but many people still take part in traditional sports such as wrestling, archery, and horseracing, having learned these skills as children.

The carpeted interior of this Mongolian *ger* is as warm and comfortable as a house. Tents similar to this may be seen across Central Asia and are often known as yurts.

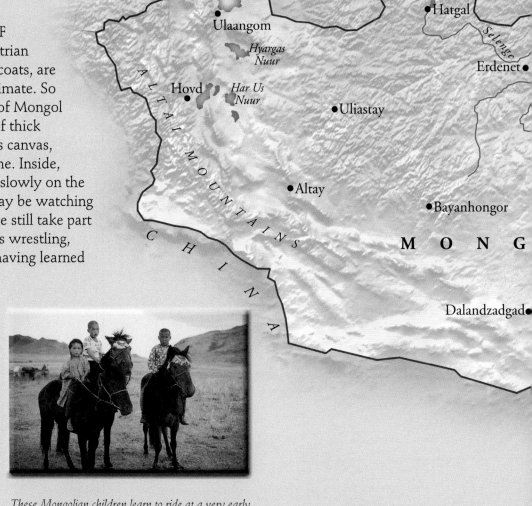

DISCOVER MORE

• *Mongolia is the most sparsely populated country in Asia, with just five people per sq mi (two people per sq km).*

• *The deserts of Mongolia are famous for fossils of dinosaurs, such as Protoceratops. It was here that American scientists discovered dinosaur eggs and nests during an expedition in 1922.*

These Mongolian children learn to ride at a very early age. Horses were first tamed by humans on the steppe grasslands of Asia.

Map labels: SAYAN MTS · Hövsgöl Nuur · Hatgal · Ulaangom · Hyargas Nuur · Selenge · Erdenet · Hovd · Har Us Nuur · ALTAI MOUNTAINS · Uliastay · CHINA · Altay · Bayanhongor · M O N G · Dalandzadgad

1 | 2 | 3 | 4 | 5

A Mongolian woman provides water for Bactrian camels at a well. These tough animals are used for transporting goods and people. They can withstand the extreme temperatures of the Gobi Desert.

Where in the world?

7 A.M.   noon   8 P.M.
Washington, DC   GMT   Ulaanbaatar

Washington, DC to Ulaanbaatar	Ulaanbaatar lies on
✈ 6,341 mi (10,350 km) 12 hr 10 min	47° 55'N latitude 106° 53'E longitude

Life facts

How long do people live?

U.S.A.   76 years

Mongolia   62 years

How many people in 100 own cars?

48

1

Cattle are brought in over grasslands, against a backdrop of sand dunes near Hyargas Nuur, along a distance of 150 miles (240 km).

RUSSIAN FEDERATION

●Darhan

HENTIYN MOUNTAINS

Kerulen   ●Choybalsan

Buyr Nuur

Ulaanbaatar ⊛

L I A   ▲Saynshand ●

G o b i D e s e r t

C H I N A

200 miles

300 km

Mongolia

Country facts

	Area sq mi (sq km)	Population	Language	Religion	Currency
Mongolia	604,247 (1,565,000)	2,617,379	Khalka Mongol	Tibetan Buddhist	Tugrik

Search and find

Western China

Western China

SLOWLY ACROSS THE WORLD'S highest plateaus, shaggy oxen called yaks meander like black dots in distant fields of snow. Trucks jolt past jagged mountain ranges, glaciers, and trackless sand dunes. They follow the ancient trading routes leading westward from China into Central and Western Asia.

The western half of China is made up of three vast but sparsely populated regions. The far west is a good source of minerals and timber, and the parched lowlands of the Turpan Depression have been irrigated to allow the production of crops such as grapes and melons.

A great many people in the west of the country do not belong to the Chinese ethnic group, although many people from the east are now beginning to settle in these remote regions too. Uygur, Kazakh, and Uzbek farmers and herders all live in the Xinjiang region in the northwest. They are Muslim peoples, speaking languages that are related to Turkish. The Tibetan people follow Buddhist beliefs. Their mountaintop monasteries and shrines are filled with the deep chanting of monks, and are lit by the flickering flames from yak-butter lamps. The Tibetan city, Lhasa, is dominated by the awe-inspiring palace of the Potala.

KAZAKHSTAN
Fuhai
• Karamay
Ebinur L.
MONGO
Yining
Dzungaria
• Ürümqi
KYRGYZSTAN
TIAN SHAN MOUNTAINS
Bosten L.
Turpan
Depressio
• Aksu
Kashi
TAJIKISTAN
Taklimakan Desert
ALTUN MTS
C H I N
PAKISTAN
▲ K2 28,250 ft (8,611 m)
• Hotan
KUNLUN M
INDIA
Plateau of Tibet
Lhasa
NEPAL
• Xigazê
HIMALAYA
Mt Everest
BHUTAN

DISCOVER MORE

• *Mount Everest, on the Tibet-Nepal border, is the world's highest peak at 29,078 ft (8,863 m) above sea level. Tibet is often called "Roof of the World."*

• *One name for the Xinjiang desert is Taklimakan, which means "enter and never return"—a name that has often proved to be appropriate.*

Tajik people inhabit the far west of China and also the neighboring countries of Tajikistan and Afghanistan. Many of them herd sheep, goats, and camels in remote, bleak valleys. They live in large, round tents called yurts.

Country facts					
	Area sq mi (sq km)	Population	Language	Religion	Currency
China	3,696,527 (9,573,998)	1,250,066,000	Mandarin Chinese	Atheist	Renminbi

1   2   3   4   5

Highest mountains

Mount Everest
29,078 ft
(8,863 m)

Mount McKinley
20,320 ft
(6,194 m)

Where in the world?

7 A.M.   noon   8 P.M.
Washington, DC GMT   Lhasa

Washington, DC to Lhasa
7,652 mi (12,314 km)
14 hr 45 min

Lhasa lies on
29° 41'N latitude
91° 12'E longitude

Life facts

How long do people live?

U.S.A.
76 years

China
70 years

How many people in
100 own cars?

48

0.4

Hami

Yumen

QILIAN MTS

Qinghai L.

Xining

Huang He

Gyaring L.

Ngoring L.

BAYAN HAR MTS

Chang Jiang

TANGGULA MTS

Qamdo

Mekong

Salween

I N D I A

M Y A N M A R   (B U R M A)

Xiaguan

LAOS

A

China

High on the Tibetan plateau, the Potala palace towers over the city of Lhasa. Approached by 1,000 steps, it was formerly the home of Tibet's chief religious leaders, the Dalai Lamas.

200 miles

300 km

N
W   E
S

Search and find

Eastern China

Eastern China

Qiqiha

Running across the north of China is the Great Wall, built originally to keep out invaders about 2,220 years ago. Its main course alone is about 2,260 mi (3,640 km) in length, which makes it the longest such structure on Earth.

AT DAWN, GROUPS OF CHINESE people gather in the peaceful Park of Tiantan to practice the graceful exercises known as tai chi. Later, schoolchildren stop to watch a man fly a paper kite in the gusting wind. Their teacher takes them into the Hall of Good Harvests, where in the old days the emperors came to pray. The wooden roof and pillars dazzle the eye with patterns of scarlet, gold, blue, and green. Outside the park, minibuses and bicycles pass the high-rise buildings of Beijing, China's capital.

China is the most populous country in the world, and most of its people live in the eastern region. These lands contain cold forests, grasslands, misty valleys, and lakes. The fertile plains of the east are crossed by great rivers. The Huang He (Yellow River) winds through northern China, taking its name from the windblown soil that clouds its waters. The Chang Jiang River enters the sea near the port of Shanghai. The south is hot and humid, with paddy fields of rice. Here is the seaport of Guangzhou, the skyscrapers of Hong Kong —a center of international business—and the Portuguese colonial buildings of Macao.

Small offshore islands include another state called Taiwan. Its people are of Chinese origin. Rice terraces are carved from the island's mountain slopes, but two-thirds of the islanders live in the coastal towns.

DISCOVER MORE

• *More people speak standard Mandarin Chinese than any other language in the world.*

• *Shanghai is China's biggest city. It is the world's largest non-capital city, with a total population of 13.5 million.*

The tiled roofs of the old Imperial Palace give way to modern skyscrapers in Beijing. The palace became known as the Forbidden City because it was out-of-bounds to Chinese citizens for 500 years.

GREATER HINGGAN RANGE

LESSER

RU

M O N G O L I A

YIN MTS

Baotou

Beijing

Tianjin

Mu us -Desert

Shijiazhuang

Taiyuan

Jina

QILIAN MTS

Qinghai L.

Xining

Huang He

Lanzhou

Huang He

Zhengzhou

Xi'an

C H I N A

Huang He

BAYAN HAR MTS

Wuhar

Chang Jiang

Yichang

Dongting L.

Chengdu

Red Basin

Chongqing

Changsha

HENGDUAN MTS

Leshan

Luzhou

DALOU MTS

Hengyang

Guiyang

NAN LI

MYANMAR (BURMA)

Salween

AILAO MTS

Xiaguan

Liuzhou

Kunming

Nanning

Mekong

Pingxiang

LAOS

VIETNAM

Zhanjiang

Gulf of Tonkin

Haiko

Hainan

A

B

C

D

E

F

G

V FEDERATION

AN RANGE

Harbin

Mudanjiang

Jilin

Changchun

Tonghua

Fushun

Shenyang

Anshan

NORTH KOREA

Dalian

Korea Bay

Bo Gulf

Weihai

Yantai

YELLOW SEA

Zibo

Qingdao

Weishan L.

Xuzhou

Nanjing

Hao L.

Shanghai

Zhoushan I.

Shaoxing

Hangzhou

EAST CHINA SEA

Poyang L.

Nanchang

Fuzhou

Zhangzhou

Xiamen

Taiwan Strait

Taipei

TAIWAN

Shantou

P'eng-hu Is

Kao-hsiung

Guangzhou

Hong Kong

Macao

SOUTH CHINA SEA

Tiananmen Gate is the main entrance to the imperial palace in Beijing, over which is a portrait of the Chinese communist leader Mao Zedong (1893–1976).

Longest rivers

Nile	4,145 mi (6,670 km)
Chang Jiang	3,964 mi (6,380 km)
Mississippi	3,741 mi (6,020 km)

The city of Hong Kong spreads over a number of small islands and part of the mainland, linked by tunnels and ferries. Most of its high-rise offices were built when the city was a British colony, before 1997.

200 miles

300 km

Where in the world?

7 A.M. — noon — 8 P.M.
Washington, DC — GMT — Beijing

Washington, DC to Beijing	Beijing lies on
6,941 mi (11,170 km)	39° 56'N latitude
✈ 13 hr 20 min	116° 24'E longitude

Life facts

How long do people live?	How many people in 100 own cars?
U.S.A. 76 years	48
China 70 years	0.4
Taiwan	not available

Search and find

Eastern China

Capital: Beijing	C5	Nanning	F5
Anshan	C6	Pingxiang	G5
Baotou	C5	Qingdao	D6
Changchun	B6	Qiqihar	B6
Changsha	E6	Shanghai	D7
Chengdu	E4	Shantou	F7
Chongqing	E5	Shaoxing	E7
Dalian	C6	Shenyang	C6
Fushun	C6	Shijiazhuang	D5
Fuzhou	E7	Taiyuan	D5
Guangzhou	F6	Tianjin	C6
Guiyang	F5	Tonghua	C7
Haikou	G6	Weihai	D7
Hangzhou	E7	Wuhan	E6
Harbin	B6	Xi'an	D5
Hengyang	F6	Xiaguan	F4
Hong Kong	F6	Xiamen	F7
Jilin	B6	Xining	D4
Jinan	D6	Xuzhou	D6
Kunming	F4	Yantai	C6
Lanzhou	D4	Yichang	E5
Leshan	F4	Zhangzhou	F7
Liuzhou	F5	Zhanjiang	G6
Luzhou	E5	Zhengzhou	D5
Macao	F6	Zibo	D6
Mudanjiang	B7	**Taiwan**	
Nanchang	E6	*Capital*: Taipei	E7
Nanjing	D6	Kao-hsiung	F7

Country facts

China

Taiwan

	Area sq mi (sq km)	Population	Language	Religion	Currency
China	3,696,527 (9,573,998)	1,250,066,000	Mandarin Chinese	Atheist	Renminbi/HK Dollar
Taiwan	13,969 (36,179)	22,113,250	Min/Mandarin Chinese	Daoism/Buddhist	Taiwan Dollar

A

Korean Peninsula

NORTH KOREA, SOUTH KOREA

The industrial city of Seoul is the capital of South Korea. It is built in the valley of the Han River and is served by the coastal port of Inch'ŏn, on the Yellow Sea.

North Korea

South Korea

THE KOREAN PENINSULA extends from northeastern China toward Japan. It divides the Sea of Japan from the Yellow Sea. The land is occupied by a single people, the Koreans, but today is divided into two separate countries.

North Korea is a land of mountains, descending to plains around the capital, P'yŏngyang. The rocks are rich in silver, iron ore, and uranium. In the bitterly cold winters, snow drives across the crumpled, brown landscape. In summer the land thaws out and becomes green, with high temperatures and heavy rains—ideal conditions for growing rice.

The mountains continue into South Korea. Most people live in the west and south, where the ragged coast breaks up into thousands of small islands. The South Korean landscape is a patchwork of fields growing rice or soybeans. Cities are linked with the capital, Seoul, by expressways and railroads. Palaces and temples from the ancient Chosŏn kingdom can still be seen around Seoul. South Korea is a major international economic power, with factories producing computers, electrical goods, and cars.

Laborers plant rice in the flooded paddy fields, their heads shaded against the heat of the Sun.

With a swirl of color, Korean girls perform a dance wearing traditional costume.

DISCOVER MORE

• The Korean Peninsula is surrounded by over 3,000 small islands. Most of them are uninhabited.

• Two-thirds of the Korean Peninsula is covered by forest.

North Korea   South Korea

Country facts					
	Area sq mi (sq km)	Population	Language	Religion	Currency
North Korea	46,540 (120,539)	21,386,109	Korean	Non religious/traditional beliefs	Won
South Korea	38,023 (98,480)	46,884,800	Korean	Non religious/Buddhist	Won

RUSSIAN FED.

Najin

Ch'ŏngjin

Hyesan

Kapsan

Kilchu

Kanggye

NANGNIM MTS

Changjin

Tanch'ŏn

Sinŭiju

Tŏkch'ŏn

Hamhŭng

Sinp'o

Hŭngdŏki

Anju

...mi I.

Sunch'ŏn

Yŏnghŭng

NORTH KOREA

SEA OF JAPAN

Korea Bay

Wŏnsan

P'yŏngyang

Imjin

Namp'o

Kosŏng

Sariwŏn

Haeju

Kaesŏng

Ch'ŏrwŏn

Yanggu

Ch'unch'ŏn

Seoul

Puch'ŏn

Inch'ŏn

Suwŏn

Han

Samch'ŏk

Ullung I.

Ch'ungju

SOUTH KOREA

Chŏngju

Andong

Anmyŏn I.

Yŏndŏk

YELLOW SEA

Taejon

Sangju

P'ohang

Kunsan

Chonju

Naktong

Taegu

Ulsan

Chinju

Kwangju

Masan

Pusan

Mokp'o

Chin I.

Korea Strait

Cheju Strait

Cheju

Cheju I.

100 miles

150 km

Where in the world?

7 A.M.
Washington, DC

noon
GMT

9 P.M.
Seoul

Washington, DC to Seoul
6,950 mi (11,186 km)
13 hr 20 min

Seoul lies on
37° 35'N latitude
127° 3'E longitude

Life facts

How long do people live?

How many people in 100 own cars?

U.S.A.
76 years — 48

North Korea
51 years — n.a.

South Korea
74 years — 15

Search and find

North Korea		South Korea	
Capital: P'yŏngyang C7		*Capital*: Seoul ..D7	
Anju	C7	Andong	E8
Ch'ongjin	B9	Cheju	G7
Haeju	D7	Chinju	F8
Hamhŭng	C8	Chŏngju	E8
Hŭngdŏki	C8	Chonju	F7
Hyesan	B8	Ch'ŏrwŏn	D8
Kaesŏng	D7	Ch'unch'ŏn	D8
Kanggye	B7	Ch'ungju	E8
Kapsan	B8	Inch'ŏn	D7
Kilchu	B9	Kunsan	F7
Kosong	D8	Kwangju	F7
Najin	A9	Masan	F8
Namp'o	D7	Mokp'o	F7
Sariwŏn	D7	P'ohang	E9
Sinp'o	C8	Puch'ŏn	E7
Sinŭiju	C6	Pusan	F8
Sunch'ŏn	C7	Samch'ŏk	E8
Tanch'ŏn	C8	Sangju	E8
Tokch'ŏn	C7	Suwŏn	D7
Wŏnsan	C8	Taegu	F8
Yŏnghŭng	C8	Taejon	E8
		Ulsan	F9
		Yanggu	D8
		Yŏndŏk	E9

A B C D E F G

Japan

Japan

SOME OLD JAPANESE PAINTINGS and woodcuts show beautiful islands set in blue seas, the snowy slopes of Mount Fuji, or cherry blossoms in the spring. Others depict glowing paper lanterns, temples and shrines, or simply furnished but beautiful wooden houses. People dressed in silk robes, called *kimonos*, or farmers planting rice are shown in still other paintings and woodcuts.

A photographer visiting Japan today is able to record many of the same scenes. However, modern additions might include the bright lights of Tokyo; flashing pinball arcades; a high-speed train streaking across the landscape; factories assembling cars and computers; traders at a busy fish market; or a suited businessman eating a packed lunch of cold rice, pork, egg, and pickles with chopsticks.

Japan, snowy in the far north and semitropical in the far south, is made up of a chain of islands on the earthquake-prone rim of the Pacific Ocean. It is a mountainous land, and most of its people live in the cities of the narrow lowlands near the coasts.

Two traditional crops, rice and tea, remain important today. Japan has few mineral resources, and must import large amounts of oil for its industries. Japanese-owned companies operate worldwide.

Japanese religions include Shinto and various forms of Buddhism. Many beautiful temples can be seen throughout the country.

Owls and bears make up just one of the figures sculpted from snow at a festival in Sapporo, on the northern island of Hokkaido, which experiences harsh winters.

DISCOVER MORE

• *Emperor Akihito of Japan is the 125th ruler in the same Japanese royal family, or dynasty, which dates back more than 2,000 years.*

• *The Seikan Tunnel passes underneath the Tsugaru Strait, linking the Japanese islands of Honshu and Hokkaido. At 33 mi (54 km), it is the world's longest rail tunnel.*

Japan has been in the forefront of developing high-speed locomotives such as the famous Bullet train. Current track speeds can reach 186 mph (300 km/h).

Map of Japan

Soya Strait
Rebun I.
● Wakkanai
Rishiri I.

Hokkaido

Asahikawa ●
▲ *Asahi Dake 7,513 ft (2,289 m)*

Ishikari Bay
Otaru ●
Sapporo ●
● Obihiro
● Kushiro

Uchiura Bay
Hakodate ●
Cape Erimo

Tsugaru Strait

Aomori ●
Hirosaki ●
Hachinohe ●

SEA OF JAPAN

Akita ●
● Morioka

Honshū

Yamagata ●
Niigata ●
● Sendai

Sado I.
Fukushima ●
Nagaoka ●
Koriyama ●

Abukuma

Kanazawa ●
Toyama ●
J A P A N
Utsunomiya ●
● Iwaki
● Hitachi
● Mito
Takasaki ●

Shinano

Fukui ●
Matsumoto ●

Tokyo ✪
Kawasaki ●
● Chiba

L. Biwa
Gifu ●
▲ *Mt Fuji 12,388 ft (3,776 m)*
● Yokohama

ōto
Toyota ●
Nagoya ●
Shizuoka ●
Osaka ●
Toyohashi ●
Hamamatsu ●
Sakai ●
Wakayama ●

Miyake I.

PACIFIC OCEAN

Hachijo I.
Amami I.

Okinawa I.

Sakishima Is

Japan

Life facts

How long do people live?

U.S.A. — 76 years
Japan — 80 years

How many people in 100 own cars?

U.S.A. — 48
Japan — 37

Search and find

Country facts

	Area sq mi (sq km)	Population	Language	Religion	Currency
Japan	145,882 (377,834)	126,182,077	Japanese	Buddhist/Shinto	Yen

150 miles
150 km

Indian Ocean
and Islands

THE WORLD'S THIRD BIGGEST OCEAN COVERS AN area of 28,350,500 square miles (73,427,000 sq km), meeting the Atlantic Ocean off South Africa and merging with the Pacific Ocean off Southeast Asia and Australia. The long, thin arm of the Red Sea is linked to the Mediterranean Sea by the Suez Canal. The Indian Ocean is tropical, washing over coral reefs and white sands bordered by coconut palms. Moisture from the ocean is picked up by seasonal winds called monsoons and falls as torrential rain over southern Asia.

Madagascar, off Africa's east coast, is the fourth largest island in the world. Its people are partly of Southeast Asian origin and partly African. It is a land of mountains and plateaus, and its forests are home to many unique wild animals, such as lemurs. Smaller African islands have been created by volcanic activity or by coral formation. They include the Comoros, the Seychelles, Mauritius, and Réunion.

Asian islands include the Laccadive Islands and the Maldives, a long necklace of coral islands strung across the ocean, southwest of India. They are so low-lying that any future rise in the level of the ocean would submerge most of them. In the northeastern Indian Ocean are the Andaman and Nicobar islands, while far to the southeast lie Christmas Island and the Cocos Islands, which are territories of Australia.

RED SEA

ARABIA SEA

Socotra (YEMEN)

AFRICA

SEYCHELLES

Amirante Is

Providence Is

COMOROS   Farquhar Is   Agalega Is

Mozambique Channel

MADAGASCAR   MAURITIUS

Réunion (FRANCE)

DISCOVER MORE

- *The Indian Ocean plunges to an amazing depth of 23,376 ft (7,125 m) in the Java Trench.*

- *Monsoon rains from the Indian Ocean are the heaviest on Earth. The island of Réunion received the rainfall record for one day, 74 in (1,870 mm).*

- *The island of Madagascar is home to the strange aye-aye, an endangered animal that is similar in appearance to a lemur.*

Coconut palms line the beach on La Digue Island in the Seychelles. Located in the Indian Ocean, this group of 115 islands makes up an independent African nation. The economy is based upon tourism, copra (dried coconut), spices, fruit, and small industries.

200 miles

300 km

Prince Edward Is (SOUTH AFRICA)

Crozet Is (FRANCE)

Kerguelen Is (FRANCE)

Madagascar
 Sri Lanka
 Mauritius
 Comoros
Seychelles
 Maldives

A S I A

Bay of
Bengal

Andaman Is
(INDIA)

ccadive Is
(INDIA)

**SRI
LANKA**

Nicobar Is
(INDIA)

MALDIVES

Chagos Archipelago
(U.K.)

Christmas I.
(AUSTRALIA)

Cocos Is
(AUSTRALIA)

N D I A N   O C E A N

AUSTRALIA

*Some of the world's
biggest tortoises live on
the Indian Ocean islands of
Mauritius and the Seychelles.
Males have been known to weigh
over 660 lb (300 kg).*

Amsterdam I.
(FRANCE)

St. Paul I.
(FRANCE)

Where in the world?

7 A.M.   noon   7 P.M.
Washington, DC GMT Christmas I.

Washington, DC to Christmas I.
5,616 mi (9,038 km)
10 hr 50 min

Christmas I. lies on
01° 59'N latitude
157° 22'W longitude

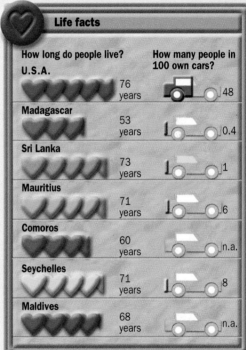

Life facts

	How long do people live?	How many people in 100 own cars?
U.S.A.	76 years	48
Madagascar	53 years	0.4
Sri Lanka	73 years	1
Mauritius	71 years	6
Comoros	60 years	n.a.
Seychelles	71 years	8
Maldives	68 years	n.a.

Country facts

	Area sq mi (sq km)	Population	Language	Religion	Currency
Madagascar	226,656 (587,039)	14,873,387	Malagasy	IB*	Franc
Sri Lanka	25,332 (65,610)	18,933,558	Sinhali	Buddhist	Rupee
Mauritius	788 (2,041)	1,182,212	English	Hindu	Rupee
Comoros	719 (1,862)	562,723	Arabic	Sunni Muslim	Franc
Seychelles	176 (456)	76,164	English	Catholic	Rupee
Maldives	116 (300)	300,220	Divehi	Sunni Muslim	Rufiyaa

*Indigenous beliefs

Search and find

Africa

A | B | C | D | E | F | G

A SMALL BOY IS RUNNING, SPINNING ALONG A hoop he has made from a bent bicycle wheel and hammered straight. He runs past a market where stalls are heaped with mangoes. He cuts across the palm-lined beach, calling to the fishermen as they haul up their boats. He crosses the dusty main road, swerving between honking buses, then sprints out of the sunshine into a shady back alley. Africa is a continent of young people—44 percent of the population is under fifteen years of age. Many people live in the big, bustling cities, but others still live in small villages, following ancient customs and learning to herd, hunt, cook, and farm in the traditional way. Africa is the world's second largest continent and lies between the Atlantic and Indian oceans and the Mediterranean Sea. It has huge deserts, such as the Sahara and the Kalahari, dripping tropical rain forests, and great rivers such as the Nile and the Congo. Snowcapped mountains rise on the equator. Africa is the home of many of the last big wild animals on Earth—lions hunt zebra on the grasslands, while crocodiles and hippotamuses feed in the lakes.

Many parts of Africa are poor, and some have suffered for many years from natural disasters, such as the spread of the Sahara desert southward. However, the continent also has many rich resources, including diamonds, gold, and oil.

MEDITERR

MOROCCO
TUNISIA
ALGERIA
L
Western Sahara
MAURITANIA
MALI
NIGER
CAPE VERDE
SENEGAL
GAMBIA
BURKINA FASO
GUINEA-BISSAU
GUINEA
NIGERIA
SIERRA LEONE
IVORY COAST
GHANA
TOGO
BENIN
LIBERIA
EQUATORIAL GUINEA
CAMEROON
SÃO TOMÉ & PRÍNCIPE
GABON
REP OF CONG

ATLANTIC OCEAN

500 miles

500 km

AN

NAMIBIA

DISCOVER MORE

• *The Great Rift Valley is a huge crack in the earth's crust which runs through Ethiopia to Mozambique. It is more than 4,350 mi (7,000 km) long and, in places, more than 6,000 ft (1,829 m) deep.*

• *The Victoria Falls, on the Zambezi River between Zambia and Zimbabwe, form a wall of white water 5,495 ft (1,675 m) high.*

A zebra foal gallops with its mother across the savanna, the dry grassland of East Africa. Wildlife reserves protect spectacular herds of wildlife and attract tourists from all over the world.

1 | 2 | 3 | 4 | 5

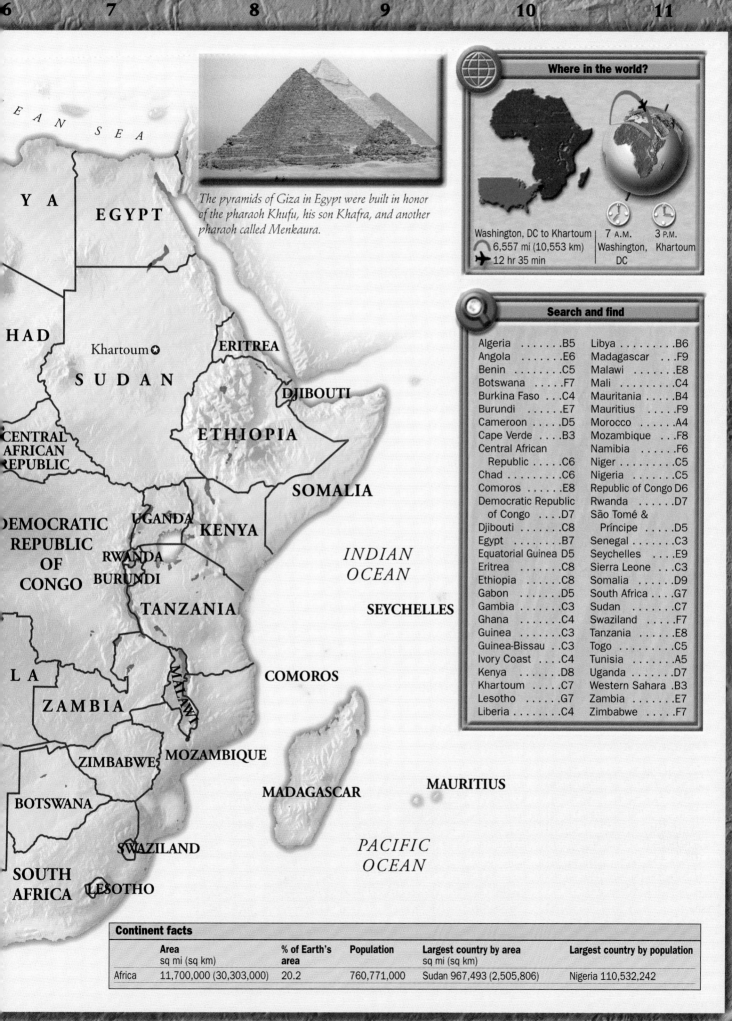

The pyramids of Giza in Egypt were built in honor of the pharaoh Khufu, his son Khafra, and another pharaoh called Menkaura.

Where in the world?

Washington, DC to Khartoum
6,557 mi (10,553 km)
12 hr 35 min

7 A.M. Washington, DC

3 P.M. Khartoum

Search and find

Algeria B5	Libya B6
Angola E6	Madagascar . . .F9
Benin C5	Malawi E8
Botswana F7	Mali C4
Burkina Faso . . .C4	Mauritania B4
Burundi E7	Mauritius F9
Cameroon D5	Morocco A4
Cape Verde B3	Mozambique . . .F8
Central African	Namibia F6
Republic C6	Niger C5
Chad C6	Nigeria C5
Comoros E8	Republic of Congo D6
Democratic Republic	Rwanda D7
of Congo D7	São Tomé &
Djibouti C8	Príncipe D5
Egypt B7	Senegal C3
Equatorial Guinea D5	Seychelles E9
Eritrea C8	Sierra Leone . . .C3
Ethiopia C8	Somalia D9
Gabon D5	South Africa G7
Gambia C3	Sudan C7
Ghana C4	Swaziland F7
Guinea C3	Tanzania E8
Guinea-Bissau . .C3	Togo C5
Ivory Coast C4	Tunisia A5
Kenya D8	Uganda D7
Khartoum C7	Western Sahara .B3
Lesotho G7	Zambia E7
Liberia C4	Zimbabwe F7

Continent facts

	Area sq mi (sq km)	% of Earth's area	Population	Largest country by area sq mi (sq km)	Largest country by population
Africa	11,700,000 (30,303,000)	20.2	760,771,000	Sudan 967,493 (2,505,806)	Nigeria 110,532,242

Northeast Africa

LIBYA, EGYPT

Many tourists visit Luxor, a city on the Nile River in southern Egypt, to see the ancient temples of Luxor and Karnak.

WELCOME TO THE SEAPORT OF Alexandria, in Egypt. White buildings and domes rise up above the harbor. Bustling crowds pack the dockside as passengers step ashore. Many of the men wear long white shifts, while women wear gowns of black or patterned cotton. They are Muslims and wear long headscarves as a mark of their faith.

A train takes travelers south across the delta of the Nile River. This is lush farmland, crisscrossed by waterways. In the narrow streets of Cairo, Egypt's capital, old men drink coffee and students argue about religion and politics. There are fine old mosques alongside modern hotels and offices. On the edge of the city are the pyramids, massive royal tombs built more than 4,500 years ago.

Upstream, southward from Cairo, the Nile flows past ancient temples and industrial towns until it reaches the Aswān Dam. Wooden sailing ships float by. The Nile is bordered by a wide strip of green fields and date palms, beyond which lies a vast desert. It stretches eastward to the Red Sea and westward into Libya.

The sweltering deserts of Libya record some of the fiercest temperatures on Earth. Crops are grown at a few water sources, called oases, but most farming takes place along the coast. The chief source of wealth is oil. Most Libyans live in coastal cities such as Tripoli and Benghazi. The people are Muslim Arabs.

DISCOVER MORE

• *At 100 mi (162 km), the Suez Canal is one of the longest canals in the world built to carry large ships. It links the Mediterranean with the Red Sea.*

• *The world's highest temperature, 136°F (58°C) taken in the shade, was recorded at Al Azizyah in Libya in 1922.*

Food is sold at this stall in the back streets of Cairo. Egyptian food includes mashi *(a mixture of various vegetables including tomatoes, cabbage, and stuffed eggplants),* fuul *(beans),* hummus *(chickpea paste), macaroni, lamb, and fish.*

About 2,000 years ago, Libya and Egypt were part of the Roman Empire, which controlled vast areas of Europe, western Asia, and North Africa. Roman ruins such as Coastal Curia at Sabrata can still be seen.

Where in the world?

7 A.M.
Washington, DC
noon
GMT
2 P.M.
Tripoli

Washington, DC to Tripoli
4,865 mi (7,829 km)
9 hr 20 min

Tripoli lies on
32° 50'N latitude
13° 13'E longitude

Life facts

How long do people live?

U.S.A. — 76 years
Libya — 66 years
Egypt — 62 years

How many people in 100 own cars?

U.S.A. — 48
Libya — 10
Egypt — 2

Longest rivers

Nile — 4,145 mi (6,670 km)
Mississippi — 3,741 mi (6,020 km)

Nefertiti, a queen of ancient Egypt, died in 1340 B.C. This bust was found by archaeologists at Tell el-'Amârna. It shows her wearing cosmetics and a royal crown.

300 miles

500 km

Libya

Egypt

Country facts

	Area sq mi (sq km)	Population	Language	Religion	Currency
Libya	679,358 (1,759,537)	4,992,838	Arabic	Sunni Muslim	Dinar
Egypt	385,299 (997,743)	67,273,906	Arabic	Sunni Muslim	Pound

Search and find

Libya
Capital: Tripoli . . C4
Az-Zāwiyah C4
Benghazi C6
Derna C6
Ghadāmis C3
Misurata C5
Surt C5

Egypt
Capital: Cairo . . . C8

Alexandria C8
Aswān E9
Asyūt D8
El Mahalla
   El Kubra C8
Giza C8
Luxor D8
Port Said C8
Suez C8
Tanta C8

Northwest Africa

ALGERIA, MOROCCO, TUNISIA

Algeria is Africa's second largest country, after Sudan. Eighty percent of the land area is the Sahara Desert, where rocks blasted with windblown sand have been eroded into unusual shapes.

THE SUN IS HIGH OVER THE square of Jemaa el-Fna, in the Moroccan city of Marrakech. Countrywomen sell finely woven baskets, while a street vendor in a broad-brimmed hat sells cupfuls of cool, refreshing water from his goatskin flask. There are people selling oranges, dates, pumpkins, and beans. There are dancers, drummers, boxers, fortune-tellers, snake charmers, and performing monkeys. As evening approaches, the sun sets behind the Koutoubia mosque. Lanterns are lit and stalls sell sizzling snacks of fish and lamb.

The Arabs call Morocco *Maghreb*, which means "the west," a term that is now extended to include the neighboring countries of Algeria, Tunisia, and the small state of Western Sahara (claimed by Morocco). The Maghreb lands are also home to another people, named the Berbers.

Africa's Mediterranean coast, just 8 miles (13 km) south of Spain across the Strait of Gibraltar, is a land of olive groves, whitewashed villages, and large ports such as Oran, Algiers, and Tunis. The land rises through foothills to the crumpled rocks and snow-streaked ridges of the Atlas Mountains. Beyond, camel caravans and four-wheel-drive vehicles follow tracks into the endless, baking wasteland of the Sahara Desert, where rocks, gravel, and high, windblown sand dunes stretch toward Central Africa.

In the medina, or old city center, in Marrakech, Morocco, this souk, or market, sells an enormous variety of olives.

DISCOVER MORE

• The fennec fox, native to the Sahara Desert, is the world's smallest fox, standing just 8 in (20 cm) at the shoulder. Its enormous ears, which help it to lose body heat, add almost another 6 in (15 cm) to its height.

1   2   3   4   5

Highest mountains

Mount McKinley
20,320 ft
(6,194 m)

Mount Toubkal
13,665 ft
(4,165 m)

This Berber girl comes from the Atlas Mountains of Morocco. The Berbers are North African people.

Where in the world?

7 A.M.   noon   1 P.M.
Washington, DC   GMT   Algiers

Washington, DC to Algiers
4,241 mi (6,826 km)
8 hr 10 min

Algiers lies on
36° 42'N latitude
03° 13'E longitude

Life facts

How long do people live?

U.S.A.	76 years
Algeria	69 years
Morocco	69 years
Tunisia	73 years

How many people in 100 own cars?

U.S.A.	48
Algeria	2
Morocco	4
Tunisia	3

MEDITERRANEAN SEA

Algiers
Blida
Bejaïa   Skikda
Ech-Cheliff
Constantine
di Bel Abbès   Batna

Annaba   Bizerte
★Tunis
Sousse
Kairouan
Sfax

TUNISIA

Ghardaïa

SAHARAN ATLAS MTS

G E R I A

L I B Y A

In Salah

A H A G G A R

Tahat Peak
▲ *9,573 ft (2,918 m)*

Tamanrasset

S a h a r a

N I G E R

Algeria

Morocco

Tunisia

Search and find

Algeria
Capital: Algiers .C7
Adrar E6
Annaba C8
Batna C8
Béchar D6
Bejaïa C7
Blida C7
Constantine C8
Ech-Cheliff C7
Ghardaïa D7
In Salah E7
Oran C6
Sidi Bel Abbès . .C6
Skikda C8
Tamanrasset . . .F7
Tindouf E4

Casablanca C5
Fez C5
Kenitra C4
Marrakech D4
Meknès D5
Oujda C6
Safi D4
Tangier C5
Tarfaya E4
Tétouan C5

Tunisia
Capital: Tunis . . .C8
Bizerte C8
Kairouan C8
Sfax C8
Sousse C8

Morocco
Capital: Rabat . .C5
Agadir D4

Western Sahara
Dakhla E3
El Aaiún E3

Country facts

	Area sq mi (sq km)	Population	Language	Religion	Currency
Algeria	919,595 (2,381,751)	31,133,486	Arabic	Sunni Muslim	Dinar
Morocco	177,117 (458,733)	29,661,636	Arabic	Sunni Muslim	Dirham
Tunisia	63,170 (163,610)	9,513,603	Arabic	Sunni Muslim	Dinar

West Africa

NIGER, MALI, MAURITANIA, NIGERIA, IVORY COAST, BURKINA FASO, GUINEA, GHANA, SENEGAL, BENIN, LIBERIA, SIERRA LEONE, TOGO, GUINEA-BISSAU, GAMBIA, CAPE VERDE

A WEST AFRICAN JOURNEY MIGHT START on the Gulf of Guinea, where Atlantic surf pounds sandy beaches lined with palms. The Guinea coast is naturally covered in tropical forest, and remains so around the oil fields of the Niger River delta. Elsewhere it is taken up by plantations producing cocoa, peanuts, natural rubber, or palm oil.

On the coast are large, modern cities; Lagos, Nigeria, is one. This city is extremely hot and humid, and is often jammed solid with traffic. Transportation north might be a crowded train or an overloaded minibus or truck, painted with humorous or religious motifs and slogans.

To the north, the landscape changes, with cultivated grasslands becoming drier and drier toward

1 Niger	9 Senegal
2 Mali	10 Benin
3 Mauritania	11 Liberia
4 Nigeria	12 Sierra Leone
5 Ivory Coast	13 Togo
6 Burkina Faso	14 Guinea-Bissau
7 Guinea	15 Gambia
8 Ghana	16 Cape Verde

the plateaus and desert fringes of the north. A cool, seasonal desert wind, the *harmattan*, blows dust southward from the Sahara Desert over dried-up riverbeds and towns of dried mud brick.

Hundreds of different ethnic groups live in West Africa—among them the Ashante, Ibo, Yoruba, Hausa, and Fulani.

Niger

Mali

Mauritania

Nigeria

Ivory Coast

Burkina Faso

Guinea

Ghana

Senegal

Benin

Liberia

Sierra Leone

Togo

Guinea-Bissau

Gambia

Cape Verde

1 2 3 4 5

Country facts

	Area sq mi (sq km)	Population	Language	Religion	Currency
Niger	496,900 (1,286,971)	9,962,242	Hausa	Muslim	CFA Franc
Mali	428,077 (1,108,719)	10,429,124	Babara	Muslim	CFA Franc
Mauritania	397,953 (1,030,698)	2,581,738	Arabic	Muslim	Ouguiya
Nigeria	356,668 (923,770)	113,828,587	Hausa	Muslim	Naira
Ivory Coast	124,502 (322,460)	15,818,068	French	Muslim	CFA Franc
Burkina Faso	105,869 (274,201)	11,575,898	Mossi	Muslim	CFA Franc
Guinea	94,927 (245,861)	7,538,953	Fulani	Muslim	Franc
Ghana	92,100 (238,539)	18,887,626	Hausa	Indigenous	Cedi
Senegal	75,749 (196,190)	10,051,930	Wolof	Muslim	CFA Franc
Benin	43,483 (112,621)	6,305567	Fon	Indigenous	CFA Franc
Liberia	38,250 (99,068)	2,923,725	Creole	Traditional	Dollar
Sierra Leone	27,699 (71,740)	5,296,651	Creole	Muslim	Leone
Togo	21,927 (56,791)	5,080.413	Ewe	Indigenous	CFA Franc
Guinea-Bissau	13,946 (36,120)	1,234,555	Portuguese	Indigenous	CFA Franc
Gambia	4,363 (11,300)	1,336,320	Malinke	Muslim	Dalasi
Cape Verde	1,556 (4,030)	405,748	Creole/ Portuguese	Catholic	Escudo

Where in the world?

7 A.M. noon noon
Washington, DC GMT Nouakchott

Washington, DC to Nouakchott
3,904 mi (6,282 km)
7 hr 30 min

Nouakchott lies on
18° 06'N latitude
15° 57'E longitude

Life facts

How long do people live?

How many people in 100 own cars?

Country	Years	Cars per 100
U.S.A.	76 years	48
Niger	42 years	0.4
Mali	47 years	0.2
Mauritania	50 years	1
Nigeria	54 years	1
Ivory Coast	46 years	1
Burkina Faso	46 years	0.3
Guinea	46 years	0.2
Ghana	57 years	0.5
Senegal	57 years	1
Benin	54 years	1
Liberia	60 years	1
Sierra Leone	49 years	0.4
Togo	59 years	2
Guinea-Bissau	49 years	0.3
Gambia	54 years	1
Cape Verde	71 years	3

AÏR MOUNTAINS

LIBYA

CHAD

NIGER

GER

Zinder

L. Chad

Kano

Maiduguri

NIGERIA

Benue

CAMEROON

500 miles

800 km

Search and find

Niger
Capital: Niamey .E5
Maradi E6
Zinder E6

Mali
Capital: Bamako .E4
Ségou E4
Sikasso E4
Tombouctou
  (Timbuktu) . . .D4

Mauritania
Capital:
  Nouakchott D2

Nigeria
Capital: Abuja . . .F6
Abeokuta F5
Ibadan F5
Ilorin F5
Kaduna E6
Kano E6
Lagos F5
Maiduguri F7
Ogbomosho F5
Oshogbo F6
Onitsha F6
Port Harcourt . .G6
Zaria F6

Ivory Coast
Capital:
  Yamoussoukro .F4
Abidjan F4
Bouaké F4
Daloa F4

Burkina Faso
Capital:
  Ouagadougou . .E4

Bobo Dioulasso .E4

Guinea
Capital:
  Conakry F3
Kankan F3

Ghana
Capital: Accra . . .F5
Kumasi F4
Tamale F5

Senegal
Capital: Dakar . .E2
Thiès E2

Benin
Capitals:
  Cotonou F5
  Porto-Novo . . .F5

Liberia
Capital:
  Monrovia F3
Harbel F3

Sierra Leone
Capital:
  Freetown F3

Togo
Capital: Lomé . . .F5

Guinea-Bissau
Capital: Bissau .E2

Gambia
Capital: Banjul . .E2

Cape Verde
Capital: Praia . . .D1

A
B
C
D
E
F
G

Northern Central Africa

SUDAN, CHAD, CENTRAL AFRICAN REPUBLIC, CAMEROON

These court musicians from Cameroon blow long horns. The musical tradition of Africa is rich, with a wide range of drums, flutes, bells, xylophones, and stringed instruments.

ARRIVING AT WADI HALFA OFF the Lake Nasser steamer, travelers board dusty train coaches to cross the scorching Nubian Desert. Khartoum, the Sudanese capital, is built where two rivers, the Blue and White Nile, join to form the single Nile River. Sudan is an Islamic country, of mosques and camel markets, of long-robed, turbanned men sipping tea or coffee, of old colonial buildings and flat-roofed mud-brick dwellings. However, many days' journey onward through Africa's largest country, by gear-grinding truck or by rusty Nile riverboat from the town of Kosti, lead to the swamps of the Sudd and the southern mountains. Here, in the lands of the Dinka, Nuer, and Shilluk peoples, the villages consist of round thatched huts, with stockades for cattle. Customs in the southern part of Sudan are African or Christian, a world away from the Islamic north.

Chad, too, has an Islamic north and a Christian south. Thin savanna grasslands border Chad's desert, a poverty-stricken zone where drought and famine are common. More fertile lands border the Chari and Logone rivers and the shallow waters of Lake Chad. Savanna extends southward into the Central African Republic (C.A.R.) and the plateaus of Cameroon, on the Atlantic coast. The far south of this region includes the great rain forests of central Africa. These extend from southern Cameroon and southwestern C.A.R. across the basin of the Congo River.

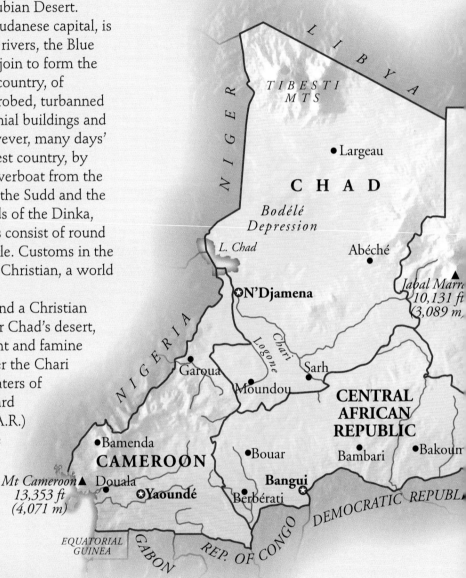

LIBYA

TIBESTI MTS

NIGER

• Largeau

CHAD

Bodélé Depression

L. Chad

Abéché

▲ Jabal Marra 10,131 ft (3,089 m)

●N'Djamena

Chari

Logone

NIGERIA

Garoua

Moundou

Sarh

CENTRAL AFRICAN REPUBLIC

•Bamenda
CAMEROON

•Bouar

Bambari

•Bakoun

Mt Cameroon▲ 13,353 ft (4,071 m)

Douala

⊗Yaoundé

Bérbérati

Bangui☆

DEMOCRATIC REPUBL

EQUATORIAL GUINEA

GABON

REP. OF CONGO

DISCOVER MORE

• *The Sudd, in southern Sudan, is a vast swamp of 6,370 sq mi (16,500 sq km). Its area is doubled each year when the White Nile floods. Tangled with water hyacinth roots and papyrus reeds, it is home to crocodiles and hippopotamuses.*

In the center of Omdurman is the tomb of Sudan's national hero, Sheik Muhammed Ahmed, known as the Mahdi.

Fulani cattle herders collect water from a well in Kanem, a region of northwest Chad that borders the Sahara Desert. The Fulani people, known in some areas as Fulbe or Peul, live across a broad band of Central and West Africa.

Where in the world?

7 A.M. Washington, DC | noon GMT | 3 P.M. Khartoum

Washington, DC to Khartoum
6,557 mi (10,553 km)
12 hr 35 min

Khartoum lies on
15° 34'N latitude
32° 36'E longitude

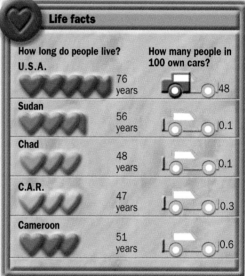

Life facts

	How long do people live?	How many people in 100 own cars?
U.S.A.	76 years	48
Sudan	56 years	0.1
Chad	48 years	0.1
C.A.R.	47 years	0.3
Cameroon	51 years	0.6

EGYPT · Libyan Desert · RED SEA · Wadi Halfa · Nubian Desert · Port Sudan · Nile · Merowe · Atbara · SUDAN · Atbara · Kassala · ERITREA · Omdurman · Khartoum · Wad Medani · El Obeid · Kosti · Blue Nile · yala · ETHIOPIA · Malakal · Bahr al-Ghazal · White Nile · Sudd · Juba · CONGO · UGANDA · KENYA

300 miles
500 km

Search and find

Sudan
Capital: Khartoum C7
Atbara C8
El Obeid D7
Juba E7
Kassala C8
Kosti D7
Malakal E7
Merowe C7
Nyala D6
Omdurman C7
Port Sudan C8
Wadi Halfa B7
Wad Medani . . .D8

Chad
Capital: N'Djamena D4

Abéché D5
Largeau C5
Moundou D4
Sarh D5

C.A.R.
Capital: Bangui .E5
Bakouma E5
Bambari E5
Berbérati E4
Bouar E4

Cameroon
Capital: Yaoundé E3
Bamenda E3
Douala E3
Garoua D4

Sudan / Chad / C.A.R. / Cameroon (flags)

There are three main national parks in the Central African Republic. International conservation groups are working with local people to preserve threatened wildlife species, including rhinoceroses.

Country facts

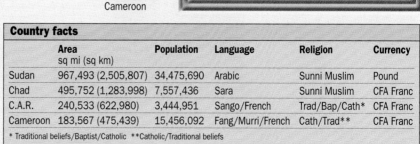

	Area sq mi (sq km)	Population	Language	Religion	Currency
Sudan	967,493 (2,505,807)	34,475,690	Arabic	Sunni Muslim	Pound
Chad	495,752 (1,283,998)	7,557,436	Sara	Sunni Muslim	CFA Franc
C.A.R.	240,533 (622,980)	3,444,951	Sango/French	Trad/Bap/Cath*	CFA Franc
Cameroon	183,567 (475,439)	15,456,092	Fang/Murri/French	Cath/Trad**	CFA Franc

* Traditional beliefs/Baptist/Catholic **Catholic/Traditional beliefs

The Horn of Africa
ETHIOPIA, SOMALIA, ERITREA, DJIBOUTI

An Ethiopian mother sits with her young daughter. Most Ethiopians live on the land, and the climate is moderate. However, droughts are common, causing harvests to fail and people to go hungry.

IN A ROUND THATCHED HOUSE made of mud and straw, an Ethiopian family rests after a hard day's work plowing the land with oxen. The evening is cold in the highlands, and the farmer pulls a woolen cloak around his body for warmth. His wife tends a stew pot that is simmering on the hearth and stacks up *injera*, pancakes of sour bread. These are made from a grain called teff.

Ethiopia is a land of mountains, rocky plateaus, and deserts, crossed by part of the Great Rift Valley and by the Blue Nile River, which tumbles over the spectacular Tisissat Falls, southeast of Lake Tana. Ethiopia has ancient palaces and rock-hewn Christian churches. Today, its modern capital, Addis Ababa, is the largest city of the region, with a population of three million. It is the headquarters of the Organization of African Unity (O.A.U.), whose member states aim to promote peace and prosperity across the continent. The city is also famous for its silverwork and other crafts.

The Horn of Africa, the peninsula that juts out south of the Red Sea, is occupied by three countries: Eritrea , Djibouti, and Somalia. All three consist largely of desert, scrub, and mountain. These lands are crossed by herders of goats and camels. Most of the population inhabits seaports on the Indian Ocean. The region includes Muslims and, in Ethiopia and Eritrea, Christians.

DISCOVER MORE
• Lake Assal, in Djibouti, is the lowest point in Africa, 512 ft (156 m) below sea level. Its waters evaporate in the hot, dry air, leaving behind islands made of salt.

• Nearly 100 different languages are spoken in Ethiopia. The country's official language is Amharic, which is spoken by about half of the population.

Traditional circular thatched huts are found mostly in the south of Somalia, where there is enough rain to support farming. In the dry desert regions, nomadic herders use portable, dome-shaped shelters instead.

A

Highest mountains

Mount McKinley
20,320 ft
(6,194 m)

Ras Dashen
15,158 ft
(4,620 m)

Eritrean girls gather at a well to fill containers with fresh water. Water is a precious resource in this dry country. Supplies are replenished by seasonal rains in the Ethiopian highlands.

Where in the world?

7 A.M.
Washington, DC

noon
GMT

3 P.M.
Addis Ababa

Washington, DC to Addis Ababa
7,168 mi (11,536 km)
13 hr 50 min

Addis Ababa lies on
09° 00'N latitude
38° 44'E longitude

B

Life facts

How long do people live?

U.S.A.		76 years
Ethiopia		41 years
Somalia		46 years
Eritrea		55 years
Djibouti		51 years

How many people in 100 own cars?

U.S.A.	48
Ethiopia	n.a.
Somalia	0.1
Eritrea	n.a.
Djibouti	3

C

D

Asseb

DJIBOUTI

sab

Djibouti

Gulf of Aden

Berbera

Cape Caseyr

Hargeisa

Harer

awa

SOMALIA

OPIA

OGADEN

Shebelē

Eyl

INDIAN OCEAN

Jubba

Baydhabo

Mogadishu

Marka

Baraawe

Kismaayo

200 miles

300 km

Ethiopia

Somalia

Eritrea

Djibouti

Search and find

Ethiopia
Capital:
  Addis Ababa ..D5
Aksum C5
Debre Markos ..D5
Dire Dawa D6
Gonder C5
Gore D4
Harer D6
Nazret D5

Somalia
Capital:
  Mogadishu ...F7
Baydhabo F7

Baraawe F7
Berbera D7
Eyl D8
Hargeisa D7
Kismaayo G6
Marka F7

Eritrea
Capital: Asmara .B5
Asseb C6
Keren B5
Massawa B5

Djibouti
Capital: Djibouti .C6

E

F

Country facts

	Area sq mi (sq km)	Population	Language	Religion	Currency
Ethiopia	435,184 (1,127,127)	59,680,383	Amharic/Oromo	EO*/Sunni Muslim	Birr
Somalia	246,201 (637,661)	7,140,643	Somali	Sunni Muslim	Shilling
Eritrea	46,842 (121,321)	3,984,723	Tigrinya	Sunni Muslim	Nakfa
Djibouti	8,494 (21,999)	447,439	French	Muslim	Franc

*Ethiopian Orthodox

G

East Africa

Tanzania, Kenya, Uganda, Burundi, Rwanda

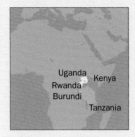

IN THE FAR WEST, VOLCANIC mountain ranges and forests descend to the lands of Rwanda, Burundi, and Uganda. These small countries lie among Africa's great lakes: Edward, Albert, Kivu, Kyoga, Victoria, and Tanganyika. Huts and houses are scattered over hillsides, where shady, green banana leaves contrast with the rich, red soil.

In Kenya, northern deserts around Lake Turkana give way to misty highlands, spread out beneath the jagged peaks of Mount Kenya. Sprawling modern cities, such as Nairobi, attract tourists, businesspeople, and poor country dwellers in search of work.

Beyond the Great Rift Valley, from Kenya across the border into Tanzania, are sweeping savanna grasslands dotted with acacia trees, with the snowcapped peaks of Kilimanjaro in the distance. In these huge, tawny landscapes, beneath blue skies and billowing white clouds, all the big animals seem very much at home.

Off the East African coast, wooden sailing ships called dhows sail between islands such as Zanzibar and Pemba, famous for their fragrant cloves. Cargo ships sail into big seaports such as Dar es Salaam and Mombasa.

DISCOVER MORE

• *Lake Victoria, within Uganda, Kenya, and Tanzania, is Africa's biggest lake, with a total area covering 26,590 sq mi (68,880 sq km). Its waves can be as high as those of the ocean.*

• *Tanzania's Kilimanjaro is the highest mountain in Africa, reaching 19,340 ft (5,895 m) above sea level. The first European explorers on first sight could scarcely believe that mountains near the equator could be covered in snow.*

Nairobi is the capital of Kenya and the chief commercial center of East Africa. In the city center, modern office and hotel buildings rise from broad, tree-lined avenues. Beyond the sprawling suburbs there are cool, green hills and, to the south and east, hot savanna grasslands.

200 miles

300 km

1   2   3   4   5

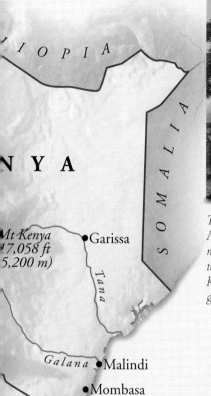

I O P I A

S O M A L I A

N Y A

Mt Kenya
17,058 ft
(5,200 m)

• Garissa

Tana

Galana • Malindi

• Mombasa

Same

Tanga •

Pemba I.

Zanzibar I.
• Zanzibar

agamoyo •

✪ Dar es Salaam

Mafia I.

ufiji

• Kilwa Kivinje

• Lindi

• Mtwara

Ruvuma

IQUE

INDIAN OCEAN

The clouds clear to reveal snowcapped Kibo and Mawenzi, the two highest points of the Kilimanjaro massif. They tower above the flat-topped acacia trees of the East African savanna. The slopes of Kilimanjaro rise through farmland, forest, mountain grasses, and snowfields.

A high collar of beaded necklaces adorns this woman of the Turkana people. The Turkana live in the arid lands of northwestern Kenya and also across the border in Sudan.

Where in the world?

7 A.M.   noon   3 P.M.
Washington, DC   GMT   Dar es Salaam

Washington, DC to Dar es Salaam	Dar es Salaam lies on
7,924 mi (12,752 km) 15 hr 15 min	06° 48'S latitude 39° 17'E longitude

Life facts

How long do people live?		How many people in 100 own cars?
U.S.A.	76 years	48
Tanzania	46 years	0.1
Kenya	48 years	1
Uganda	43 years	0.1
Burundi	46 years	0.1
Rwanda	42 years	0.1

Search and find

Tanzania
Capitals: Dar es Salaam
  (Administrative) . .E7
Dodoma
  (Legislative) D5
Bagamoyo E7
Iringa E5
Kigoma D3
Kilosa E6
Kilwa Kivinje . . .E7
Lindi F7
Mbeya E5
Mtwara F7
Mwanza C5
Njombe F5
Rungwe E5
Same D6
Shinyanga D5
Songea F5
Tabora D4
Tanga D7
Zanzibar D7

Kenya
Capital: Nairobi .C6

Garissa C7
Kakamega B5
Kericho C5
Kisumu B5
Malindi C7
Mombasa D7
Nakuru C6
Nanyuki B6
Thika C6

Uganda
Capital: Kampala B4
Arua B4
Fort Portal B4
Jinja B4
Masaka C4
Mbale B5
Moroto B5

Burundi
Capital:
  Bujumbura . . .D3

Rwanda
Capital: Kigali . .C4

Tanzania

Kenya

Uganda

Burundi

Rwanda

Country facts

	Area sq mi (sq km)	Population	Language	Religion	Currency
Tanzania	364,899 (945,088)	31,270,8209	Swahili	Trad*/Sunni Muslim	Shilling
Kenya	224,961 (582,649)	28,808,658	Swahili	Cath/Prot/Trad**	Shilling
Uganda	93,070 (241,051)	22,804,973	Swahili/Ganda	Protestant/Catholic	Shilling
Burundi	10,745 (27,830)	5,735,937	Rundi	Catholic	Franc
Rwanda	10,170 (26,340)	8,154,933	Rwanda	Catholic	Franc

*Traditional beliefs **Catholic/Protestant/Traditional beliefs

A
B
C
D
E
F
G

Equatorial Africa

DEMOCRATIC REPUBLIC OF CONGO, ANGOLA, ZAMBIA, REPUBLIC OF CONGO, GABON, EQUATORIAL GUINEA, SãoTOMÉ & PRÍNCIPE

A CROWDED RIVERBOAT, MADE up of barges hauled by a tug boat, slowly churns its way up the muddy flood of the Congo River. On deck, a woman washes out a cotton dress in a plastic bowl, while another cooks a fish stew on a stove. Radios blare out the intricate electric guitar rhythms of the late, great Franco or the sweet, lilting voice of Mbilia Bel—the king and queen of Congolese pop music. The Congo, the greatest river of Central Africa, winds between the cities of Brazzaville and Kinshasa, forming the international boundary between the Republic of Congo and the Democratic Republic of Congo.

The heart of the African continent is dense rain forest, drained by countless streams and rivers. Small bands of hunters, such as the slightly built Mbuti, live in the forest, but most people of the region are farmers or city dwellers. The forest extends westward into Gabon and Equatorial Guinea, and southward into Angola, where it gives way to plateaus, highlands, and desert.

Part of Equatorial Guinea is made up of islands. The hot, humid islands of São Tomé make up a separate country, 125 miles (200 km) west of Gabon.

DISCOVER MORE

• *The Congo River is the second longest in Africa, covering 2,900 mi (4,667 km) from its source to the Atlantic Ocean.*

• *The Congo region has one of the finest artistic traditions in Africa. The elongated and distorted features of its carved wooden masks inspired some of the world's great twentieth-century artists, such as Henri Matisse and Pablo Picasso.*

Life facts

How long do people live?	How many people in 100 own cars?
U.S.A. — 76 years	48
Dem. Rep. of Congo — 49 years	1
Angola — 48 years	1
Zambia — 37 years	2
Rep. of Congo — 47 years	1
Gabon — 57 years	2
Equatorial Guinea — 57 years	1
São Tomé & Príncipe — 64 years	n.a.

Longest rivers

Nile	4,145 mi (6,670 km)
Mississippi	3,741 mi (6,020 km)
Congo	2,900 mi (4,667 km)

This is Central Market district in Kinshasa, capital of the Democratic Republic of Congo. Kinshasa is a hot and humid city, sprawling along the banks of the Congo River opposite Brazzaville. It has a population of more than 4.5 million.

A

Where in the world?

7 A.M.	noon	1 P.M.
Washington, DC	GMT	Kinshasa

Washington, DC to Kinshasa
6,543 mi (10,529 km)
12 hr 35 min

Kinshasa lies on
04° 23'S latitude
15° 27'E longitude

B

EPUBLIC

S U D A N

Bondo

Uele

Watsa

Congo

Basoko   Kisangani

Bunia

U G A N D A

L.Edward

DEMOCRATIC
REPUBLIC
OF
CONGO

L.Kivu

Bukavu

RWANDA

BURUNDI

Lualaba

Lomami

Kananga

Mbuji-Mayi

Kalemie

T A N Z A N I A

L. Tanganyika

Kasai

Lubilash

Kamina

Bukama

L. Mweru

Mbala

Kolwezi   Likasi

Kasama

Lubumbashi

L. Bangweulu

M A L A W I

Mufulira
Kitwe

Ndola

Chipata

Z A M B I A   Kabwe

Lusaka

MOZAMBIQUE

Zambezi

Kafue

Livingstone

Z I M B A B W E

200 miles

300 km

Dem. Rep. of Congo

Angola

Zambia

Rep. of Congo

Gabon

Equatorial Guinea

São Tomé &
Príncipe

Search and find

Democratic
Republic of Congo
Capital: Kinshasa C5
Bandundu C5
Basoko B7
Bondo B7
Bukama D7
Bukavu C8
Bunia B8
Kalemie D8
Kamina D7
Kananga D6
Kikwit D5
Kisangani B7
Kolwezi E7
Likasi E7
Lubumbashi E7
Matadi D4
Mbandaka B5
Mbuji-Mayi D7
Tshikapa D6
Watsa B8

Angola
Capital: Luanda .D4
Benguela E4
Huambo E5
Lobito E4
Lubango E4
Luena E6

Namibe E4
Saurimo D6

Zambia
Capital: Lusaka .F7
Chipata E8
Kabwe E8
Kasama E8
Kitwe E7
Livingstone F7
Mbala D8
Mufulira E7
Ndola E8

Republic of Congo
Capital: Brazzaville C5
Loubomo C4
Pointe-Noire C4

Gabon
Capital: Libreville B4
Masuku C4
Port-Gentil C4

Equatorial Guinea
Capital: Malabo .B4

São Tomé &
Príncipe
Capital: São Tomé B3

C

D

E

F

Country facts

	Area sq mi (sq km)	Population	Language	Religion	Currency
D.R. of Congo	905,563 (2,345,408)	50,481,305	French/Lingala	Catholic	Congolese Franc
Angola	481,351 (1,246,699)	11,177,537	Portuguese/Umbundu	Cath/Trad*	Kwanza
Zambia	290,583 (752,610)	9,663,535	English/Bemba	Prot/Trad/Cath**	Kwacha
R. of Congo	132,046 (341,999)	2,716,814	French/Monokutuba	Catholic	CFA Franc
Gabon	103,347 (267,669)	1,225,853	French/Fang	Christian/IB***	CFA Franc
Eq. Guinea	10,830 (28,050)	465,746	Fang/Spanish	Catholic	CFA Franc
S. Tomé & Prín.	371 (961)	154,878	Portuguese	Catholic	Dobra

*Catholic/Traditional beliefs   **Protestant/Traditional beliefs/Catholic   ***Indigenous beliefs

G

Namibia to Mozambique

NAMIBIA, MOZAMBIQUE, BOTSWANA, ZIMBABWE, MALAWI

Windhoek, the Namibian capital, is a busy, modern city. Its industries include the cutting and polishing of semi-precious stones and diamonds, and meat canning.

THE GRAVEL AND SAND DUNES of the hot Namib Desert lie on the southwest African coast, bordered by the cold currents of the Atlantic Ocean. Rain is very rare, but at night sea mists roll inland, providing just enough moisture for desert plants. Few people live in Namibia's harsh landscapes, which are rich in minerals—uranium, lead, and cadmium.

The Okavango River spills over northeastern Botswana, forming vast wetlands which are the haunt of thousands of animals and birds. Southeastern Botswana is occupied by another desert, the Kalahari. The San people, who live here, are experts at desert survival. They have lived in southern Africa longer than any other people. A central plateau gives way to eastern grasslands, where most of the Tswana people live. Cattle ranching and diamond mining are the major industries.

Zimbabwe lies on a plateau to the south of the Zambezi River. Farmers grow tobacco and vegetables, often struggling during long periods of drought. The capital, Harare, is one of the major cities of southern Africa. The Zambezi River flows eastward, to enter the Indian Ocean in central Mozambique. Its capital, Maputo, has the second largest harbor in Africa. Its port also serves the landlocked nations to the east.

To the north, Malawi lies on the edge of a split in the earth's crust called the Great Rift Valley. A system of rift valleys extend throughout much of eastern Africa.

Namibia

Mozambique

Botswana

Zimbabwe

Malawi

DISCOVER MORE

• *The Okavango is a river that never reaches the sea. It forms the world's largest swamp, over 10,810 sq mi (28,000 sq km) in area. Ninety percent of its water is lost through evaporation.*

Country facts

	Area sq mi (sq km)	Population	Language	Religion	Currency
Namibia	318,694 (825,417)	1,648,270	Ovambo/English	Lutheran	Rand
Mozambique	309,494 (801,589)	19,124,335	Portuguese/Makua	Indigenous Beliefs	Metical
Botswana	224,607 (581,732)	1,464,167	English/Tswana	Traditional Beliefs/AC*	Pula
Zimbabwe	150,803 (390,580)	11,163,160	English/Shona	Ang**/Traditonal Beliefs	Dollar
Malawi	45,745 (118,480)	10,000,416	English/Chichewa	Sunni Islam/Catholic/PB	Kwacha

*African Churches **Anglican

1   2   3   4   5

T A N Z A N I A

Cape Delgado

MALAWI

GREAT RIFT VALLEY

L. Nyasa

L. Malawi

Lúrio

Lilongwe

Nacala

Zomba

Nampula

Moçambique

Zambezi

Tete

Blantyre

Victoria Falls

Quelimane

L. Kariba

Harare ✪

MOZAMBIQUE

Z I M B A B W E

Gweru   Mutare   Chimoio

Beira

Bulawayo

Save

ancistown

erowe

INDIAN OCEAN

Selibi-alapye Phikwe

Limpopo

AFRICA

Inhambane

SWAZILAND

✪**Maputo**

N
W   E
S

400 miles

600 km

A   B   C   D   E   F   G

Where in the world?

7 A.M.   noon   2 P.M.
Washington, DC   GMT   Harare

Washington, DC to Harare
7,943 mi (12,783 km)
15 hr 15 min

Harare lies on
17° 50'S latitude
31° 03'E longitude

Life facts

How long do people live?	How many people in 100 own cars?
U.S.A. 76 years	48
Namibia 41 years	4
Mozambique 45 years	0.5
Botswana 40 years	6
Zimbabwe 39 years	2
Malawi 37 years	0.5

Longest rivers

Nile   4,145 mi (6,670 km)

Mississippi   3,741 mi (6,020 km)

Zambezi   1,700 mi (2,740 km)

The thundering waters of the Victoria Falls, on the Zimbabwe-Zambia border, are at their most impressive between June and October, when the Zambezi River is in flood.

Search and find

Namibia
Capital:
   Windhoek D4
Grootfontein ...C4
Keetmanshoop ..E4
Lüderitz E4
Rehoboth D4
Swakopmund ...D4
Walvis Bay D4

Mozambique
Capital: Maputo .E7
Beira C8
Chimoio C8
Inhambane D8
Moçambique ...B9
Nacala B9
Nampula B9
Quelimane C8
Tete C8

Botswana
Capital: Gaborone D6
Francistown D6
Lobatse D6
Molepolole D6
Palapye D6
Selibi-Phikwe ...D7
Serowe D6

Zimbabwe
Capital: Harare .C7
Bulawayo C7
Gweru C7
Mutare C7

Malawi
Capitals:
   Lilongwe B8
Blantyre C8
Zomba B8

South Africa and Its Neighbors

SOUTH AFRICA, LESOTHO, SWAZILAND

A Swazi carries the traditional weapons of the warrior. The Swazi people live in Swaziland. They speak a language called siSwati, which is related to Zulu.

PASSENGERS SAILING INTO CAPE Town stare at the skyline instead of the harbor, for looming above South Africa's third largest city is the awesome sight of Table Mountain, a massive slab wreathed in white clouds beneath a blue sky.

South Africa, the continent's richest country, is a land of contrasts. There are vineyards and orchards growing in the warm sunshine of the Cape Province—on the Cape of Good Hope—dusty velds (grassland), the fortresslike walls of the Drakensberg Mountains, and deep underground shafts where miners drill for gold. There are the modern, wealthy cities of Pretoria and Johannesburg, but there are also sprawling townships such as Soweto, where young black people seek to educate themselves despite desperately poor housing conditions and little chance of employment.

South Africa is a land of many peoples. There are Zulu, Xhosa, and Ndebele, and many other black African groups. There are people of Asian and mixed descent, English-speaking city dwellers and Afrikaner farmers, who are descendants of the Dutch settlers.

South African territory surrounds two small independent kingdoms, home of the Sotho and Swazi peoples. Lesotho is a land of mountains and plateaus, grazed by sheep, while the veld of Swaziland is used for corn and cattle farming.

Longest rivers

River		Length
Nile		4,145 mi (6,670 km)
Mississippi		3,741 mi (6,020 km)
Orange		1,300 mi (2,100 km)

DISCOVER MORE

• Many South African languages include clicking sounds, which outsiders find very hard to pronounce. The Xu! language includes 48 different types of click.

• The fossilized footprints of three different types of dinosaur can still be seen on the bank of the Subeng River in Lesotho.

Miners drill for ore in a South African gold mine. Many miners come from neighboring countries, such as Lesotho, as well as from South Africa itself. South Africa is the world's biggest producer of gold.

BOT

Kalahari Desert

NAMIBIA

Upington

Kuruman

Alexander Bay

Orange

Namib Desert

Port Nolloth

Springbok

Kenhardt

Dougl

Harts

SOUTH AFRICA

ATLANTIC OCEAN

Carnarvon

Calvinia

Victoria West

Great Karoo

Clanwilliam

Beaufort West

Malmesbury

Oudtshoorn

Cape Town

Worcester

Paarl

Cape of Good Hope

Hermanus

Mosselbaai

False Bay

Cape Agulhas

The world's biggest bird is the ostrich. It cannot fly and so runs at high speed on long, powerful legs. In South Africa, ostriches are farmed for their meat and feathers.

Highest mountains

Mount McKinley
20,320 ft
(6,194 m)

Thabana Ntlenyana
11,425 ft
(3,482 m)

Where in the world?

7 A.M.   noon   2 P.M.
Washington, DC GMT Cape Town

Washington, DC to Cape Town
7,889 mi (12,696 km)
15 hr 10 min

Cape Town lies on
38° 48'S latitude
18° 28'E longitude

South Africa

Lesotho

Swaziland

Life facts

How long do people live?

How many people in 100 own cars?

U.S.A.   76 years   48

South Africa   56 years   10

Lesotho   54 years   0.6

Swaziland   39 years   3

Search and find

South Africa
Capitals: Cape Town
  (Legislative) F4
Pretoria
  (Administrative) ..D7
Alexander Bay ..E4
Aliwal North F7
Beaufort West ..F5
Bloemfontein ...E7
Burgersdorp F7
Calvinia F5
Carnarvon F5
Clanwilliam ...F4
Douglas E6
Durban E8
East London F7
Empangeni E8
Grahamstown ...F7
Hermanus G4
Johannesburg ..D7
Kenhardt E5
Kimberley E6
Kirkwood F6
Krugersdorp ...D7
Kuruman D6
Ladysmith E8
Louis Trichardt ..C8
Mafikeng D6
Malmesbury F4
Messina C8

Middelburg D8
Mosselbaai G5
Oudtshoorn ...F5
Paarl F4
Pietermaritzburg .E8
Pietersburg C8
Port Elizabeth ...F6
Port Nolloth E4
Port Shepstone .F8
Potgietersrust ..C7
Sasolburg D7
Soweto D7
Springbok E4
Sun City D7
Umtata F7
Upington E5
Vereeniging D7
Victoria West ...F5
Vryburg D6
Welkom E7
Worcester F4

Lesotho
Capital: Maseru .E7
Mafeteng E7

Swaziland
Capital:
  Mbabane D8
Manzini D8

ZIMBABWE
Messina
Louis Trichardt
Pietersburg
Potgietersrust
Sun City
Middelburg
Mafikeng
Krugersdorp
Pretoria
Johannesburg
Soweto
Sasolburg
Vereeniging
Vryburg
Mbabane
Manzini
SWAZILAND
Welkom
Kimberley
Thabana Ntlenyana
Ladysmith
Bloemfontein
Maseru
Empangeni
LESOTHO
Mafeteng
Pietermaritzburg
Aliwal North
Durban
Burgersdorp
Port Shepstone
Umtata
INDIAN OCEAN
Kirkwood
East London
Grahamstown
Port Elizabeth
Limpopo
MOZAMBIQUE
Vaal
Vaaldam
Orange
DRAKENSBERG MTS

200 miles
300 km

Country facts

	Area sq mi (sq km)	Population	Language	Religion	Currency
South Africa	471,008 (1,219,911)	43,426,386	Eng/Zulu/Xhosa	Trad/LCC*	Rand
Lesotho	11,718 (30,350)	2,128,950	Sesotho	Cath/Trad**	Loti
Swaziland	6,703 (17,361)	985,335	siSwati	LCC/Trad*	Lilangeni

*Traditional beliefs/local Christian churches **Catholic/Traditional beliefs

Oceania

OCEANIA IS THE SMALLEST OF ALL THE CONTINENTS, and most of its area is made up of deep, blue ocean, known mainly to sharks and swooping frigate birds. Even so, Oceania takes up a huge area of our planet, including Australia and the island of Papua New Guinea—the second largest island in the world. There are hundreds of smaller islands to be found within this vast expanse of water, but those most notable in size include New Zealand, the Solomon Islands, Vanuatu, and New Caledonia.

The largest country is Australia. It was first settled by Aboriginal peoples more than 50,000 years ago, but their descendants are greatly outnumbered by people of European (especially British) and Asian descent. Most Australians live in the big cities, for much of the back country consists of vast sheep and cattle stations, tropical forests, or empty desert.

The tropical island of New Guinea lies across the Torres Strait. Its western half is part of Indonesia, but its eastern half is an independent state, Papua New Guinea.

The islands of New Zealand, far across the Tasman Sea, are cool and green, largely given over to farming and raising sheep. Most New Zealanders are of European descent, or belong to a Polynesian people called the Maoris.

The didgeridoo is a traditional musical instrument played by the Australian Aborigines. It is made of a long wooden tube. Rhythmic sucking and blowing produce an eerie, reverberating sound.

DISCOVER MORE

• *It is estimated that more languages are spoken in Papua New Guinea than in any other country—at the latest count, 817.*

• *Pitcairn is a tiny island about halfway between Australia and South America. Its inhabitants are descended from the crew of a British naval ship called the* Bounty. *The sailors settled here in 1790 after organizing a mutiny.*

• *The Solomon Islands have 39 endangered or threatened animal species. As in many Pacific nations, they include corals, turtles, and shells.*

Northern Marianas (U.S.A.)

Guam (U.S.A.)

MI

PALAU

FE
OF M

MELA

Irian Jaya (INDONESIA)

**PAPUA
NEW
GUINEA**

ARAFURA SEA

GREAT BARRIER REEF

CO

AUSTRALIA

GREAT DIVIDING RANGE

*Great Australian
Bight*

2,000 miles

3,000 km

The flightless emu is Australia's biggest bird. It weighs about 88 lb (40 kg) and has long, very powerful legs. It pecks the ground for seeds, berries, flowers, and insects.

Western Australia

The skyscrapers of downtown Perth tower over green parkland. Perth, on the Swan River, has been called the world's most remote city because it is so far from other major centers of population.

Western Australia

ALONG A DESERT TRACK, A mining truck roars, kicking up a cloud of dust. A lizard, basking in the hot sunshine, scuttles for cover. A dog barks by a shack, waiting for an Aborigine child to throw sticks.

The state of Western Australia is a very thinly populated region, which takes in storm-battered coasts on the Indian Ocean, the Great Sandy Desert, the Gibson Desert, and the Great Victoria Desert. In the north are remote cattle stations and the amazing gorges of the Purnululu (or Bungle Bungle) National Park; in the south, the flat, vast expanse of the Nullarbor Plain. The far southwest is forested, and types of eucalyptus trees known as *jarah* and *karri* are felled for their hardwood. Off the coast of North West Cape is the Ningaloo Reef, an underwater spectacle of corals and fishes. The state's mineral wealth includes gold, industrial diamonds, iron ore, bauxite, coal, and oil.

Highways converge on the state capital, Perth, and its port of Fremantle, which together are home to more than one million people. The skyscrapers are a world away from the deserts of the Australian interior, known as the "outback." In the southwest, the mild climate allows fruit, grapevines, and wheat to be grown and sheep to be raised.

200 miles

300 km

DISCOVER MORE

• *The Nullarbor Plain is a railroad engineer's dream. One stretch of track between West and South Australia runs absolutely straight for 297 mi (478 km).*

• *What seem to be rocks on the shore at Hamelin Pool in Western Australia are in fact stromatolites—colonies of tiny bacteria. They have been called living fossils, and are believed to be descended from the first organisms ever to develop on Earth.*

This young Aborigine comes from the Kimberley Plateau, a remote highland region in northwestern Australia. Many Australian Aborigines decorate their faces and bodies for ceremonies and dances.

INDIAN OCEAN

Port Hedland

Dampier

Barrow I.

Fortescue

North West Cape

Ashburton

Mt Bruce 4,052 ft (1,235 m)

L. Macleod

Carnarvon

Dirk Hartog I.

Hamelin Pool

Murchison

Geraldton

Northam

Perth
Fremantle
Mandurah

Bunbur

Cape Naturaliste

Busselton

Cape Leeuwin

1   2   3   4   5

## Map labels

Joseph Bonaparte Gulf

Bonaparte Archipelago

Drysdale

Wyndham

Kimberley Plateau

Purnululu ∴

Cape Lévêque

Broome ●

Derby ●

Fitzroy

Eighty Mile Beach

Great Sandy Desert

De Grey

Gibson Desert

WESTERN AUSTRALIA

● Meekatharra

Mount Magnet

● Laverton

Great Victoria Desert

Nullarbor Plain

Kalgoorlie-Boulder

Great Australian Bight

Point Culver

Esperance ●

Archipelago of the Recherche

Albany ●

Australia

Where in the world?

7 A.M. Washington, DC GMT   noon   8 P.M. Perth

Washington, DC to Perth
11,551 mi (18,590 km)
22 hr 15 min

Perth lies on
31° 50'N latitude
116° 10'E longitude

Life facts

How long do people live?

U.S.A.   76 years

Australia   80 years

How many people in 100 own cars?

48

47

Flatlands stretch to a level horizon across the Nullarbor Plain. This vast region lies between the Great Victoria Desert and the Great Australian Bight. It is an arid land with no rivers, and its only vegetation is scrub and bush. Large parts of it are limestone rock.

Search and find

Western Australia	
Albany G6	Geraldton E5
Broome B7	Kalgoorlie-Boulder F7
Bunbury G6	Laverton E7
Busselton G6	Mandurah F6
Carnarvon D5	Meekatharra . . . E6
Dampier C5	Mount Magnet . . E6
Derby B7	Northam F6
Esperance G7	Perth F6
Fremantle F6	Port Hedland . . . C6
	Wyndham B8

Country facts

	Area sq mi (sq km)	Population	Language	Religion	Currency
Australia	2,967,893 (7,686,843)	18,783,551	English	Catholic/Anglican	Dollar

Eastern Australia

A NIGHT FLIGHT ACROSS Australia reveals very few lights. The vast landmass remains dark and mysterious. However, as the sun rises and the plane descends over Sydney, a large, sprawling city comes into view, clustered around the blue waters of its famous harbor. Most Australians live in the coastal cities of the east and south—Brisbane, Sydney, Melbourne, and Adelaide. They look outward to sandy beaches and rolling surf, rather than inland to the sparsely populated "outback." Some coastal cities have a look of London, England, about them, for modern Australia was founded by British settlers who seized the land from its original inhabitants, the Aborigines. Many of today's Australians come from other ethnic backgrounds: Greek, Italian, Lebanese, Vietnamese, and Thai.

Eastern Australia stretches from the tropical creeks and sugarcane fields of Queensland to the vineyards of South Australia, and south to the forests and cool, rocky shores of the island of Tasmania. Eastern Australia is rimmed with the mountains of the Great Dividing Range and the Australian Alps, the source of the Murray and Darling river system. The highlands enclose large areas of grassland (grazed by kangaroos and huge numbers of sheep and cattle), stands of gray-barked, fragrant eucalyptus, burning desert, and rock.

DISCOVER MORE

• *The Great Barrier Reef, running parallel to Australia's Pacific coast, is the longest coral reef in the world. Teeming with underwater life, it is more than 1,200 mi (2,000 km) long.*

• *South Australia has the world's biggest sheep station, covering more than 3,860 sq mi (10,000 sq km). Australia is the world's biggest producer of wool.*

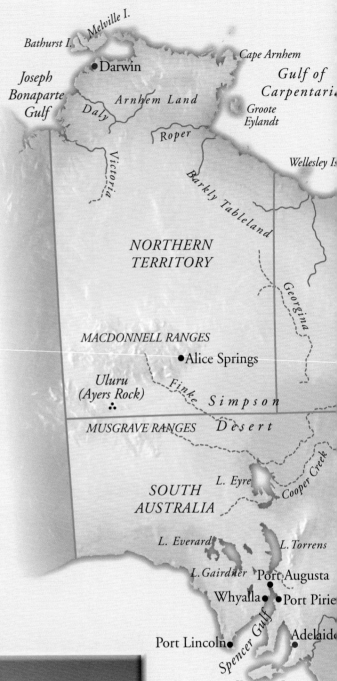

Sydney's Opera House rises like a series of sails beside the city's harbor. The beautiful building, which was completed in 1973, has become the most familiar landmark in Oceania.

1   2   3   4   5

Highest mountains

Mount McKinley
20,320 ft
(6,194 m)

Mount Kosciusko
7,310 ft
(2,229 m)

Where in the world?

7 A.M.   noon   10 P.M.
Washington, DC   GMT   Canberra

Washington, DC to Canberra
9,907 mi (15,945 km)
19 hr 5 min

Canberra lies on
35° 21'S latitude
149° 10'E longitude

Life facts

How long do people live?

U.S.A.   76 years

Australia   80 years

How many people in 100 own cars?

48

47

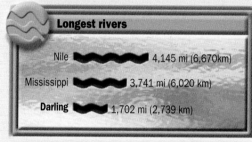

Longest rivers

Nile   4,145 mi (6,670 km)

Mississippi   3,741 mi (6,020 km)

Darling   1,702 mi (2,739 km)

Torres Strait
Cape York

Cape York Peninsula

Great Barrier Reef

Mitchell
Gilbert
Norman
Flinders

Cairns

Burdekin

Townsville

PACIFIC OCEAN

QUEENSLAND

Diamantina
Thomson
Barcoo
Belyando

Great Artesian Basin

Mackay

Cape Townsend

Rockhampton

Warrego

Bundaberg

Fraser I.

Sunshine Coast

Toowoomba   Brisbane
Gold Coast

Barwon

Grafton

NEW SOUTH WALES

Darling
Lachlan

Dubbo   Maitland
   Newcastle
   Gosford
Wagga Wagga   Sydney
   Wollongong

Murray

Canberra

Albury   AUSTRALIAN CAPITAL TERRITORY
Mt Kosciusko

Bendigo

AUSTRALIAN ALPS

VICTORIA

Ballarat
Geelong   Melbourne
   Morwell

Cape Otway
Wilson's Promontory

TASMAN SEA

Bass Strait
Flinders I.
King I.
Cape Barren I.

Burnie   Devonport
Launceston
Queenstown   TASMANIA

Hobart

South East Cape

Australia

Search and find

Eastern Australia

Capital: Canberra F7	Launceston G7
Adelaide E6	Mackay C7
Albury E7	Maitland E8
Alice Springs . . C5	Melbourne F7
Ballarat F6	Morwell F7
Bendigo F7	Mount Gambier . F6
Brisbane D8	Newcastle E8
Bundaberg D8	Port Augusta . . . E5
Burnie G7	Port Lincoln . . . E5
Cairns B7	Port Pirie E5
Darwin A4	Queenstown . . . G7
Devonport G7	Rockhampton . . C8
Dubbo E7	Sunshine Coast . D8
Geelong F7	Sydney E8
Gold Coast D8	Toowoomba D8
Gosford E8	Townsville C7
Grafton E8	Wagga Wagga . . . F7
Hobart G7	Whyalla E5
	Wollongong E8

Country facts

	Area sq mi (sq km)	Population	Language	Religion	Currency
Australia	2,967,893 (7,686,843)	18,783,551	English	Catholic/Anglican	Dollar

200 miles

300 km

A B C D E F G

New Zealand

SET SAIL SOUTHEASTWARD from Australia, across the swell of the Tasman Sea, and after some 1,240 miles (2,000 km), high, clouded peaks rise on the horizon. These are the Southern Alps, snowy mountains, whose glaciers have carved deep sea inlets into the coastline. The highest peak, Mount Cook, towers over South Island, the largest of the island group that makes up New Zealand. The Pacific Ocean ports of Christchurch and Dunedin lie on its east coast, serving the fertile Canterbury Plains and the Central Otago plateau. Most people work on the land, fruit farming or sheep-shearing.

Most New Zealanders live across Cook Strait on North Island, many of them in the cities of Wellington or Auckland. Like many other Pacific islands, New Zealand has volcanic origins. The proof lies in North Island's bubbling hot springs and gushing geysers, plumes of water turned into steam by intense heat below the surface. The energy of these natural forces is harnessed to generate power.

New Zealanders are often nicknamed "Kiwis," after a flightless bird that lives in the forests. The original New Zealanders are the Maoris, a Polynesian people who retain many of their ancient traditions, including elaborate wood carving, choral singing, and dancing. Many New Zealanders are of European, mostly British, descent. The remainder come from Asia or other Pacific islands. The Cook Islands, Niue, and the Tokelau Islands are also governed by New Zealand.

A Maori dancer wearing traditional facial markings bares his tongue as a sign of respect. New Zealand's Polynesian people have retained a strong interest in their social and cultural traditions.

Auckland, with its modern skyline, is New Zealand's biggest city. It is a seaport, built in northern North Island between the harbors of Manukau and Waitemata.

DISCOVER MORE

• New Zealanders have a passion for rugby. Their national team is called the All Blacks. It starts all international games with an ancient Maori war dance, the hakka.

• New Zealand has 15 sheep for every human.

White Island rises from New Zealand's Bay of Plenty like an angry monster, its volcanic interior rumbling and spewing out plumes of smoke.

TASMAI
SEA

Cape Foulu

Greymout

Mt Cook

Jackson Head

SOUTHERN ALP

Mt Aspiring
9,957 ft ▲
(3,036 m)

Tima

L. Wakatipu

Waitaki

L.
Te Anau

Oamar

CENTRAL
OTAGO

Clutha

Cape
Providence

Invercargill

Duned

Foveaux Strait

Stewart I.

A

B

C

D

E

F

G

Map Labels (North Island)

North Cape

Whangerei

Gt Barrier I.

Hauraki Gulf

Auckland

Bay of Plenty

Hamilton

Tauranga

RAUKUMARA RANGE

East Cape

Rotorua

Gisborne

Waikato

L. Taupo

New Plymouth

Ruapehu 9,175 ft (2,797 m)

L. Waikaremoana

Poverty Bay

Cape Egmont

Wanganui

Hawke Bay

Mahia Peninsula

Napier

Hastings

Wanganui

NORTH ISLAND

PACIFIC OCEAN

Map Labels (South Island)

Cape Farewell

Golden Bay

Palmerston North

Tasman Bay

Cook Strait

Wellington

Nelson

Cape Palliser

Blenheim

Tapuaenuku 9,465 ft (2,886 m)

Westport

SOUTH ISLAND

Pegasus Bay

Christchurch

Canterbury Plains

Banks Peninsula

Canterbury Bight

The tuatara lives on islands off the New Zealand coast. It is the only surviving species from a group of reptiles that died out about 100 million years ago.

New Zealanders are proud of their sheep-shearing skills. They have plenty of practice. Wool is among the country's chief exports.

100 miles

150 km

New Zealand

Where in the world?

7 A.M. Washington, DC   noon GMT   12 A.M. Wellington

Washington, DC to Wellington
8,746 mi (14,075 km)
16 hr 50 min

Wellington lies on
41° 15'S latitude
174° 45'E longitude

Life facts

How long do people live?

U.S.A.
76 years

New Zealand
78 years

How many people in 100 own cars?

48

47

Highest mountains

Mount McKinley
20,320 ft
(6,194 m)

Mount Cook
12,315 ft
(3,754 m)

Search and find

New Zealand
Capital:
  Wellington . . .D7
Auckland B7
Blenheim D7
Christchurch . . .E7
Dunedin F6
Gisborne C9
Greymouth E6
Hamilton B8
Hastings C8
Invercargill G5

Napier C8
Nelson D7
New Plymouth . .C7
Oamaru F6
Palmerston
  North D8
Rotorua C8
Tauranga B8
Timaru F6
Wanganui D8
Westport D6
Whangerei B7

Country facts

	Area sq mi (sq km)	Population	Language	Religion	Currency
New Zealand	107,737 (279,039)	3,662,265	English	NR/Ang/Pres*	Dollar

*Non-religious/Anglican/Presbyterian

Pacific Ocean
and Islands

FLYING FISH SKIM OVER THE BLUE OCEAN SWELL, WHILE DEEP below the surface, giant squid propel themselves through inky black waters. Extending from the Arctic in the north to the Antarctic in the south, from Asia to the west and the Americas to the east, the Pacific Ocean is circled by a "ring of fire," a danger zone for earthquakes and volcanoes. These may trigger gigantic waves called tsunamis. Covering 64,186,300 square miles (1,662,425,000 sq km), the Pacific Ocean is the largest ocean in the world.

Volcanoes and coral reefs form chains of tiny islands across the Pacific Ocean. Pacific peoples may be grouped into three main cultures: Polynesians, Melanesians, and Micronesians. There are also people of European and South Asian descent. Island crafts include carving in stone and wood, basketry, and matting. The islanders are famous for their love of song and dance.

Papua New Guinea and its islands have copper mines, and tea and coffee plantations. There are also forests, mountains, and valleys where warriors dress for festivals. Eastward are the sugarcane fields of Fiji, the barren landscape of Nauru, wasted by phosphate mining, and small islands exporting copra (dried coconut). People live by growing taro (a tuber crop), fishing, or farming.

Travel and communication between so many tiny, remote, and reef-encircled islands can be very difficult.

DISCOVER MORE

• Easter Island is famous for the huge statues carved from stone and erected by Polynesian people between A.D. 1000–1600. We do not know why they were made.

• The longest atoll on earth is Kwajalein. It is situated in the Marshall Islands, and is 175 mi (283 km) long.

BERING SEA

Aleutian Is

ASIA

NORTH PACIFIC OCEAN

Midway Is (U.S.A.)

Wake I. (U.S.A.)

Northern Mariana Is (U.S.A.)

MARSHALL ISLANDS

Johnston Atoll (U.S.A.)

Guam (U.S.A.)

MICRONESIA

PALAU

FED. STATES OF MICRONESIA

Gilbert Is

MELANESIA

NAURU

Phoenix Is

KIR

PAPUA NEW GUINEA

SOLOMON ISLANDS

TUVALU

Tokela

SAMOA

America Samoa (U.S.A

Wallis & Futuna (FRANCE)

CORAL SEA

VANUATU

New Caledonia (FRANCE)

FIJI

Niu (N.Z

TONGA

AUSTRALIA

Norfolk I. (AUSTRALIA)

Gt Barrier I.

NEW ZEALAND

Chatham Is (N.Z.)

Stewart I.

Auckland Is (N.Z.)

Campbell I. (N.Z.)

Yachts anchor in Opunohu Bay, on the island of Moorea, 12 mi (19 km) northwest of Tahiti, in French Polynesia. Moorea's warm climate makes it possible to produce coffee, vanilla, and copra.

Flags:

Papua New Guinea | Solomon Islands | Fiji | Vanuatu
Samoa | Kiribati | Tonga | Micronesia
Palau | Marshall Islands | Nauru | Tuvalu

Where in the world?

7 A.M. Washington, DC | noon GMT | 2 A.M. Hawaii

Washington, DC to Hawaii
4,835 mi (7,781 km)
9 hr 20 min

Hawaii lies on
21° 19'N latitude
157° 48'W longitude

Search and find

Aleutian Islands .B5	Nauru D5
American Samoa E6	New Caledonia . .E5
Auckland Islands .F5	New Zealand . . .F5
Australia E4	Niue E6
Campbell Island F5	Norfolk Island . .E5
Chatham Islands F5	Northern Marianas
Clipperton	Islands D4
Island D8	Palau D4
Cook Islands . . .E6	Papua New
Easter Island . .E8	Guinea D4
Federated States	Phoenix Islands .D5
of Micronesia .D5	Pitcairn Island . .E7
Fiji E5	Revilla Gigedo
French Polynesia E7	Islands C8
Galápagos	Sala y Gómez . .E8
Islands D9	Samoa D5
Gilbert Islands . .D5	Solomon Islands D5
Gt Barrier Island .F5	Stewart Island . .F5
Guam D4	Tahiti D7
Hawaii C6	Tokelau D5
Johnston Atoll . .C6	Tonga E6
Kiribati D6	Tuamotu Islands .E7
Kiritimati D6	Tubuai Islands . .E6
Marquesas	Tuvalu D5
Islands E7	Vanuatu E5
Marshall Islands D5	Wake Island C5
Midway Island . .C6	Wallis & Futuna .E5

Country facts

	Area sq mi (sq km)	Population	Language	Religion	Currency
Papua New Guinea	178,703 (462,841)	4,599,785	PidginEnglish/English	Catholic/Lutheran	Kina
Solomon Islands	10,985 (28,451)	441,039	English/PidginEnglish	Anglican	Dollar
Fiji	7,054 (18,270)	802,611	Fijian/English/Hindi	Hindu/Methodist	Dollar
Vanuatu	4,707 (12,191)	185,204	Bislama	Presbyterian	Vatu
Samoa	1,104 (2,859)	224,713	Samoan	Mormon/Cong*	Tala
Kiribati	313 (811)	83,976	English/Kiribati	Catholic	Australian Dollar
Tonga	289 (749)	108,207	Tongan	Free Wesleyan	Pa'anga
Micronesia	271 (702)	129,658	English/Chuukese	Catholic/Cong*	US Dollar
Palau	188 (487)	18,110	Palauan/English	Catholic/Trad***	US Dollar
Marshall Islands	70 (181)	63,031	Marshallese/English	Cong*/NR**/Catholic	US Dollar
Nauru	21 (54)	10,501	Nauruan	Cong*	Australian Dollar
Tuvalu	10 (26)	10,444	Tuvaluan	Church of Tuvalu	Australian Dollar

*Congregational **Non-religious ***Tradional beliefs

**Map labels:**

NORTH AMERICA

HAWAII (U.S.A.)

Revilla Gigedo Is (MEXICO)

Clipperton I. (FRANCE)

Kiritimati

Galápagos Is (ECUADOR)

K I R I B A T I

Marquesas Is

French Polynesia (FRANCE)

Tahiti

Tuamotu Is

Tubuai Is

Cook Is (N.Z.)

Pitcairn I. (U.K.)

Sala y Gómez (CHILE)

Easter I. (CHILE)

SOUTH PACIFIC OCEAN

1,000 miles

1,500 km

Antarctica

NOBODY LIVES HERE. VISITING SCIENTISTS have set up bases to study the ice, the rocks, and the climate (which in recent years has become warmer). But this is still the coldest and windiest place on Earth, a frozen wilderness where nobody would want to settle. Blizzards howl over the mountain ridges, glaciers and the great shelves of permanent ice that extend from parts of the coast. Penguins huddle together for warmth on the shores, but no wild animals survive in the interior. During the southern winter (when the northern part of the world is experiencing summer), gloom and darkness settle over the landscape. In summer, the snowfields dazzle the eye, and huge icebergs drift out to sea.

The Antarctic continent is surrounded by the southern Atlantic, Indian, and Pacific Oceans, with the Ross and Weddell seas biting in deep toward the center of the landmass and the world's most southerly point, the South Pole. Mountain ranges run across the center. In this land of ice, a fiery volcano, Mount Erebus, rises from the Ross Sea.

Many countries claim Antarctic territory, largely because of the mineral wealth that lies hidden deep beneath the ice and the rich fishing offered by its oceans. However, the future of the continent is to be decided by the international community—and no decisions have been made yet.

ATLANTIC OCEAN

South Orkney Is

South Shetland Is

Graham Land

Antarctic Peninsula

Palmer Archipelago

Palmer (U.S.A.)

Palmer Land

Alexander I.

Charcot I.

BELLINGSHAUSEN SEA

Thurston I.

AMUNDSEN SEA

Siple I.

PACIFIC OCEAN

WEDDELL SEA

Coats Land

• Halley (U.K.)

Berkner I.

Ronne Ice Shelf

PENSACOLA MTS

Ellsworth Land

▲ Vinson Massif 16,864 ft (5,141 m)

WEST ANTARCTICA

Walgreen Coast

Marie Byrd Land

Cape Norvegia

Sou Po

Ross I Shel

Roosevelt I.

Cape Colbeck

ROS SEA

Scott I.

DISCOVER MORE

• *The thickest parts of the Antarctic ice cap are more than 3 mi (5 km) thick.*

• *Seventy percent of the world's freshwater is locked up in the ice of Antarctica.*

• *The coldest temperature ever recorded was –192°F (–89°C), at the Vostok base in Antarctica in 1983.*

In Antarctica, one can still get some idea of what the world must have been like before its habitation by plants, animals, and people.

## Map labels

Average permanent extent of sea ice

INDIAN OCEAN

200 miles

300 km

Queen Maud Land

Syowa (JAPAN)

Enderby Land

Mac. Robertson Land

Cape Darnley

Amery Ice Shelf

Lambert Glacier

AMERICAN HIGHLAND

EAST ANTARCTICA

mundsen-Scott ● (U.S.A.)

Queen Mary Land

Shackleton Ice Shelf

Vostok (RUSSIAN FEDERATION)

Knox Coast

TRANSANTARCTIC MOUNTAINS

Wilkes Land

Cape Poinsett

McMurdo (U.S.A.)

▲ Mt Erebus 12,448 ft (3,795 m)

Victoria Land

George V Land

Adélie Coast

Oates Land

Cape Adare

Balleny Is

Where in the world?

Washington, DC to Mount Erebus

⌒ 9,203 mi (14,811 km)
✈ 17 hr 40 min

7 A.M.	12 A.M.
Washington, DC	Mount Erebus

Emperor penguins form large colonies around the ice-bound Antarctic coast. The adult birds recognize the call of their own chicks when they return after a long swimming expedition in search of food.

Antarctica

Search and find

Alexander Island C3	Roosevelt Island E6
Amundsen-Scott .D6	Scott Island F6
Balleny Islands . .F7	Siple Island E4
Berkner Island . .C5	South Orkney
Charcot Island . .C3	Islands A4
Halley B5	South Shetland
McMurdo E6	Islands B3
Palmer C3	Syowa B8
Palmer	Thurston Island .D4
Archipelago . . .C3	Vostok D7

Continent facts

	Area sq mi (sq km)	% of Earth's area	Population
Antarctica	5,400,000 (13,986,000)	9.3	uninhabited

Arctic Ocean
and Islands

AN EXPLORER BATTLES ACROSS THE ARCTIC ICE, heading for the North Pole. His feet drag with exhaustion, his beard is rimed with frost. He is not crossing land, but the thick ice of the Arctic Ocean. Here it is so cold that the sea is permanently frozen over. Summer nights remain bright, while winter days are dark, lit only by the flickering patterns of the Northern Lights.

The edges of the great ice cap break up into floes, which drift in bitterly cold waters. Arctic seas are home to whales, fish, walrus, and seals, hunted by polar bears. In recent years, the world's climate has become warmer, and scientists fear that the ice cap is melting and that arctic wildlife will possibly soon be threatened.

Arctic Ocean islands include nine in the Norwegian territory of Svalbard. Greenland is a land of ice, settled only in coastal areas. Belonging to the North American continent, it is a self-governing Danish territory. The arctic mainland is made up of Alaska, Canada, Scandinavia, and Russia. Most of it is tundra, a deep-frozen, treeless plain, covered in snow and ice for most of the year.

Over the ages, humans have settled these harsh lands and learned to survive by hunting or by herding reindeer. They include the Inuit and related peoples of North America, the Saami of Scandinavia, the Nenets, Chukchi, and other peoples of Arctic Russia.

In recent years many Arctic peoples have had to adapt to a more modern way of life but at the same time try to protect their traditions. They have demanded greater control over their own affairs.

DISCOVER MORE

• *Greenland is generally considered to be the biggest island in the world, with an area of 840,000 sq mi (2,175,600 sq km). That's nearly one-quarter the size of the United States. Beneath its 1.8-mi (3-km)-thick cap of ice, Greenland is actually made up of three islands of rock.*

**MAP LABELS:**
Bering Strait
ALASKA (U.S.A.)
CHUKCH[I]
Barrow
Point Barrow
BEAUFORT SEA
CANADA
Cape Bathurst
Banks I.
M'Clure Strait
Victoria I.
Melville I.
Prince of Wales I.
North Magnetic Pole
Devon I.
Ellesmere I.
LINCOL[N] SEA
Foxe Basin
Baffin I.
Baffin Bay
Davis Strait
GREENLAND (DENMARK)
Denmark Strait
ICELAND

Arctic icebergs break off, or calve, from glaciers in Alaska and Greenland and float out to sea. They pose a danger to ships sailing in the area.

A

B

C

D

E

F

G

200 miles

300 km

Search and find

Ambarchik

EAST
SIBERIAN
SEA

RUSSIAN FEDERATION

New Siberian
Is

LAPTEV
SEA

Nordvik

ARCTIC
OCEAN

Severnaya
Zemlya

North
Pole

Average permanent extent of sea ice

Dikson

Franz
Josef
Land

KARA
SEA

Novaya
Zemlya

Svalbard

GREENLAND
SEA

BARENTS
SEA

North Cape

Murmansk

NORWEGIAN
SEA

NORWAY   SWEDEN   FINLAND

Arctic Circle

At the top of the world, the sun is still shining at
midnight in midsummer.

The polar bear, an excellent
swimmer, is perfectly adapted
to its environment, with its
thick, white coat.

Dependencies

A dependency is a territorial unit under the jurisdiction of another state, but not formally annexed to it. Some territories are too small to appear on the atlas maps. Their approximate positions are given here.

Territory	Administered by	Area sq mi (sq km)	Population	Language	Religion	Currency	Page number
American Samoa	U.S.A.	77 (199)	62,100	Samoan/English	Congregationalist	Dollar	191, 198
Anguilla	U.K.	37 (96)	12,400	English/Creole	Anglican	East Caribbean dollar	60 mi NW of St. Kitts & Nevis (73)
Aruba	Netherlands	75 (193)	89,000	Dutch/Papiamento	Catholic	Aruban florin	41, 73
Ashmore & Cartier Is	Australia	2 (5)	uninhabited	–	–	–	off N coast of western Australia (193)
Bermuda	U.K.	21 (54)	62,100	English	Anglican/Methodist	Bermuda dollar	41, 88
Bouvet I.	Norway	23 (59)	uninhabited	–	–	–	89
British Indian Ocean Territory	U.K.	23 (60)	2,900 (military)	English	–	Dollar	Indian Ocean (124)
British Virgin Is	U.K.	59 (153)	16,800	English	Anglican/Catholic/ Methodist	Dollar	60 mi E of Puerto Rico (41)
Cayman Is	U.K.	100 (259)	35,000	English	Anglican/Catholic	Cayman Is dollar	72
Christmas I.	Australia	52 (135)	2,500	English/Chinese	Buddhist/Taoist	Australian dollar	169
Clipperton I.	France	3 (7)	uninhabited	–	–	–	199
Cocos Is	Australia	6 (14)	590	English/Malay	Sunni Islam	Australian dollar	169
Cook Is	New Zealand	92 (237)	18,000	English/Cook Islands Maori	Cook Is Christian Church	New Zealand dollar	191, 196, 199
Coral Sea Is Territory	Australia	5 (8)	3*	–	–	–	off NE coast of Australia (195)
Falkland Is	U.K.	4,698 (12,170)	2,600	English	Anglican	Falkland pound	75, 86, 88
Faroe Is	Danish	540 (1,399)	43,800	Faeroese/Danish	Evangelical Lutheran	Faeroese krona	89, 90
French Guiana	France	33,399 (86,503)	169,000	French/Creole	Catholic	Euro	74, 79
French Polynesia	France	1,544 (4,000)	228,000	French/Tahitian	Evangelical Church of Polynesia	Euro	191, 199
Gibraltar	U.K.	2.5 (6.5)	27,100	English	Catholic	Gibraltar pound	90, 100
Greenland	Denmark	840,000 (2,175,600)	56,300	Greenland Inuit/ Danish	Evangelical Lutheran	Danish krona	41, 88
Guadeloupe	France	687 (1,779)	434,000	French/Creole	Catholic	Euro	41, 68, 73
Guam	U.S.A.	209 (541)	148,000	English/Chamorro/ Filipino	Catholic	Dollar	190, 198
Guernsey	U.K.	30 (79)	61,700	English	Anglican/Catholic	Pound	94
Heard & McDonald Is	Australia	161 (417)	uninhabited	–	–	–	310 mi SE of Kerguelen I. (168)
Howland, Baker & Jarvis Is	U.S.A.	2 (5)	–	–	–	–	NW and E of Phoenix Is (198)
Isle of Man	U.K.	221 (572)	72,600	English	Anglican	Pound	94
Jersey	associated with U.K.	45 (116)	85,600	English/French patois	Anglican	Pound	94
Johnston Atoll	U.S.A.	0.5 (1.3)	1,200 (service personnel)	–	–	–	191, 198
Kingman Reef	U.S.A.	0.1 (0.3)	uninhabited	–	–	–	500 mi NW of Christmas I. (169)
Martinique	France	436 (1,129)	399,000	French/Creole	Catholic	Euro	41, 73
Mayotte	France	145 (376)	128,000	French/Mahorian	Sunni Islam	Euro	168
Midway I.	U.S.A.	2 (5)	military	–	–	–	191, 198
Montserrat	U.K.	38 (98)	3,500	English	Anglican/Methodist	East Caribbean dollar	41, 73
Navassa I.	U.S.A.	2 (5)	uninhabited	–	–	–	90 mi E of Jamaica (73)
Netherlands Antilles	Netherlands	309 (800)	213,000	Dutch/Papiamento/ English	Catholic	Netherlands Antilles guilder or florin	41, 73

Territory	Administered by	Area sq mi (sq km)	Population	Language	Religion	Currency	Page number
New Caledonia	France	7,172 (18,576)	204,000	French/Melanesian	Catholic	Euro	191, 198
Niue	New Zealand	100 (259)	1,710	English/Niuean	Cong. Niue Church	New Zealand dollar	191, 198
Norfolk I.	Australia	13 (34)	1,770	English/Norfolk Island	Anglican	Australian dollar	191, 198
Northern Mariana Is	U.S.A.	184 (477)	66,600	English/Chamorro/Filipino	Catholic	Dollar	190, 198
Pitcairn I.	U.K.	5 (14)	44	English/Pitkern	Seventh Day Adventist	New Zealand dollar	191, 199
Puerto Rico	U.S.A.	3,515 (9,104)	3,808,610	Spanish/English	Catholic	Dollar	73
Réunion	France	982 (2,542)	692,000	French/Creole	Catholic	Euro	168
St. Helena	U.K.	159 (411)	7,040	English	Anglican/Baptist	Pound (local issue)	89
St. Pierre & Miquelon	France	93 (242)	6,800	French	Catholic	Euro	40 mi S of Newfoundland (65)
South Georgia & South Sandwich Is	U.K.	1,580 (4,091)	military	–	–	–	88, 89
Tokelau	New Zealand	5 (13)	1,500	English	Congregationalist	New Zealand dollar	191, 198
Turks & Caicos Is	U.K.	166 (430)	13,800	English	Anglican/Methodist	Dollar	72
Virgin Is of the U.S.A.	U.S.A.	136 (352)	118,000	English/Spanish	Baptist/Catholic	Dollar	41, 73
Wake I.	U.S.A.	3 (8)	military	–	–	–	191, 198
Wallis & Futuna Is	France	106 (274)	14,100	French/Wallisian/Futunian	Catholic	Euro	191, 198

*meteorological station

Disputed and other territories

The following are dependencies that are disputed. Various states claim them.

Territory	Claimed by	Area sq mi (sq km)	Population	Language	Religion	Currency	Page number
Argentine Antarctic Territory	Argentina	475,314 (1,231,064)	research bases	–	–	–	200
Australian Antarctic Territory	Australia	2,333,500 (6,043,700)	research bases	–	–	–	200
British Antarctic Territory	United Kingdom	700,000 (1,800,000)	research bases	–	–	–	200
Chilean Antarctic Territory	Chile	490,240 (1,269,723)	research bases	–	–	–	200
French Southern and Antarctic Territories	France	169,806 (439,797)	research bases	–	–	–	200
Golan Heights	Syria/Israel	444 (1,150)	29,000	Hebrew/Arabic	Sunni Islam/Jewish	New Israeli shekel	134, 136
Paracel Is	China/ Vietnam	62 (160)	military	–	–	–	220 mi E of Vietnam (153)
Peter I Island	Norway	69 (180)	–	–	–	–	200
Queen Maud Land	Norway	–	research bases	–	–	–	200
Ross Dependency	New Zealand	282,000 (730,000)	research bases	–	–	–	200
Spratly Is	China/Vietnam/Philippines/Taiwan/Brunei/Malaysia	undefined	–	–	–	–	250 mi NW of Brunei (154)
Sovereign Military Order of Malta	Sovereign Roman Catholic Order	2 acres (1.2 hectares)	30	Italian	Catholic	Scudo	106
Western Sahara	Morocco/Polisario guerilla movement	97,344 (252,120)	281,000	Arabic	Sunni Islam	Moroccan dirham	170, 174

The following statistics relate to territory controlled by the Palestinian Authority on July 23, 2000

Territory	Claimed by	Area sq mi (sq km)	Population	Language	Religion	Currency	Page number
Palestinian Entity	–	10,160 (26,314)	2,897,000	Arabic/Hebrew	Sunni Islam	New Israeli shekel	136

Glossary

altitude the height of land above sea level.

archipelago a group of islands that are close together.

basin 1. a bowl-shaped area of land that is lower than the surrounding area. 2. an area of land through which a river flows.

bay an inlet in the coastline of an ocean or lake, normally eroded by the waves.

bayou a shallow stretch of water that flows very slowly through a marshy or boggy area.

bluff a steep cliff.

border 1. the edge of an area of land or vegetation. 2. the area between two countries. 3. a boundary.

boundary an imaginary line that separates one country or area of land from another.

butte a steep-sided rock that stands on its own and rises sharply above the land around it.

canal a human-made waterway used for transportation or irrigation.

canyon a deep valley, with steep sides, which often has a river flowing through it.

cape a large region of land that projects from the coastline into a sea or ocean.

capital a location officially designated as the chief city of a nation, state, province, or territory, often the center of government.

channel a narrow stretch of water between two areas of land.

cinder cone a cone-shaped volcano that is made from layers of dust and tiny pieces of rock.

climate the pattern of weather conditions normally recorded in any one place or region.

coast the land that borders a sea or ocean.

compass rose the points of the compass, as displayed on a map.

continent a landmass or part of a landmass, making up one of the seven major geographical divisions of the world.

coral hard rock that is made from the shells and skeletons of tiny sea creatures.

crag a steep, rough rock formation.

crater 1. a large opening or depression at the top of a volcano. 2. a hollow in the land caused when a meteor crashes to Earth.

crust the thin layer of rock that covers Earth's surface.

current the movement of water over long distances in seas, oceans, and rivers.

delta an area in which a river splits into several separate waterways before entering the sea. It is normally created by deposits of mud or sand. The name comes from the triangular shape of such a region, which looks like the Greek letter delta (Δ).

desert an area of land that has very little or no rain.

divide a ridge or line of crests separating two drainage areas.

earthquake a shaking of the ground that happens when sections of Earth's crust move.

elevation the height above sea or ground level.

Equator an imaginary horizontal line around the middle of the globe, halfway between the North Pole and the South Pole.

estuary a river mouth, where freshwater meets and mixes with the salt water from an ocean or sea.

ethnic group a group of people sharing common descent, language, or culture.

fault line a fracture in Earth's surface along which sections of crust are forced together, or slide past each other, sometimes causing earthquakes.

fjord a long, deep-sea inlet, formed by glaciers in prehistoric times.

floodplain the flat land on either side of a river that is covered by water when the river floods.

forest any large area of dense woodland.

geyser jets of hot water and steam that gush up into the air. They are formed when rainwater seeps into the rocks and is heated by volcanic forces deep underground.

glacier a large body of ice that moves slowly along a valley or down a mountain.

gorge a narrow valley, with steep rocky sides, through which a river runs.

Greenwich mean time the mean solar time of the Greenwich Meridian, used throughout the world as the basis of standard time.

Greenwich Meridian the line of longitude (0°) from which distances to the east or west are measured. It passes through Greenwich, England. Also called the Prime Meridian.

grid a crisscross network of lines used to locate places on a map.

gulf an area of seawater that reaches into the land. A gulf is usually wide, with a narrow opening into the sea.

harbor a natural or human-made sea inlet that protects boats at their moorings.

hemisphere the globe divided into two halves, either north and south or east and west.

hill land that rises from the ground around it but is not as high as a mountain.

iceberg a large chunk of ice that floats in seas and oceans. Most of the iceberg lies hidden beneath the water's surface.

inlet a narrow stretch of water that cuts into the land from a sea or a river.

International Date Line an imaginary line drawn north to south across the Pacific Ocean, which notes where one day ends and another begins. For instance, if it were Monday on the west side of the line, it would be Sunday on the east side of the line.

island an area of land completely surrounded by water.

isthmus a narrow stretch of land connecting two larger bodies of land.

lagoon a body of salt water that is separated from the sea by a strip of land.

lake a body of water that is surrounded by land.

landlocked surrounded by land on all sides, with no coastline.

latitude the location of a place north or south of the Equator, that is measured in degrees. Measurements are determined using imaginary horizontal lines that circle the globe, parallel to the Equator.

lava the hot liquid rock that pours out of a volcano during an eruption.

levee a wall that is built along a riverbank to stop the river from flooding.

longitude the location of a place east or west of the Greenwich Meridian, measured in degrees. Measurements are determined using imaginary vertical lines, called meridians, which run from the North Pole to the South Pole.

marsh an area of very wet land that is usually low lying.

mesa a rocky hill or mountain with a flat top and steep sides.

mineral a natural substance that is formed inside the earth, for example gold and copper.

monsoon a strong wind that brings heavy rains in the summer months in the Indian Ocean and southern Asia.

moor an area of rough, open, high ground, often boggy.

mountain a very high area of land.

mountain pass a passageway from one side of a mountain to the other.

mountain range a chain of high peaks and ridges.

mountain system a chain of mountain ranges, or ranges sharing the same geological origins.

oasis a place in the desert where there is water and some vegetation.

ocean a very large area of salt water on Earth's surface.

paddy a flooded field in which rice plants are grown.

pampas the grasslands of South America.

peak the highest point of a mountain.

peninsula a strip of land that sticks out into the sea and is almost completely surrounded by water.

pinnacle a column of rock, eroded to a slender point.

plain a large area of flat land.

plateau an area of high ground that is usually very flat.

population the people or the number of individuals living in a given place.

prairie the flat, grass-covered lands of North America.

rain forest forests with dense, evergreen vegetation fed by very high rainfall. The term normally refers to tropical forests, but can also be applied to similar forests in temperate regions.

reef a platform of rocks or coral just below the surface of the sea.

ridge a long, thin stretch of high ground.

rift valley a long valley created by movement along a fault line in Earth's crust.

river a moderate to large body of water draining off the land and normally flowing between banks toward the sea or ocean.

salt flat a large area of flat land that is covered with crystals of salt.

sand dune a hill of sand that is formed by the wind.

savanna a wide grassy plain with a few scattered trees.

scale a distance on a map shown in proportion to the real distance.

scrub an area of land that is thickly covered with low-growing trees and shrubs.

sea a body of salt water, making up an arm or region of an ocean.

solar energy energy that is produced using the sun's rays.

steppe a wide area of flat grass-covered land in eastern Europe and central Asia.

strait a narrow stretch of water connecting two larger bodies of water.

subtropics the regions bordering the tropics.

swamp an area of wet and muddy land.

territory 1. an area of land that does not have the status of an independent nation. 2. a province or region within a nation.

time zone a large area where every place has the same time. The world is divided into 24 different time zones. The time in each zone is one hour behind or in front of the time in the neighboring zones.

tree line the point above which trees do not grow due to poor soil and climate conditions.

tributary a stream or river that flows into another one during its journey to the ocean.

Tropic of Cancer a line of latitude (23.5° north of the Equator) marking the northernmost point reached by the overhead sun on July 21.

Tropic of Capricorn a line of latitude (23.5° south of the Equator) marking the southernmost point reached by the overhead sun on December 22.

tropics the warm regions between the Tropic of Cancer and the Tropic of Capricorn near the Equator.

tundra cold bare land where the soil is frozen for long periods of each year. Only small, low-lying plants can grow on the tundra.

valley a low-lying area, eroded from the land by a river or glacier between two hills or mountains.

veldt the open, grassy plains of southern Africa.

volcano a weak point in the Earth's crust, where molten lava bursts through the surface. Past eruptions of lava may build up to form a mountain.

wetland an area of wet ground.

Index

Numbers in **bold** type refer to main entries. Numbers in *italics* refer to illustrations.

Bjelovar Croatia 113 C6
Black (river) Vietnam 152 B6
Black Forest (mountain range) Germany 102 F5, 102
Black Hills South Dakota, U.S.A. 25
Black River Vietnam 152
Black Sea 90, 110, 120, 128; map: 91, 111, 120, 122, 124, 128, 132
Blackpool U.K. 94 E5
Blanc, Mont (mountain) France 99 E7, 99
Blanca Bay Argentina 86 D5
Blanco, Cape Oregon, U.S.A. 59 C7
Blanco, Cape Peru 88 G5
Blantyre Malawi 187 C8
Blenheim New Zealand 197 D7
Blida Algeria 175 C7
block mountains 25
Bloemfontein South Africa 189 E7
Blue Mosque Turkey 132
Blue Nile (river) Ethiopia/Sudan 178, 179 D8, 180 D5, 180
Bo Gulf China 163 C6
Bobo Dioulasso Burkina Faso 176 E4
Bodélé Depression Chad 178 C4
Bodø Norway 92 C5
Bodrum Turkey 132 E3
Bogotá Colombia 76 C5, 76, 77
Bohemian Forest Czech Republic/Germany 103 E7, 108 E3, 108
Bohol (island) Philippines 157 E8
Bohol Sea 157
Boise Idaho, U.S.A. 56 C4
Bolívar, Pico (mountain) Venezuela 76 B6
Bolivar currency Venezuela 77
Bolivia 74 D6, 84–85, 85
Bologna Italy 106 B5
Bolsena, Lake Italy 106 C5
Bolzano Italy 106 A5
Bombay see Mumbai
Bonaire (island) Netherlands Antilles 73 F7
Bonaparte Archipelago Australia 193 A7
Bonaparte, Napoleon 98
Bondo Democratic Republic of Congo 185 B7
Bonifacio, Strait of Corsica 99 G7, 106 D4
Bonn Germany 102 D4
Bonneville Salt Flats Utah, U.S.A. 56 D4, 56
Borås Sweden 92 F5
Bordeaux France 98 E4
Borgarnes Iceland 92 C3
Borgholm Sweden 92 F5
Borneo (island) Indonesia 154 C6, 154
Bornholm (island) Denmark 92 G5
borscht soup 126
Bosna (river) Bosnia-Herzegovina 113 D8
Bosnia-Herzegovina 11, 91 E6, 112–113, 112
Bosnian Muslim religion Bosnia-Herzegovina 112
Bosporus (river) Turkey 132 C4
Bosporus Sea Turkey 132
Bosten, Lake China 160 C5
Boston Massachusetts, U.S.A. 44, 45 D7
Bothnia, Gulf of 91 C6, 92 D6
Botrange (mountain) Belgium 97 E8
Botswana 170 F7, 186–187
Bouaké Ivory Coast 176 F4
Bouar Central African Republic 178 E4
Boulder Colorado, U.S.A. 57 D7
Boulogne France 98 B5
Bourg-en-Bresse France 99 D7
Bourges France 98 D5
Bournemouth U.K. 94 F6
Bouvet Island Atlantic Ocean 89 G8
Bozeman Montana, U.S.A. 56 B5
Brac (island) Croatia 113 F6
Bradford U.K. 94 E6
Braga Portugal 100 C3

Brahman cattle 84
Brahmaputra (river) Bangladesh 150 B6, 150
Brăila Romania 111 D8
Branco (river) Brazil 80 B5
Brandenburg Germany 103 C7
Brandon Manitoba, Canada 67 F7
Brasília Brazil 81 D7, 81
Brașov Romania 111 D8
Bratislava Slovakia 108 F5, 109
Bratsk Russian Federation 126 D6
Braunau Austria 105 C7
Brazil 16, 22, 74, 75 C7, 80–81, 100
Brazil Current Atlantic Ocean 88
Brazilian Highlands 81 D7
Brazos (river) Texas, U.S.A. 51 C9
Brazzaville Republic of Congo 184 C5, 184, 185
Brčko Bosnia-Herzegovina 113 D8
Breda Netherlands 97 D7
Bregenz Austria 104 D5
Bremen Germany 102 B5
Bremerhaven Germany 102 B5
Brenner Austria 104 D6
Brescia Italy 106 B5
Brest France 98 C3
Breton language France 98
Bridgeport Connecticut, U.S.A. 45 E6
Bridgetown Barbados 73 E9
Brig Switzerland 104 E4
Brigham City Utah, U.S.A. 56 D5
Brighton U.K. 95 F7
Brindisi Italy 107 D8
Brisbane Australia 194, 195 D8
Bristol U.K. 94 F6
Bristol Bay Alaska, U.S.A. 61 C6
British Columbia (province) Canada 62, 66–67
British Isles 28, 89 B7, 94–95; see also United Kingdom
British people Canada 66
British rule
    Australia 194
    Guyana 78, 78
    Hong Kong 163
Brittany France 98 C3
Brno Czech Republic 108 F4
Broadway U.S.A. 44
Brook Range Alaska, U.S.A. 61 A7
Broome Australia 193 B7
Brownsville Texas, U.S.A. 51 E8
Bruce, Mt Australia 192 D6
Bruck Austria 105 C9
Bruges Belgium 96 D6, 96
Brunei 125 F8, 154 B6, 154–155
Brunswick Germany 102 C6
Brussels Belgium 96, 97 E7
Bryansk Russian Federation 122 D4
Bucharest Romania 110, 111 D8, 111
Budapest Hungary 110 C4, 110, 110
Buddhist religion
    Asia 124, 125, 146
    China 160
    Japan 166, 167
    Mandalay 150
    Mongolia 159
    Myanmar 150
    Nepal 148
    Singapore 155
    Southeast Asia 152, 152, 153
    South Korea 164
    Sri Lanka 149
    Taiwan 163
Buenos Aires Argentina 86 D6, 86, 87
Buenos Aires, Lake Argentina 86 F4
Buffalo New York, U.S.A. 44 D4
Bug (river) Poland/Ukraine 109 C7, 120 D3
Bujumbura Burundi 182 D3
Bukama Democratic Republic of Congo 185 D7
Bukavu Democratic Republic of Congo 185 C8
Bukhara Uzbekistan 130 F5

Bulawayo Zimbabwe 187 C7
Bulgaria 11, 91 E7, 110–111, 110, 114
Bulgarian language Bulgaria 111
Bulgarian Slavic people Bulgaria 110
Bullet train Japan 166
bullfighting 100
Bunbury Australia 192 G6
Bundaberg Australia 195 D8
Bungle Bungle Australia 192
Bungo Channel Japan 166 F5
Bunia Democratic Republic of Congo 185 B8
Buraydah Saudi Arabia 138 C5
Burdekin (river) Australia 195 C7
Burgas Bulgaria 111 E8
Burgersdorp South Africa 189 F7
Burgos Spain 100 C5
Burgundy France 98 D5
Burias (island) Philippines 157 D7
Burkina Faso 170 C4, 176–177
Burlington Vermont, U.S.A. 44 C6
Burma see Myanmar
Burmese people Myanmar 150
Burnie Australia 195 G7
Bursa Turkey 132 D4
Buru (island) Indonesia 155 C8
Burundi 171 E7, 182–183
Bushehr Iran 144 E6
Busrā ash-Shām Syria 134 G4
Busselton Australia 192 G6
Butte Montana, U.S.A. 56 B5
buttes 56
Butuan Philippines 157 E9
Buurgpiaatz (mountain) Luxembourg 97 F8
Buyr Nuur (lake) Mongolia 159 D9
Bydgoszcz Poland 108 C5
Bytom Poland 108 E5
Byzantine conquest Central Europe 112

C

CN Tower Toronto, Canada 62
Cabanatuan Philippines 157 B7
Čačak Yugoslavia 114 C5
cacao beans 83
Cáceres Spain 100 D4
cactuses 30, 100
Cadiz Philippines 157 D8
Cádiz Spain 100 F4
Cádiz, Gulf of Spain 100 F4
Caen France 98 C4
Cagayan de Oro Philippines 157 E8
Cagliari Italy 106 E4
Cagliari, Gulf of 106 E4
Cairns Australia 195 B7
Cairo Egypt 172, 172, C8 173
Calais France 98 B5
Calamian Group (islands) Philippines 157 D6
Calapan Philippines 157 C7
Calayan (island) Philippines 157 A7
Calbayog Philippines 157 D8
Calcutta India 124, 149 D7
Calgary Alberta, Canada 62 E5, 66 F5
Cali Colombia 76 D4
Calicut India 148 F4
California (state) U.S.A. 13, 25, 40, 42 D4, 42, 59–60
California, Gulf of 26, 40 E5, 68 B4
Callao Peru 82 E5, 82
Caltanissetta Italy 107 F6
Calvinia South Africa 188 F5
Camagüey Cuba 72 D4
Cambodia 125 E7, 152–153
Cambridge U.K. 95 F7
Cambridge Bay (Iqaluktuutiak), Nunavut, Canada 66 C6
camels
    Africa 174, 180
    Arabia 138, 140
    Asia 134
    Baghdad 144
    Central Asia 130
    China 160
    Gulf States 142
    Jordan 136

camels (continued)
    Mongolia 158, 159
    Sudan 178
Cameroon 170 D5, 178–179, 178
Cameroon, Mt Cameroon 178 E3
Camiguin (island) Philippines 157 A7
Camiguin (island) Philippines 157 E8
Campbell Island New Zealand 191 F7, 198 F5
Campeche, Bay of 69 E8
Campo Grande Brazil 80 E6
Campobasso Italy 107 D7
Campos Brazil 81 E8
Can Tho Vietnam 153 E7
Canada 21, 40, 40–41, 41, 62–67
    Arctic Ocean 202
    East 64–65
    Great Lakes 27
    North 66–67
    U.S.A. 42, 44, 52, 54, 56
    West 66–67
Canada geese 40
Canadian people Canada 64
Canadian Shield Canada 64 C4, 65 C6, 66 C6
canals 90, 96, 96
Canary Islands (island group) Atlantic Ocean 88, 89 A7, 174 D3
Canberra Australia 195 F7
Cancún Mexico 69 D9
Cannes France 99 F7
Cantabrian Mountains Spain 100 B4, 100
Canterbury U.K. 95 F7
Canterbury Bight New Zealand 197 F6
Canterbury Plains New Zealand 196, 197 E6
canyons 56
Cap Haïtien Haiti 72 D6
Cape Barren Island Australia 195 F7
Cape Canaveral Florida, U.S.A. 43 E8, 49 D7, 49
Cape Cod Massachusetts, U.S.A. 45 D7, 45, 88 C5
Cape Girardeau Missouri, U.S.A. 53 E7
Cape Province South Africa 188
Cape Town South Africa 188 F4, 188, 189
Cape Verde 89 D7, 170 B3, 176–177
Cape York Peninsula Australia 195 A6
Capitol Building, Washington, U.S.A. 43, 46
Cappadocia Turkey 132 D5, 132
Capri (island) Italy 106 C5
Captain Cook Hawaii, U.S.A. 61 G8
Caquetá (river) Colombia 76 E5
car industry 54, 54, 124, 166
Caracas Venezuela 76, 76, 77 B7
carbon dioxide 23
Carcassonne France 98 F5
Cardiff U.K. 94 F5
Cardigan Bay U.K. 94 F5
Caribbean Islands 42, 72–73
Caribbean plate 18
Caribbean Sea 72, 74, 88; map: 41, 71, 74, 76, 88
caribou 60
Carlisle U.K. 94 D5
Carlsbad New Mexico, U.S.A. 51 C6
Carlsbad Caverns U.S.A. 50
Carmarthen U.K. 95 F5
Carnarvon Australia 192 D5
Carnarvon South Africa 188 F5
carnivals 72, 80, 102
Caroline plate 18
Caroní River Venezuela 75
Carpathian Mountains Romania 90, 110, 111 C7
Carpentaria, Gulf of Australia 194 A6
carpets 130, 130, 145
Carpi Italy 106 B5
Carrao River Venezuela 75
Carrara Italy 106 B4

Carrauntoohil (mountain) Ireland 94 F3
Carson City Nevada, U.S.A. 56 D3
Cartagena Colombia 76 B4
Cartagena (river) Spain 101 E7
Casablanca Morocco 174 C5
Cascade Mountains U.S.A. 40, 58, 59
Cascade Range U.S.A. 59 C7
Caseyr, Cape Somalia 181 C9
casinos 56, 98
Casper Wyoming, U.S.A. 57 C6
Caspian Sea 17, 90, 128, 130, 144; map: 91, 122, 124, 129, 130
Cassai (river) Angola 184 E6
cassava 78, 80
Castellón de la Plana Spain 101 D7
Castres France 98 F5
Castries St. Lucia 73 E9
Catalán language France 98
Catalán people Spain 100
Catamarca Argentina 86 C4
Catanduanes (island) Philippines 157 C8
Catania Italy 107 F7
Catania, Gulf of Italy 107 F7
Catanzaro Italy 107 E7
Catholic religion
    Africa 177, 179, 185, 189
    Alps 105
    Andes 82
    Australia 193, 195
    Baltic States 118, 120
    Canada 62
    Caribbean 72
    Central America 71
    Central Europe 109, 112, 113
    East Timor 155
    France 98
    Germany 103
    Hungary 111
    Iberian Peninsula 101
    Indian Ocean 169
    Italy 106
    Lithuania 119
    Low Countries 96
    Malawi 186
    Pacific Ocean 199
    Philippines 156, 156
    South America 74, 77, 79, 81, 83, 84, 87
    U.K. 95
    U.S.A. 42
cattle farming 45, 50, 190
Cauca (river) Colombia 76 B4
Caucasus Mountains Asia/Europe 90, 122 F4, 122, 122, 124, 128 B4, 128–129, 129
caves 16, 27
caviar 144
Cayenne French Guiana 79 D9
cayenne peppers 78
Cayman Islands Caribbean Sea 72 E4
Cebu Philippines 157 E8
Cebu (island) Philippines 157 E8
Cedar (river) Iowa, U.S.A. 53 C7
Cedar City Utah, U.S.A. 56 E5
Cedar Rapids Iowa, U.S.A. 53 C7
cedar of Lebanon Asia 134, 135
Cedi currency West Africa 177
Cedros Island Mexico 68 C3
Celebes Sea map: 125, 155, 157
Celje Slovenia 112 B5
Central African Republic 171 C6, 174, 178–179
Central America 40, 70–71, 140
Central Asia 130–131
Central Europe 110, 112–113
    Northern 108–109
Central Otago New Zealand 196 F5
Central Otago Plateau New Zealand 196
Central Siberian Plateau Russian Federation 126 C5, 126
Cephalonía (island) Greece 116 D4
Ceram (island) Indonesia 155 C9
Ceram Sea 155

209

Credits

The publishers would like to thank the following sources for the use of their photographs: Page 10 (c) Ann Ronan Picture Library, (b/c) Michael Maslan Historic Photographs/Corbis; 15 (t/c) N.A.S.A.; 16 (c) Galen Rowell/Corbis, (b/r) Hanan Isachar/Corbis; 17 (c) James L. Amos/Corbis, (b/l) Andrey Zvoznikov/Hutchison Library, (b/r) Yann Arthus Bertrand/Corbis; 19 (c/r) AFP/Corbis; 20 (t/r) Ralph White/Corbis; 21 (b/l) Paul A. Souders/Corbis; 24 (b/l) Peter Lillie/Gallo Images/Corbis; 25 (b/l) Jim McDonald/Corbis; 26 (t/r) The Purnell Team/Corbis, (t/r) Craig Lovell/Corbis, (b/l) Philip Gould/Corbis; 27 (b/l) James Marshall/Corbis; 28 (t/r) Yann Arthus Bertrand/Corbis, (t/r) Paul Almasy/Corbis; 29 (c) Yann Arthus Bertrand/Corbis; 30 (c) Eric Lawrie/Hutchison Library, (b/r) Andrey Zvoznikov/Hutchison Library; 31 (t/r) Nigel Smith/Hutchison Library, (c/r) David Muench/Corbis; 33 (t/l) Jo Brewer, (t/l) Richard Hamilton Smith/Corbis, (t/l) Robert Francis/Hutchison; 34 (c/r) Hulton-Deutch Collection/Corbis, (c/r) Nik Wheeler/Corbis; 35 (t/r) Keren Su/Corbis, (c) Chicago Department of Aviation, (c/r) Roger Ressmayer/Corbis, (b/l) Steve Chen/Corbis; 45 (t) Peter Finger/Corbis, (c/r) James P. Blair/Corbis; 46 (t/r) Nathan Benn/Corbis, (b/r) Farrell Grehan/Corbis; 47 (b/l) Bob Krist/Corbis, (c/l) Richard T. Nowitz/Corbis; 51 (b/l) Bill Ross/Corbis; 52 (b/c) Buddy Mays/Corbis; 54 (b) Sandy Felsenthal/Corbis; 55 (t/l) Dallas & John Heaton/Corbis, (c) Kevin Morris/Corbis; 57 (c/r) Dean Conger/Corbis; 60 (t/r) Lowell Georgia/Corbis; 68 (b) Robert Frerck/Odyssey/Chicago/Robert Harding Picture Library; 70 (b/c) Galen Rowell/Corbis; 71 (t/c) J.G. Fuller/Hutchison Library; 73 (t/l) Robert Harding Picture Library, (b/r) Robert Francis/Hutchison Library; 75 (b/r) Charles Bowman/Robert Harding Picture Library; Cover, 77 (b/r) Jeremy Horner/Corbis; 78 (b/c) J. Henderson/Hutchison Library; 79 (t/l) Adam Woolfitt/Corbis; 82 (b) Roman Soumar/Corbis; Cover, 83 (c) Owen Franken/Corbis; 84 (b/l) Buddy Mays/Corbis; 85 (t/l) Graham Neden/Ecoscene/Corbis, (b/r) Bettman/Corbis; 86 (b/l) Dave G. Houser/Corbis; 87 (c) R. McLeod/Robert Harding Picture Library, (b/l) Pern/Hutchison Picture Library; 88 (b) Tony Aruzza/Corbis; 89 (t/r) Corbis, (c/r) D. Lomax/Robert Harding Picture Library; 92 (t/r) Kim Hart/Robert Harding Picture Library; 93 (c) Bernard Regent/Hutchison Picture Library; 96 (c/r) Sancez/Explorer/Robert Harding Picture Library; 98 (t/r) G. Hellier/Robert Harding Picture Library; 100 (b/c) Charles Bowman/Robert Harding Picture Library; 101 (t/c) Robert Frerck/Robert Harding Picture Library, (b/c) Michael Russelle/Robert Harding Picture Library; 102 (t/r) Gavin Hellier/Robert Harding Picture Library; 103 (t/c) Nigel Blythe/Robert Harding Picture Library, (b/c) Bob Krist/Corbis; 106 (b/c) Charles & Josette Lenars/Corbis; 108 (b/c) Norman Froggard/Hutchison Library; 109 (c) Adam Woolfitt/Corbis, (b/c) Gavin Hellier/Robert Harding Picture Library; 110 (c) Sandra Vanninil/Corbis, (b/c) Regent/Hutchison Library; 112 (t/r) Hans Georg Roth/Corbis; 113 (t/c) Crispin Hughes/Hutchison Library; 114 (b/c) Arne Hodalic/Corbis; 115 (t/c) AFP/Corbis, (c) Melanie Friend/Hutchison Library, (b/c) Jeremy Horner/Panos Pictures; 118 (b/c) Ludovic Maisant/Corbis; 120 (b/c) Reuters Newmedia Inc./Corbis; 121 (t/c) Nik Wheeler/Corbis; 122 (b/c) Dean Conger/Corbis; 123 (b/c) Dean Conger/Corbis; 124 (b/c) Arthur Thévenart/Corbis; 126 (b/c) Dean Conger/Corbis; 127 (b/l) Wolfgang Kaehler/Corbis; Cover, 128 (c) John Egan/ Hutchison Library, (b/c) Brian Goddard/Panos Pictures; 129 (t/c) J.C. Tordai/Hutchison Library; 130 (t/r) Janet Wishnetsky/Corbis, (b/l) Audrey Zvoznikov/Hutchison Library; 131 (t/c) Brian Vikander/Corbis; 132 (t/r) Adam Woolfitt/Robert Harding Picture Library, (b/c) Philip Wolmuth/ Hutchison Library; 133 (t/r) Robert Harding Picture Library, (b/l) Hutchison Library; 134 (t/r) Paolo Koch/Robert Harding Picture Library; Cover, 134 (c) K.M. Westermann/Corbis; 135 (t/l) K.M. Westerman/Corbis, (b/r) Paolo Koch/Robert Harding Picture Library; 136 (b/l) J.C. Tordai/Panos Pictures; 137 (t/l) E. Simanor/Robert Harding Picture Library; 138 (b/l) T. Maugher/Robert Harding Picture Library; 139 (t/l) Robert Harding Picture Library, (b/r) Mohamed Amin/Robert Harding Picture Library; 140 (t/r) Juliet Highet/Hutchison Library; Cover, 142 (t/r) Adam Woolfitt/Corbis; 143 (b/r) Charles & Josette Lenars/Corbis; 144 (t/r) David Lomax/Robert Harding Picture Library, (b/c) Lister/Hutchison Library; 145 (t/c) Trygve Bolstad/Panos Pictures; 146 (b/l) David Cumming/Corbis; 147 (b/r) Charles & Josette Lenars/Corbis; 148 (t/r) Hutchison Library; 150 (t/r) Jean-Leo Dugast/Panos Pictures, (b/r) Trygve Bolstad/Panos Pictures; 151 (b/r) Richard Bickel/Corbis; 152 (b/c) Jermey Horner/Hutchison Library; 153 (t/c) Steve Raymer/ Corbis; 155 (b/l) Robert Harding Picture Library; 156 (c/r) Caroline Penn/Panos Pictures, (b/c) John Watt/Hutchison Library; 157 (c/r) Chris Stowers/ Panos Pictures; 158 (t/r) Adam Woolfitt/Corbis, (b/l) Hutchison Library; 159 (t/l) Robert Harding Picture Library, (b/r) Hutchison Library; 160 (b/l) John R. Jones, Papilio/Corbis; 162 (b/l) Wolfgang Koehler/Corbis; 163 (t/c) Wolfgang Koehler/Corbis, (c) Nocholas Hall/Robert Harding Picture Library; 164 (b/l) Stephanie Maze/Corbis; 166 (t/r) Paul Quayle/Panos Pictures, (b/l) Craig Lovell/Corbis; 168 (b/l) The Stock Market; 169 (b/l) Nik Wheeler/ Corbis; 172 (b/c) Liba Taylor/Hutchison Library; 173 (t/l) Sandro Vannini/Corbis; 174 (b/c) Jeremy Horner/Hutchison Library; 175 (t/c) M. Jelliffe/ Hutchison Library; 178 (t/r) Michael & Patricia Fogden/Corbis, (b/l) Paul Almasy/Corbis; 179 (t/l) Jacques Jangoux/Tony Stone Images; Cover, 180 (t/r) Sarah Errington/Hutchison Library, (b/c) Liba Taylor/Hutchison Library; 181 (t/c) Coroline Penn/Corbis; 182 (b/l) Pemberton/Hutchison; Cover, 183 (c) Adrian Arbib/Corbis; 185 (t/l) Marc Schlossman/Panos Pictures; 186 (t/r) Yann Arthus-Bertrand/Corbis; 188 (t/r) Philip Perry/Frank Lane Picture Agency/Corbis, (b/c) Hutchison Library; 189 (t/l) Charles O'Rear/Corbis; 190 (t/r) Charles & Josette Lenars/Corbis; 192 (t/r) John Lamb/Tony Stone Images; Cover, 192 (b/c) Paul Chesley/Tony Stone Images; 193 (c/r) Roger Garwood & Trish Ainslie/Corbis; 196 (t/r) The Stock Market, (c/r) The Stock Market, (b/c) AFP/Corbis; 197 (t/c) Kevin Schafer/Corbis, (b/c) Jack Fields/Corbis; 198 (b/c) The Stock Market. All other photographs from MKP Archives. In addition the publisher would like to thank: The Flag Institute; and the following artists for their contribution – Rob Jakeway and Martin Saunders.

The publisher has made every effort to contact all copyright holders, but apologizes if any source remains unacknowledged.